FLASH Review

for

English Grammar

Blanche Ellsworth

John Higgins

Janice Wiggins-Clarke

Addison
Wesley

Boston San Francisco New York
London Toronto Sydney Tokyo Singapore Madrid
Mexico City Munich Paris Cape Town Hong Kong Montreal

Vice President and Publisher: Alison Pendergast
Senior Acquisitions Editor: Steven Rigolosi
Senior Production Manager: Bob Ginsberg
Project Coordination, Text Design, and Electronic Page Makeup: TechBooks
Cover Design Manager: Barbara Atkinson
Cover Design: Night & Day Design
Manufacturing Buyer: Lucy Hebard
Printer and Binder: Courier Corporation
Cover Printer: Phoenix Color Corporation

Library of Congress Cataloging-in-Publication Data

Ellsworth, Blanche, (date)-
    Flash review for english grammar / Blanche Ellsworth, John Higgins, Janice Wiggins-Clarke.
        p. cm.
    ISBN 0-321-10188-X
        1. English language--Grammar. 2. English language--Grammar--Problems, exercises,
    etc.   I. Higgins, John A. II. Wiggins-Clarke, Janice. III. Title.
    PE1112.E44 2002
    428.2'076--dc21

                                                                        2001038871

Please visit our web site at http://www.flashreview.com

ISBN 0-321-10188-X

45678910-CRK-080706

CONTENTS

FOREWORD

Dear College Student:

Congratulations on purchasing your *Flash Review*. The fact that you purchased it indicates that you know there's an easier way to make good grades in college—and that you have decided to pursue it. This is the first and most important step you can take to start excelling in your academic efforts.

You see, making good grades in college has more to do with your attitude, determination, and knowledge of how to excel academically than with your level of raw intelligence. I am living proof of that principle.

How a Struggling High School Student Became a College Star

As a high school senior, I had no desire to do well in school, and my grades reflected my bad attitude. As a freshman I had tried to study and make good grades, but my test scores were always disappointing. After my sophomore year I essentially gave up. After all, spending time with my friends was a lot more fun than staying home and studying. As a result, I graduated at the bottom of my class—497th in a class of 512 students. In fact, my poor academic performance almost kept me from graduating altogether.

My parents constantly reminded me how important my education was. They often told me it would determine what types of jobs I would get and how much money I would make. My education would even affect how happy I was, they said. Unfortunately, their advice fell on deaf ears. I was having fun with my friends, and homework seemed like a waste of time.

I underwent an attitude adjustment after high school. I took odd jobs such as shoveling asphalt to fill potholes, offloading semi trucks at a loading dock, flipping burgers at a fast-food joint, and delivering stacks of newspapers to paperboys on street corners. Now don't get me wrong—there's nothing wrong with good, honest hard work. I felt, though, that I was capable of doing more.

When I turned 27, I decided it was time to get a college education, so I took some refresher classes at a local community college to boost my grades. Eventually, I was accepted into a four-year college. Five years later I graduated at the top of my class with bachelor's and master's degrees in business. How did I do it? I learned how to be a smart student rather than a student who is smart.

Study the Habits of the Best Students

I knew I couldn't compete with the top students in terms of raw intelligence, so I started observing their study habits. Then I began to use all the tips, tool, and tactics they used to get straight A's. I asked a friend who was a great student to let me in on his secret. He said, "David, you need to look at your education as though it were a full-time job." He went on to ask, "Are you ever late for your regular job?" I wasn't. "Do you ever just skip work because you don't feel like going?" I didn't. Then he asked, "When your boss gives you an assignment, do you ever just blow it off?" Of course not—I'd get fired. "Exactly," he concluded. "You'd get fired. Why should your job be any different from your college education?"

That very day I decided I would take my education seriously and treat it as though it were a full-time job. I never skipped another class; I arrived on campus at 7:30 AM and didn't leave until I finished my work for the day; and I turned in every assignment that was given to me, even all the optional and extra-credit assignments.

I continued to gather information about study techniques from many other sources and started to figure out what worked for me and what didn't. Finally, I condensed all the advice into a few effective techniques, and I implemented them one by one. For example, I learned that studying in the same place at the same time every day helps one focus and get more done. So I found a spot in the corner of the campus library and made it my "office." Sure enough, I was able to concentrate better and get my work done faster.

Another powerful tip helped me boost my math and science scores. While most study-skills books tell you to stop studying a couple of hours before a test to clear your mind and help you relax, this technique had never worked for me. A friend advised me to do just the opposite—to spend the hour before the test memorizing the formulas. "Forget about how to apply them," he said. "Just organize them and write them down on paper several times. Keep studying them until the test starts. When the test begins, pull out a fresh piece of paper and write down all the formulas, just like you've been doing for the past hour." I tried this technique, and it worked. At the start of my next math exam, I had all the formulas I needed right in front of me—it was almost like an open-book test. That one tip increased my math and science test scores by a full grade.

Flash Review will help you put this tip into practice because it provides all the formulas in one compact, easy-to-study place. With *Flash Review*, you'll breeze through quick, comprehensive reviews before taking your tests.

Academic Success Is Mainly a Function of Knowing How to Make Good Grades

When my scores started to improve, I began to realize that academic success has more to do with knowing how to make good grades than with being a genius. Let me explain. When I started college I spent hours on end studying in the library. I tried to memorize information and cram for tests, but my grades were mediocre. I became frustrated and depressed.

Then a friend taught me some techniques for memorizing facts and figures using word-picture associations. I began to practice these and suddenly started to ace my daily quizzes. Then I bought an organizer and began to schedule my time and develop daily to-do lists. My productivity soared, and I was completing tasks in half the time they took previously. I formed a couple of study groups for some of my harder classes and found myself teaching others the material I was learning. My comprehension of the material improved dramatically. I started to visit my professors during office hours and developed trusting relationships. As a result, they always went the extra mile to help me when I had trouble. I went to the academic skills office and took a short course on taking tests. The course gave me a host of test-taking techniques, and my grades started to improve immediately.

Are you getting the picture? You must learn *how* to be a good student. Most of you will be in college for at least two years; some will be in college for more than eight years. That's a long time. Doesn't it make sense to invest some time in learning how to be an exceptional student?

Using *Flash Review* Will Help You Grasp Topics Quickly

Flash Review is an excellent study tool to help you learn your assigned topic quickly and easily. It is also an effective tool to use when preparing for exams. I'll never forget when I was assigned to do a report on Shakespeare's classic work *The Taming of the Shrew*. I read the first twenty pages and was completely lost. I kept trying to follow the story, but it was useless—I just wasn't getting it.

Finally, I decided to talk to the teacher's assistant, and he suggested that I buy a study guide similar to *Flash Review*. After reading the first few pages, the mystery unfolded, and I finally understood what the story was about. I went on to get an A in that class. After that experience, I purchased a study guide for every topic my classes covered.

Using *Flash Review* will help you grasp difficult and complex topics in record time. It will make you more productive, and when used in conjunction with your regular reading and homework assignments, it will help you master the material you are studying.

Flash Review has also developed a companion Web site that will dramatically improve your comprehension of the materials and shave time off your learning curve. The *Flash Review* Online Study Center (*http://www.flashreview.com*) is a fully interactive learning environment that allows you to take practice quizzes. It provides immediate feedback, enabling you to use your time wisely. Interactive quizzes are only one example of what the *Flash Review* Online Study Center offers to help you learn the material and become a top student. I urge you to visit Flashreview.com and start benefiting from its rich set of interactive learning tools.

I wish you success in your academic endeavors.

David Frey
Author, *Make Straight A's in School: 50 Proven Secrets for Making the Grade!*

INTRODUCTION

How to Use *Flash Review for English Grammar*

This book has four main sections to help you succeed in your grammar course. They are:

1. **Exploring English Grammar**—a basic overview of grammar along with material to help you build your grammar confidence. This section also shows you how good grammar skills can help you succeed in college, on the job, and in everyday life.

2. **Your English Grammar Course and You**—a section filled with tips designed to help you succeed in your grammar course.

3. **Flash Web Links for English Grammar**—a section that features Internet resources to help you master grammar skills.

4. **Grammar Review**—five units of grammar-related content that features basic guidelines, examples, and practice exercises to improve your grammar skills.

In addition, non-native speakers of English will find several sections—marked with ESL icons—that focus on their special needs.

Who Uses *Flash Review for English Grammar?*

This book is for all students taking courses that focus on grammar. You can also use this book for writing courses such as: freshman composition, expository writing, paragraph writing, essay writing, and ESL classes. Students will find it useful on its own, in conjunction with instructors' assigned texts or customized texts, and in distance learning courses.

What Grammar Review Is Provided?

The section **"Grammar Review,"** offers five units of study divided into short subsections that cover basic grammar, punctuation and mechanics, word choice, and a brief subsection on writing paragraphs. Clear and easy-to-follow guidelines, examples, and practice exercises are provided for most sections of the book. With some variation in sequence, the content and progression of sections generally match the way most grammar-focused courses are taught.

Throughout this book, you will find the following helpful resources:

 **Flash Focus**   Unit objectives and list of core concepts

Flash Summary   Clear and concise overview of key topics

 Flash Test   Practice questions with multiple-choice or fill-in answers. Answers are included at the end of the section. For more quiz practice visit the Flash Review Online Study Center at http://www.flashreview.com

What *Flash Review for English Grammar* Can Do for You

Now you are ready to begin the next section, which looks at grammar—and your relationship to it—in more depth. In closing this introduction, we urge you to consider that using this book should enable you to:

✓ Impress your instructor favorably.
✓ Participate intelligently in class.
✓ Take better class notes.
✓ Work productively with classmates.
✓ Organize and study effectively.
✓ Ace your exams.
✓ Find what you need on the Internet.
✓ Write your research paper painlessly and well.
✓ Acquire meaningful new knowledge that you can use in your life.
✓ Get a better grade.

EXPLORING ENGLISH GRAMMAR

Grammar: What It Is and How It Works

Grammar is a set of rules and guidelines for effective writing. We use grammar throughout our daily lives—to write a college term paper, business memo, e-mail to a friend, or note to a neighbor. However, you'll need to do more than just memorize a set of grammar rules and guidelines. You'll also need to:

✓ Understand and identify the parts of speech and know when and where to apply them.

✓ Write clear, complete sentences that express your thoughts and ideas.

✓ Understand when and how to use capitalization and punctuation.

In a nutshell, you need to learn how to make grammar work for you, and this book can show you how to accomplish that goal.

Getting Over Your Fear of Grammar

Does the word "grammar" strike fear in your heart? Do you break out into a cold sweat when you have to write a term paper, a letter of application for a job, or an e-mail to a college professor about an assignment? These are just a few common grammar fears. In fact, most people have some degree of fear about grammar. However, you don't have to let fear hold you back from understanding and mastering grammar. Here are a few do's and don'ts to keep in mind:

DO:	Relax. Take your time and enjoy getting to know how grammar works.	**DON'T:**	Try and memorize each of the grammar rules and guidelines in one or two sittings. The rules will have more meaning if you understand them within context.
DO:	Work through the practice exercises that end most subunits.	**DON'T:**	Skip over the practice exercises. They will help build your overall grammar skills and make you more comfortable with applying them in your writing.
DO:	Ask questions in class.	**DON'T:**	Be afraid that your questions are "dumb." Odds are that some of your classmates have the same questions.
DO:	Read as much as you can—newspapers, magazines, textbooks, novels, etc.	**DON'T:**	Rush. Take your time when you read so that you can see how grammar works in writing and to reinforce the skills that you are learning in class.
DO:	Let go of any concerns about making mistakes—it's the only way you'll learn.	**DON'T:**	Be hard on yourself when you make a mistake.

How Grammar Can Help You Succeed in School, at Work, and in Life

Like it or not, good grammar skills will help you succeed throughout your college career, at work, and in your everyday life.

Using Grammar in College Writing

The ability to write clear, complete sentences that are grammatically correct is essential in college writing. Consider, for example, all of the work that goes into preparing a term paper. You may spend hours in the library and on the Internet researching a topic and have clear ideas about what you want to say about that topic. However, if your paper isn't grammatically correct, your ideas could seem meaningless and all the time you spent conducting research could go right down the drain. In the end, all you'll have for your hard work is a low grade.

Using Grammar on the Job

One of the most valuable skills in the work world is the ability to write well. Most jobs require some form of writing—a twenty-page proposal on a new computer system, a few paragraphs describing your thoughts on ways to make your division more profitable, a letter to your boss requesting a pay increase, or an e-mail to a colleague about meeting after work. In fact, your ability to write well on the job can affect whether you'll get a promotion, a pay increase, or credit for an idea you have proposed.

Using Grammar in your Everyday Life

A mastery of grammar skills is also important in your everyday life. You may not be aware of it, but you are constantly writing—a letter to a company about a defective product you received, a note to your parents asking for more money for school, an e-mail to a friend you haven't seen in a long time, a note on the refrigerator telling your kids to clean up their rooms, etc. Understanding the rules of grammar and how to apply them can make writing in your personal life more effective by allowing you to write clear sentences that express how you feel.

Glossary of Grammatical Terms

Action Verb: A verb that tells what the subject *does, did,* or *will do.*

Adjective: An adjective modifies a noun (or occasionally a pronoun).

Adverb: An adverb usually modifies a verb. It describes *how, when, where, or to what degree* the action of a verb is done.

Antecedent: The noun that a pronoun stands for is called the antecedent of that pronoun.

Auxiliary (Helping) Verbs: Verbs that convey some condition of the main verb, such as tense or mood.

Compound Sentence: A sentence that has two or more independent clauses.

Complex Sentence: A sentence that has one independent clause and one or more dependent clauses.

Conjunction: A conjunction joins other words or word groups. There are two kinds of conjunctions: a coordinating conjunction and a subordinating conjunction.

Conjunctive Adverb: An adverb used as a conjunction. For example: *however, thus,* and *therefore.*

Coordinating Conjunction: A conjunction (*and, but, or, nor, for, yet, so*) that joins words or word groups of the same kind or same importance.

Clause: A group of related words containing a subject and a verb.

Demonstrative Pronoun: A pronoun that specifies a particular referent: *this* is the page; take any one of *these; that* is her office.

Dangling Modifier: A modifier (usually a phrase) "dangles" when there is no word in the sentence to which it can logically or grammatically refer.

Dependent Clause: A clause that, although containing a subject and verb, cannot stand alone grammatically.

Direct Object: A noun (or pronoun) that tells *whom* or *what* after an action verb.

Independent Clause: A clause that sounds complete and makes sense when it stands alone.

Indirect Object: A noun (or pronoun) that appears after certain action verbs that tells *to* or *for whom* or *to* or *for what* the action of the verb is done.

Intransitive Verb: A verb that does not need a direct object to complete its meaning. It expresses an action that does not have a receiver: the meeting *adjourned;* the chairperson *stayed* after the meeting.

Linking Verb (State-of-Being, Copulative): A verb that expresses no action at all. It merely expresses state of being; it indicates a link of identity or description between the subject and the subjective complement following the verb: Borneo *is* an island; her cousin *became* a minister.

Noun: A word that names a person, place, or thing (including a quality or an idea).

Objective Complement: A noun that follows a direct object and renames or explains it.

Preposition: A connecting word such as *in, on, of, for,* or *into* that shows how a noun is related to the sentence containing it: the plane flew *into* the clouds.

Pronoun: A word that takes the place of (stands for) a noun.

Simple Sentence: A sentence with one independent clause.

Subject: The part of a sentence that names the person or thing the sentence refers to.

Subjective Complement (also called a *predicate nominative*): A noun (or pronoun) that follows a linking verb and renames or explains the subject.

Subordinating Conjunction: A conjunction (*if, because, although, when, unless,* etc.) that joins a dependent (subordinate) clause to an independent (main) clause.

Transitive Verb: A verb that needs a direct object to complete its meaning: red lights *stop* traffic; Dr. Hourani *removed* the tumor.

Verb: A verb asserts something about the subject of a sentence.

YOUR ENGLISH GRAMMAR COURSE AND YOU

Making the Most of Your Grammar Course

Prepare Yourself for What's Ahead

In order to get off to a strong start in your grammar course, follow these steps and ask these questions:

Find out what the course objectives are. What are you expected to learn in the course?

Find out how the course will be organized. How will your instructor structure the course? What portions will be lecture, conferences, discussion, etc.?

Find out how you will be tested. What kinds of exams, quizzes, and assignments will you receive? When are tests scheduled? When are assignments due? What are the penalties for turning in late assignments? Can you take a make-up exam if necessary?

Find out how your instructor will determine your grade. How much do tests, attendance, class participation, and extra credit work count?

Find out when your instructor is available outside of class. What are your instructor's office hours? What is his/her telephone number and e-mail address?

Examine the syllabus for your course. What is the schedule for assignments and tests? What kinds of materials (textbooks, dictionary, thesaurus, etc.) will you need for the course?

Get to know your classmates. Who would you feel comfortable working/studying with?

Get to know your campus resources. Is there a writing center that provides tutorial assistance? Is there a computer lab available for student use? Where is the library and what are its hours of operation?

Throughout your grammar course, ask yourself the following questions:

✓ Do I understand the course content? If not, am I asking my professor for extra help?

✓ Am I getting more comfortable with my writing skills? If not, am I paying attention in class and doing the practice assignments?

✓ Am I staying actively involved in class? Am I asking questions? Am I working with my classmates?

✓ Am I taking advantage of my campus resources? Have I visited the writing lab and/ or computer lab?

Take Notes

You will cover a lot of ground in your grammar course, so it will be important that you develop good note-taking skills. Here are a few strategies to follow:

1. Preview your class assignments so that you know ahead of time what your instructor will cover in class.

2. Create a shorthand system that allows you to keep up with the instructor during lectures. Abbreviate words if the instructor goes too fast, then go back and fill in the blanks. If you are still missing information, ask your instructor or a classmate to fill in the blanks.

3. Ask the instructor to repeat information if you did not have a chance to copy down everything.

4. Summarize the main points of the class lecture. Your instructor will communicate the main points of a lecture in a number of ways, for example, by:

   Writing on the chalkboard

   Listing and numbering key points

   A change in voice or rate of speech

   A direct announcement ("A noun is....")

5. Copy down examples so that you can refer back to them in your writing.

6. Review and edit your notes after class. (See the next section on using a computer to store class notes.)

Keep a Computerized Notebook

Create a separate file for your grammar course. Transfer your class notes into your file as soon as you can after each class. This process automatically contributes to your learning the information.

As you transfer your notes, edit and reorganize them in terms of the following questions:

✓ How can I use this information?

✓ How does this information fit in with previous lectures?

✓ How does this information fit in with the reading assignment?

✓ What does this all mean? How can I summarize it?

✓ What additional information do I need? What don't I understand?

✓ Use the highlighter function or an icon from clip art to mark notes you find difficult to grasp and questions you have.

✓ Develop your own system, such as bolding or italicizing or bulleting, to identify main points, definitions, and examples.

✓ Save your work to disk. Print out a copy of your notes and take them to class so that you can refer to them during the next lecture.

✓ Use the cut and paste function to integrate text notes with lecture notes.

Highlight and Mark Your Textbook

Highlighting and marking your textbook will help you to:

✓ Refer to key terms and examples.

✓ Stay focused during class.

✓ Remember what you have read.

Here are a few strategies for highlighting a textbook:

✓ First, read the material in a particular section, then go back and highlight the most important information. Pay attention to terms/concepts that are in boldface.

✓ After reading the section, go back and highlight the parts of the section that express the main ideas or important points to remember.

✓ Highlight just the right amount of information so that the main terms, explanations, and examples are clear to you. If you highlight too much, you won't be able to easily see the most important information of the section. You'll also miss important information if you highlight too little.

Here are a few strategies for marking a textbook:

✓ Circle terms, definitions, and examples that you don't understand. Next to the circled item (or in the margin) place a "?". You can discuss this material with your instructor or a classmate.

✓ Mark items that may appear on a test.

✓ Draw arrows to show the relationship between different concepts, terms, and examples.

Prepare for Exams

Taking exams can be extremely stressful for college students; however, it doesn't have to be. If you take time to prepare for an exam, you will see that your stress level will be reduced.

Here a few strategies for preparing for exams:

✓ Get organized. Plan and schedule the time you'll need to effectively study the material on the exam. It's best if you start your review at least a week before the exam (maybe more, if you are having difficulty grasping the material).

✓ Identify what will be covered on the exam. To find out what material will be covered, you should review all textbook chapters that have been assigned; lecture notes, exams, and quizzes; classroom handouts; and outside assignments. Also talk to your instructor and classmates about what would most likely be covered in the exam.

✓ Develop methods for learning the material. Refer to your notes, to material in your book that you have highlighted and/or marked, prepare index cards with important concepts, etc.

Here are a few strategies for taking exams:

Be prepared. Bring the necessary materials to class, arrive on time, do a quick review of the exam and familiarize yourself with what it contains, and plan the time you'll need to devote to the various sections of the exam.

Read the directions. Be sure you are clear about what is being asked of you. If you have questions, ask your instructor to explain the directions.

Stay calm. Test anxiety is natural; however, it can affect how you perform. To alleviate anxiety, be sure that you are prepared for the exam. Become familiar with the testing location, conditions, and time allotment. Think positively, and take time to compose yourself before taking the exam. Also, start with the questions that you feel most comfortable answering; this will boost your confidence.

Mapping *Flash Review for English Grammar* to Other Grammar-Focused Texts

A set of tables that map the sections contained in **Flash Review for English Grammar** to similar sections of five commonly used grammar-focused texts are provided on the next pages. (There are, however, many other grammar-focused texts that can also be mapped to **Flash Review for English Grammar**.) The five textbooks presented here are:

Choy et al., **Basic Grammar and Usage,** **Fifth Edition**

Fawcett and Sandberg, **Grassroots,** **Seventh Edition**

Langan and Goldstein, **English Brushup,** **Second Edition**

Langan, **Sentence Skills,** **Sixth Edition**

Winkler and McCuen, **Grammar Talk**

Flash Review for English Grammar	Choy et al., *Basic Grammar and Usage*
Unit I: Sentences and Grammar	
1–3. The Sentence and Its Parts	Ch. 1—Sentences with One Subject and One Verb
4–9. The Parts of Speech: A Survey	Unit 1—Identifying Subjects and Verbs (all four chapters in unit)
10–11. Using Nouns	Ch. 1—Sentences with One Subject and One Verb
12–15. Using Verbs	Ch. 1—Sentences with One Subject and One Verb; Ch. 4—Main Verbs and Helping Verbs; Ch. 25—Irregular Verbs
16–17. Using Adjectives and Adverbs	Ch. 1—Sentences with One Subject and One Verb
18–20. Using Pronouns	Ch. 1—Sentences with One Subject and One Verb; Unit 5—Pronoun Usage (all four chapters in unit)
21–22. Recognizing Phrases and Clauses	Ch. 9—Compound Sentences; Ch. 10—Complex and Compound-Complex Sentences; Ch. 15—Restrictive and Nonrestrictive Clauses
23–24. Agreement	Unit 2—Subject-Verb Agreement (all four chapters in unit)
25–27. Effective Sentences	Unit 3—Identifying and Punctuating the Main Types of Sentences (all four chapters in unit); Ch. 23—Misplaced and Dangling Modifiers; Ch. 24—Parallel Structure
Unit II: Punctuation	
28–30. The Comma [,]	Unit 3—Identifying and Punctuating the Main Types of Sentences (all four chapters in unit); Unit 4—Punctuation that "Sets Off" or Separates (all four chapters in unit)

31–32. The Period [.]	Ch. 11—Avoiding Run-On Sentences and Comma Splices; Ch. 12—Correcting Fragments
33–34. The Question Mark [?]	_____
35–36. The Exclamation Point [!]	_____
37. The Semicolon [;]	Ch. 9—Compound Sentences; Ch. 11—Avoiding Run-On Sentences and Comma Splices
38–40. The Apostrophe [']	Ch. 22—More Punctuation
41. Italics (Underlining)	Ch. 22—More Punctuation
42–46. Quotation Marks [""]	Ch. 22—More Punctuation
47–48. The Colon [:]	Ch. 22—More Punctuation
49. The Dash [—]	Ch. 22—More Punctuation
50–51. Parentheses [()]	_____
52. Brackets [[]]	_____
53. The Hyphen [-]	_____
54. The Slash (Virgule) [/]	_____
Unit III: Mechanics and Spelling	
55. Manuscript Form	_____
56–58. Capitalization	Ch. 21—Capitalization
59. Syllabication	_____
60–62. Numbers	_____
63–64. Abbreviations	_____
65–69. Spelling	_____
Unit IV: Word Choice	
70–73. Word Choice	_____
Unit V: Paragraphs	
74–75. Paragraphs	_____

Flash Review for English Grammar	Fawcett/Sandberg, *Grassroots*, 7e
Unit I: Sentences and Grammar	
1–3. The Sentence and Its Parts	Ch. 6—Subjects & Verbs
4–9. The Parts of Speech: A Survey	Ch. 6—Subjects & Verbs; Ch. 20—Nouns; Ch. 21—Pronouns; Ch. 22—Adjectives and Adverbs; Ch. 23—Prepositions (and check index)
10–11. Using Nouns	Ch. 20—Nouns
12–15. Using Verbs	Ch. 6—Subjects & Verbs; Ch. 7—Avoiding Sentence Fragments; Unit 3—Using Verbs Effectively (all five chapters in unit)
16–17. Using Adjectives and Adverbs	Ch. 17—Conjunctive Adverbs; Ch. 22—Adjectives and Adverbs
18–20. Using Pronouns	Ch. 18—Relative Pronouns; Ch. 21—Pronouns
21–22. Recognizing Phrases and Clauses	————————
23–24. Agreement	Ch. 8—Present Tense (Agreement)
25–27. Effective Sentences	Ch. 7—Avoiding Sentence Fragments; Ch. 13—Coordination; Ch. 14—Subordination; Ch. 15—Avoiding Run-Ons and Comma Splices; Unit 6—Revising for Consistency and Parallelism (all three chapters in unit)
Unit II: Punctuation	
28–30. The Comma [,]	Ch. 28—Commas
31–32. The Period [.]	Ch. 30—Direct and Indirect Quotations
33–34. The Question Mark [?]	Ch. 30—Direct and Indirect Quotations
35–36. The Exclamation Point [!]	Ch. 30—Direct and Indirect Quotations
37. The Semicolon [;]	Ch. 16—Semicolons
38–40. The Apostrophe [']	Ch. 29—Apostrophes
41. Italics (Underlining)	————————
42–46. Quotation Marks [""]	Ch. 30—Direct and Indirect Quotations
47–48. The Colon [:]	————————
49. The Dash [—]	————————
50–51. Parentheses [()]	————————

52. Brackets [[]]	_____
53. The Hyphen [-]	_____
54. The Slash Virgule [/]	_____
Unit III: Mechanics and Spelling	
55. Manuscript Form	Ch. 1 (Part C—Guidelines for Submitting Written Work)
56–58. Capitalization	Ch. 27—Capitalization
59. Syllabication	_____
60–62. Numbers	_____
63–64. Abbreviations	_____
65–69. Spelling	Ch. 31—Spelling
Unit IV: Word Choice	
70–73. Word Choice	_____
Unit V: Paragraphs	
74–75. Paragraphs	Ch. 3—Developing Effective Paragraphs; Ch. 4—Improving Your Paragraphs; Ch. 5—Moving from Paragraph to Essay

Flash Review for English Grammar	**Langan/Goldstein,** *English Brushup,* **2e**
Unit I: Sentences and Grammar	
1–3. The Sentence and Its Parts	Ch. 1—Subjects and Verbs
4–9. The Parts of Speech: A Survey	Ch. 1—Subjects and Verbs; Ch. 2—More About Verbs; Ch. 4—Sentence Types; Ch. 20—Adjectives and Adverbs; Ch. 23—More About Subjects and Verbs
10–11. Using Nouns	Ch. 1—Subjects and Verbs; Ch. 23—More About Subjects and Verbs
12–15. Using Verbs	Ch. 1—Subjects and Verbs; Ch. 2—More About Verbs; Ch. 23—More About Subjects and Verbs; Ch. 24—Even More About Verbs
16–17. Using Adjectives and Adverbs	Ch. 20—Adjectives and Adverbs
18–20. Using Pronouns	Ch. 7—Pronouns; Ch. 19—Pronoun Types

21–22. Recognizing Phrases and Clauses	Ch. 4—Sentence Types
23–24. Agreement	Ch. 3—Subject-Verb Agreement; Ch. 25—More about Subject-Verb Agreement
25–27. Effective Sentences	Ch. 4—Sentence Types; Ch. 5—Fragments; Ch. 6—Run-Ons
Unit II: Punctuation	
28–30. The Comma [,]	Ch. 8—Comma; Ch. 27—More About the Comma
31–32. The Period [.]	Ch. 11—Other Punctuation Marks
33–34. The Question Mark [?]	Ch. 11—Other Punctuation Marks
35–36. The Exclamation Point [!]	Ch. 11—Other Punctuation Marks
37. The Semicolon [;]	Ch. 11—Other Punctuation Marks; Ch. 30—More About Punctuation Marks
38–40. The Apostrophe [']	Ch. 9—Apostrophe; Ch. 28—More About the Apostrophe
41. Italics (Underlining)	Ch. 30—More About Punctuation Marks
42–46. Quotation Marks [""]	Ch. 10—Quotation Marks; Ch. 29—More About Quotation Marks
47–48. The Colon [:]	Ch. 11—Other Punctuation Marks
49. The Dash [—]	Ch. 11—Other Punctuation Marks; Ch. 30—More About Punctuation Marks
50–51. Parentheses [()]	Ch. 11—Other Punctuation Marks; Ch. 30—More About Punctuation Marks
52. Brackets [[]]	————————
53. The Hyphen [-]	Ch. 11—Other Punctuation Marks; Ch. 30—More About Punctuation Marks
54. The Slash (Virgule) [/]	————————
Unit III: Mechanics and Spelling	
55. Manuscript Form	Ch. 17—Paper Form
56–58. Capitalization	Ch. 13—Capital Letters; Ch. 32—More About Capital Letters
59. Syllabication	————————
60–62. Numbers	Ch. 21—Numbers and Abbreviations

63–64. Abbreviations	Ch. 21—Numbers and Abbreviations
65–69. Spelling	Ch. 18—Spelling
Unit IV: Word Choice	
70–73. Word Choice	Ch. 14—Word Choice; Ch. 33—More About Word Choice
Unit V: Paragraphs	
74–75. Paragraphs	—————————

Flash Review for English Grammar	Langan, *Sentence Skills,* 6e
Unit I: Sentences and Grammar	
1–3. The Sentence and Its Parts	Part 2, Section 1 (Subjects & Verbs)
4–9. The Parts of Speech: A Survey	Part 2, Section 1 (Subjects & Verbs) (Adjectives & Adverbs) also see index.
10–11. Using Nouns	Part 2, Section 1 (Subjects & Verbs)
12–15. Using Verbs	Part 2, Section 1 (Standard English Verbs), (Irregular Verbs), (Consistent Verb Tense), (Additional Information about Verbs)
16–17. Using Adjectives and Adverbs	Part 2, Section 1 (Adjectives & Adverbs)
18–20. Using Pronouns	Part 2, Section 1 (Pronoun Reference, Agreement, and Point of View), (Pronoun Types)
21–22. Recognizing Phrases and Clauses	Part 4 (Four Traditional Sentence Patterns), (Other Patterns That Add Variety to Writing)
23–24. Agreement	Part 2, Section 1 (Subject-Verb Agreement)
25–27. Effective Sentences	Part 4, (Four Traditional Sentence Patterns); Part 2, Section 1 (Fragments), (Run-Ons)
Unit II: Punctuation	
28–30. The Comma [,]	Part 2, Section 3 (Comma)
31–32. The Period [.]	Part 2, Section 3 (End Marks)
33–34. The Question Mark [?]	Part 2, Section 3 (End Marks)
35–36. The Exclamation Point [!]	Part 2, Section 3 (End Marks)
37. The Semicolon [;]	Part 2, Section 3 (Other Punctuation Marks)

38–40. The Apostrophe [']	Part 2, Section 3 (Apostrophe)
41. Italics (Underlining)	_____
42–46. Quotation Marks [""]	Part 2, Section 3, (Quotation Marks)
47–48. The Colon [:]	Part 2, Section 3, (Other Punctuation Marks)
49. The Dash [—]	Part 2, Section 3, (Other Punctuation Marks)
50–51. Parentheses [()]	Part 2, Section 3 (Other Punctuation Marks)
52. Brackets [[]]	_____
53. The Hyphen [-]	Part 2, Section 3 (Other Punctuation Marks)
54. The Slash (Virgule) [/]	_____
Unit III: Mechanics and Spelling	
55. Manuscript Form	Part 2, Section 2 (Paper Format)
56–58. Capitalization	Part 2, Section 2 (Capital Letters)
59. Syllabication	_____
60–62. Numbers	Part 2, Section 2 (Numbers and Abbreviations)
63–64. Abbreviations	Part 2, Section 2 (Numbers and Abbreviations)
65–69. Spelling	Part 2, Section 4 (Spelling Improvement)
Unit IV: Word Choice	
70–73. Word Choice	Part 2, Section 4 (Effective Word Choice)
Unit V: Paragraphs	
74–75. Paragraphs	Part 1, Effective Writing

Flash Review for English Grammar	**Winkler/McCuen, *Grammar Talk***
Unit I: Sentences and Grammar	
1–3. The Sentence and Its Parts	Unit 1—The Basic Sentence
4–9. The Parts of Speech: A Survey	Unit 1—The Basic Sentence Unit 4—Verbs—An Overview Unit 8—Using Pronouns Correctly Unit 10—Distinguishing Between Adjectives & Adverbs

10–11. Using Nouns	Unit 1—The Basic Sentence Unit 2—Building Sentences
12–15. Using Verbs	Unit 4—Verbs—An Overview Unit 5—Regular and Irregular Verbs Unit 7—Problems with Verbs
16–17. Using Adjectives and Adverbs	Unit 10—Distinguishing Between Adjectives & Adverbs
18–20. Using Pronouns	Unit 8—Using Pronouns Correctly Unit 9—Pronoun Problems
21–22. Recognizing Phrases and Clauses	Unit 2—Building Sentences
23–24. Agreement	Unit 6—Subject-Verb Agreement
25–27. Effective Sentences	Unit 2—Building Sentences Unit 3—Avoiding Non-Sentences
Unit II: Punctuation	
28–30. The Comma [,]	Unit 13—Punctuation You Can Hear
31–32. The Period [.]	Unit 13—Punctuation You Can Hear
33–34. The Question Mark [?]	Unit 13—Punctuation You Can Hear
35–36. The Exclamation Point [!]	Unit 13—Punctuation You Can Hear
37. The Semicolon [;]	Unit 14—Punctuation You Can't Hear
38–40. The Apostrophe [']	Unit 13—Punctuation You Can Hear
41. Italics (Underlining)	_____
42–46. Quotation Marks [""]	Unit 14—Punctuation You Can't Hear
47–48. The Colon [:]	Unit 14—Punctuation You Can't Hear
49. The Dash [—]	Unit 14—Punctuation You Can't Hear
50–51. Parentheses [()]	Unit 14—Punctuation You Can't Hear
52. Brackets [[]]	_____
53. The Hyphen [-]	_____
54. The Slash Virgule [/]	_____
Unit III: Mechanics and Spelling	
55. Manuscript Form	_____

56–58. Capitalization	_____
59. Syllabication	_____
60–62. Numbers	_____
63–64. Abbreviations	_____
65–69. Spelling	_____
Unit IV: Word Choice	
70–73. Word Choice	_____
Unit V: Paragraphs	
74–75. Paragraphs	_____

FLASH WEB LINKS FOR ENGLISH GRAMMAR

Listed below are general online resources to help you throughout your grammar and writing courses. Use links at these sites to find additional information; be sure to bookmark or record your finds. Keep in mind that URLs frequently change or disappear. If you can't find a site, use a search engine to look for it by name.

Purdue Online Writing Lab (OWL)

http://owl.english.purdue.edu/

 Visit this site for a complete list of resources, handouts, and exercises about grammar and editing. The site also offers grammar advice for ESL writers.

Grammar Now

http://grammarnow.com/
At this web site, you can ask grammar-related questions.

Good Grammar, Good Style

www.protrainco.com/info/noframes/grammar.htm
This is another web site where you can ask grammar-related questions.

Pop-Up Grammar

http://www.brownlee.org/durk/grammar/
Pop-Up Grammar is an online testing, instruction, and assessment site. To test your grammar skills, take several interactive grammar quizzes. The site will then evaluate your strengths and weaknesses.

Common Grammatical Errors

http://www.wisc.edu/writetest/Handbook/CommonErrors.html
This site contains a checklist that covers common grammatical problems, including comma splices.

Sentence Review

http://owl.english.purdue.edu/handouts/index2.html
This web site offers a comprehensive overview of the parts of speech and sentence construction.

Sentence Structure

http://www.uottawa.ca/academic/arts/writcent/hypergrammar/bldsent.html
This site covers sentence structure and options and also includes review exercises.

How to Write Clear Sentences

http://www.wisc.edu/writetest/Handbook/ClearConciseSentences.html
This site offers guidance on writing clear, concise sentences.

What is a Sentence Fragment?

http://info2.harper.cc.il.us/writ_ctr/fragmnt.htm
This web site includes examples, suggestions, and links to two simple tests for detecting sentence fragments.

Using Adjectives

http://www.edunet.com/english/grammar/adjectiv.html
This site offers a discussion of adjectives, and other grammatical terms.

Using Adverbs

http://www.edunet.com/english/grammar/adverbs.html
This site offers a discussion of adverbs, and other grammatical terms.

Dictionary Online

http://www.m-w.com/dictionary.htm
This site offers a free, online dictionary.

Roget's Online Thesaurus

http://www.thesaurus.com
This web site offers the entire *Roget's Thesaurus* online.

A Word A Day

http://www.wordsmith.org/awad/
This web site helps you build your vocabulary by sending you a new vocabulary word every day.

Punctuation Made Simple

http://chuma.cas.usf.edu/~olson/pms/
This web site offers a comprehensive overview of punctuation.

End Punctuation

http://www.uottawa.ca/academic/arts/writcent/hypergrammar/endpunct.html
This web site offers guidance on punctuation that ends sentences.

When to Use—and Not to Use—Quotation Marks

http://www.wilbers.com/quotes.htm
This web site offers rules and instructions for using quotation marks.

Mindy McAdams' Spelling Test

http://www.sentex.net/~mmcadams/spelling.html
This interactive spelling test of fifty of the most commonly misspelled words in American English will tabulate your score automatically. The site also offers advice on ways to become a better speller and some words of encouragement for those who find spelling to be a challenge.

Overcoming Hyphenphobia

http://www.superconnect.com/wordsmit/hyphens.htm
This web site offers practical advice on how to use hyphens as well as tips on writing and common error patterns.

Using Commas

http://owl.english.purdue.edu/writers/by-topic.html#Punctuation
This site presents a discussion of the primary uses of the comma. The site also contains proofreading strategies and exercises.

Using Pronouns

http://www.uottawa.ca/academic/arts/writcent/hypergrammar/pronouns.html
This web site provides a comprehensive overview of pronouns and their proper uses.

Using Semicolons

http://www.wisc.edu/writetest/Handbook/Semicolons.html
This site offers a guide to using semicolons.

Using Colons

http://www.uottawa.ca/academic/arts/writcent/hypergrammar/colon.html
This site offers guidance on using the colon.

Dangling Modifiers

http://stripe.colorado.edu/~cuwrite/dangtut.html
This web site offers a worksheet containing a simple three-step process for recognizing dangling modifiers as well as two options for fixing them.

Coordination/Subordination

http://students.itec.sfsu.edu/ised783/Writing/coord.html
This web site, from San Francisco State University, offers guidance on how to use coordination and subordination effectively in writing.

GRAMMAR REVIEW

UNIT I: SENTENCES AND GRAMMAR (SECTIONS 1–27)

 FLASH FOCUS

When you complete Unit I, you should be able to:

✓ Understand basic grammar concepts

✓ Understand the main parts of a sentence

✓ Create clear, correct, and effective sentences

> "Always write (and read) with the ear, not the eye. You should hear every sentence you write as if it was being read aloud or spoken."
> —C.S. Lewis

> "The maker of a sentence launches into the infinite and builds a road into chaos and old night, and is followed by those who hear him with something of wild, creative delight."
> —Ralph Waldo Emerson

 FLASH TEST

Before you begin studying the sections in Unit I, take the diagnostic tests on sentences and grammar to test your knowledge. If you answer eight or more questions incorrectly in either of the diagnostic tests, be sure to note where you need extra help or explanation, and pay close attention to those particular sections in Unit I.

DIAGNOSTIC TEST: SENTENCES

In the blank after each sentence,

Write **S** if the boldfaced expression is **one complete, correct sentence.**

Write **F** if it is a **fragment** (incorrect: less than a complete sentence).

Write **R** if it is a **run-on** (incorrect: two or more sentences written as one—also known as a **comma splice** or **fused sentence**).

EXAMPLE: The climbers suffered from hypothermia. **Having neglected to bring warm clothing.** ___F___

1. Calcium is the most abundant mineral in the body. **However, many Americans are not getting enough of it in their diets.** 1. _____

2. Stock prices rose slightly yesterday. **The Dow Jones average up 16.9 points and the NASDAQ index up 3.2.** 2. _____

3. **In Russia, pork is sold for 465 rubles a pound that amount is equivalent to the average monthly salary.** 3. _____

4. The Yankees made two big trades after the season had begun. **First for a shortstop and then for a center fielder.** 4. _____

5. The African American Society put Martina Jones in charge of the Multicultural Festival. **A responsibility that appealed to her.** 5. _____

6. **The boys are learning traditional Irish dancing, they really seem to enjoy their dance class.**   6. _____

7. The President eventually seemed happy to retire from politics. **His family looking forward to spending more time with him.**   7. _____

8. Although American society may seem uncaring, more people are volunteering to help with the homeless.   8. _____

9. **The reason for her shyness being that she knew no one at the party except her hostess.**   9. _____

10. **The experiment to produce nuclear fusion was both controversial and exciting, scientists all over the world attempted to duplicate its results.**   10. _____

11. **Scientists have learned that sick bison can infect livestock with a serious bacterial disease.**   11. _____

12. She loved all styles of art. **She said she particularly loved the impressionists, she had studied them in Paris.**   12. _____

13. We walked over to the lost-and-found office. **To see whether the bag had been turned in.**   13. _____

14. **The shift lever must be in neutral only then will the car start.**   14. _____

15. Buenos Aires, Argentina, is a lively city, the streets are safe at all times. Movie theaters stay open all night.   15. _____

16. **If you want an unusual form of exercise, learn to play the bagpipes.**   16. _____

DIAGNOSTIC TEST: GRAMMAR

In the blank,

> Write **C** if the boldfaced expression is used **correctly**.
>
> Write **X** if it is used **incorrectly**.

EXAMPLE: There **was** dozens of dinosaur bones on the site.   _____X_____

1. We need to keep this a secret between you and **I**.   1. _____

2. Bill was fired from his new job, **which** made him despondent.   2. _____

3. Each member will be responsible for **their** own transportation.   3. _____

4. There **was** at least five computers in the office.   4. _____

5. Several of **us** newcomers needed a map to find our way around.   5. _____

6. Every administrator and faculty member **was** required to attend the orientation program.   6. _____

7. The graduate teaching assistant and **myself** met for a review session.   7. _____

8. Surprisingly enough, presidential candidate Joan Smith was leading **not only** in the cities **but also** in the rural areas.   8. _____

9. In each sack lunch **were** a cheese sandwich, an apple, and a soda.   9. _____

10. Leave the message with **whoever** answers the phone.   10. _____

11. **Having made no other plans for the evening,** Tony was glad to accept the invitation.   11. _____

12. Everyone in the Hispanic Society **was** urged to join the movement to bring more Hispanic faculty to campus.   12. _____

13. If I **were** driving to Pennsylvania this weekend, I would take along my sketch pad.   13. _____

14. I bought one of the printers that **were** on sale.   14. _____

15. There **were** five different Asian student organizations on campus. 15. _____

16. The prosecutor demanded that the witness tell her **when did she hear the shot.** 16. _____

17. The director, as well as the choir members, **has** agreed to appear on television. 17. _____

18. The supervisor is especially fond of arranging training programs, working on elaborate projects, and **to develop budgets.** 18. _____

19. A faux pas **is when you commit a social blunder.** 19. _____

20. **Who** do you think mailed the anonymous letter to the editor? 20. _____

Answers to Diagnostic Test on Sentences

1. S	5. F	9. F	13. F
2. F	6. R	10. R	14. R
3. R	7. F	11. S	15. R
4. F	8. S	12. R	16. S

Answers to Diagnostic Test on Grammar

1. X	5. C	9. C	13. C	17. C
2. X	6. C	10. C	14. C	18. X
3. X	7. X	11. C	15. C	19. X
4. X	8. C	12. C	16. X	20. C

1–3 The Sentence and Its Parts

FLASH SUMMARY

The sentence is our basic unit of spoken or written thought. In writing, a sentence begins with a capital letter and ends with a period, question mark, or exclamation point. Every sentence consists of two essential parts, the **subject** and the **predicate.**

1. The Two Parts of a Sentence

A. **The Subject.** The subject part of a sentence (called the **complete subject**) names the person or thing the sentence refers to. That person or thing itself is called the **simple subject** (usually shortened to just **subject**). In the examples below, the complete subject is boxed, and the simple subject is in **bold print.**

A vicious **tornado** swept through the valley.

Three **friends** from high school rented a room in Houston.

American foreign **policy** toward Asia was a lively topic.

Frank Sinatra has left an indelible mark on popular music.

Note: Only the most common kind of sentence, the kind that *tells,* is shown here. In section 3A are sentences that *ask, command,* and *exclaim.* For simplicity, most sentence discussions in this book will deal with sentences that tell (declarative sentences).

B. **The Predicate.** The predicate part of a sentence (called the **complete predicate**) tells what the subject *does (did, will do)* or what or how the subject *is (was, will be).* The key word(s) in the predicate—the word(s) stating the actual doing or being—is called the **simple predicate,** or **verb.** In the examples below, the complete predicate is boxed and the simple predicate, or verb, is in **bold.**

A vicious tornado **swept** through the valley.

Three friends from high school **rented** a room in Houston.

American foreign policy toward Asia **was** a lively topic.

Frank Sinatra **has left** an indelible mark on popular music.

Some complete predicates contain **complements** (words needed to complete the verb's meaning):

Three friends rented a *room* . . .

American foreign policy . . . was a lively *topic*.

Frank Sinatra has left an indelible *mark* . . .

Subjects and complements are explained fully in section 11, page 34; verbs are explained in sections 12–15, pages 37–47.

Note: A subject, verb, or complement may be **compound;** that is, it may have two or more parts joined by *and, or,* or *but;*

SUBJECT   PREDICATE   COMPLEMENT

Poems and *stories delight* and *edify children, teenagers,* and *adults.*

2. The Sentence Pattern

Subject, verb, and **complement(s)** usually occur in a standard order or pattern: **S V (C) (C).** This means that the subject **[S]** comes first, then the verb **[V]**, then—perhaps— one or two complements **[C]**.

              S   V
The risky mission succeeded perfectly.

            S   V   C
Such rocks emit radiation.

         S   V   C   C
That noise from the street gave her a headache.

This normal order is altered in most questions (*What did they see?* [→*They did see what*]) and exclamations (*Such a fool I was!* [→*I was such a fool*]), and in sentences such as *Never had the company faced such losses* [→*The company had never faced such losses*] and *There were no seats left* [→*No seats were left*].

3. Ways of Classifying Sentences

A. By Purpose

DECLARATIVE (a statement): The day dawned clear.

INTERROGATIVE (a question): Did the day dawn clear?

IMPERATIVE (a command or request): Wake up and greet the day. [*You* is understood to be the subject.]

EXCLAMATORY (an expression of emotion, usually beginning with *how* or *what*): What a clear day this is! How far we can see!

B. By Structure, according to the number and kinds of clauses they contain. A sentence may be **simple, compound, complex,** or **compound–complex.** Section 22C, pages 72–73, explains these categories in detail.

FLASH TEST

PART 1

In the blank, write the number of the place where the **complete subject** ends and the **complete predicate** begins.

EXAMPLE: Immigrants (1) to the United States (2) have helped greatly (3) in building the country.   2

1. The Statue of Liberty (1) was restored (2) and reopened (3) in 1988.   1. _____

2. Many of the abandoned railroad stations (1) of America and Canada (2) have been restored (3) for other uses.   2. _____

3. The junction (1) of the Allegheny (2) and Monongahela rivers (3) creates (4) the Ohio River.   3. _____

4. The editor (1) wrote a kind note (2) after the long list of changes (3) to be made before final printing.   4. _____

5. The United States, (1) Mexico, (2) and Canada (3) now have (4) a free-trade agreement.   5. _____

6. I (1) recently completed (2) a twenty-page research paper (3) on the new common currency for European countries.   6. _____

7. Which (1) of the three word-processing software packages (2) has (3) the best thesaurus?   7. _____

8. Rarely would she drive her car after the earthquakes.
[This inverted-word-order sentence, rewritten in subject-predicate order, becomes: She (1) would rarely (2) drive (3) her car (4) after the earthquakes.]   8. _____

9. None (1) of the polls (2) shows Stanton (3) winning.   9. _____

10. When did the committee select the candidate for comptroller?
[Rewritten in subject–predicate order:
The committee (1) did select (2) the candidate (3) for comptroller when?]   10. _____

FLASH TEST

PART 2

Write **S** if the boldfaced word is a **subject** (simple subject or part of a compound subject).

Write **V** if it is a **verb** (simple predicate).

Write **C** if it is a **complement** (or part of a compound complement).

EXAMPLES:

Wendell played a superb game.   S

Wendell **played** a superb game.   V

Wendell played a superb **game.**   C

1. **All** perform their tragic play.   1. S

2. All perform their tragic **play.**   2. C

3. Champion athletes **spend** much time training and competing.   3. V

4. Champion athletes spend much **time** training and competing.   4. C

5. **Sue** and Janet enjoy gardening.   5. S

6. Sue and Janet enjoy **gardening.**   6. C

7. Many **athletes** worry about life after the pros. 7. _____ S

8. Many athletes **worry** about life after the pros. 8. _____ V

9. The populist **theme** from the last election may survive until the next election. 9. _____ S

10. The populist theme from the last election **may survive** until the next election. 10. _____ V

11. The **neighborhood** worked hard to clean up the local playground. 11. _____ S

12. The neighborhood **worked** hard to clean up the local playground. 12. _____ V

13. The clustered lights far below the plane were **cities.** 13. _____ C

FLASH TEST

PART 3

In each sentence, fill in the blank with a word of your own that makes sense. Then, in the blank at the right, tell whether it is a **subject** (write **S**), **verb** (write **V**), or **complement** (write **C**).

EXAMPLE: The builders needed a <u>ladder</u> for the new job. _____ C

1. Beautiful _____*flowers*_____ grow in our garden. 1. _____ S

2. We grow beautiful _____*roses*_____ in our garden. 2. _____ C

3. Cabbages, onions, and _____*radishes*_____ grow in our garden. 3. _____ S

4. Three students in English 101 _____*flunked*_____ their final examination. 4. _____ V

5. The instructor was a _____*fool*_____. 5. _____ C

6. With the ball on the ten-yard line, the crowd _____*roared*_____. 6. _____ V

7. Shaw wrote a _____*play*_____ about a speech professor and an un-educated young woman. 7. _____ C

8. The crisp, clear _____*drink*_____ refreshed us. 8. _____ S

9. Too many people in this country _____*are*_____ unconcerned about their health. 9. _____ V

10. Materials necessary for this course include a(n) _____*book*_____ and a calculator. 10. _____ C

Answers to Exercises for: The Sentence and Its Parts

Part 1

1. 1	**3.** 3	**5.** 3	**7.** 2	**9.** 2
2. 2	**4.** 1	**6.** 1	**8.** 1	**10.** 1

Part 2

1. S	**4.** C	**7.** S	**10.** V	**13.** C
2. C	**5.** S	**8.** V	**11.** S	
3. V	**6.** C	**9.** S	**12.** V	

Part 3
(Words will vary.)

1. roses	S	**5.** tyrant	C	**9.** remain	V
2. roses	C	**6.** cheered	V	**10.** protractor	C
3. beets	S	**7.** play	C		
4. failed	V	**8.** air	S		

4–9 The Parts of Speech: A Survey

FLASH SUMMARY

Every word performs one of five functions: *naming, expressing doing or being, modifying, connecting,* or *expressing emotion*. In traditional grammar, these functions are classified into eight **parts of speech**: *noun, pronoun, verb, adjective, adverb, preposition, conjunction,* and *interjection*.

4. Words That Name

A. Nouns. A noun is a word that names a person, place, or thing (including a quality or idea):

PERSON: woman, Sandra, poet, Sylvia Plath

PLACE: kitchen, city, park, Lincoln Park

THING: tree, ship, U.S.S. *Iowa,* cereal

QUALITY OR IDEA: love, height, democracy, motion

See sections 10–11, pages 33–35, for details about nouns.

B. Pronouns (*pro-* means "for" or "instead of"). As its name suggests, a pronoun takes the place of (stands for) a noun. The noun that a pronoun stands for is called the **antecedent** of that pronoun:

[antecedent in *italics;* pronoun in **bold**]

Rosa brought a friend with **her** to the rally.

If space *shuttles* cannot land in Florida, **they** land in California.

See sections 18–20, pages 61–66, for details about pronouns.

5. Words That Express Doing or Being: Verbs

A verb asserts something about the subject of a sentence. An **action verb** tells what the subject *does, did,* or *will do*. A **linking verb** tells that the subject *is, was,* or *will be* something.

ACTION: Hummingbirds *fly* up to sixty miles per hour. [tells what the subject, *Hummingbirds,* does]

LINKING: The hummingbird *is* nature's helicopter. [tells that the subject is something]

Some verbs consist of several words—a **main verb** preceded by one or more **auxiliary** (helping) **verbs:**

[auxiliary verbs in *italics;* main verb in **bold**]

Hummingbirds *will* **explore** almost anything red.

They *have* even *been* **attracted** to red ribbons.

The verb in a sentence is also called the **simple predicate.** See sections 12–15, pages 37–47, for details about verbs.

Note: Besides asserting (in a declarative or exclamatory sentence), a verb can also *ask* (in an interrogative sentence), or *command or request* (in an imperative sentence).

6. Words That Modify

To *modify* means "to change." A word that modifies changes or clarifies our concept of another word.

A. **Adjectives.** An adjective modifies a noun (or occasionally a pronoun). It describes that noun or limits its meaning. **Descriptive adjectives** tell *what kind: small* car (what kind of car?), *green* rug, *unimaginable* brutality, *odoriferous twenty-cent* cigar. **Limiting adjectives (determiners)** tell *which one* or *how many.* There are several kinds of limiting adjectives.

POSSESSIVE: *my* auto, *her* grades, *their* policy [which auto, grades, policy?]

DEMONSTRATIVE: *this* auto, *those* grades, *that* policy

INDEFINITE: *any* auto, *either* grade, *many* policies

INTERROGATIVE: *which* auto? *whose* grades? *what* policy?

NUMERICAL: *one* auto, *two* grades, *third* policy

ARTICLES: *an* auto, *the* grades, *a* policy

As these examples show, an adjective usually appears directly before the noun it modifies. A descriptive adjective can also appear after a linking verb (as a complement). Such an adjective describes the subject to which the verb links it:

     S   V   C

That song is *lively.* [*Lively* describes the subject, *song.*]

The statistics seemed *reliable.*

B. **Adverbs.** An adverb usually modifies a verb. It describes *how, when, where,* or *to what degree* the action of a verb is done. There are several kinds of adverbs:

MANNER: Pat dances *gracefully.* [dances how?]

TIME: Pat danced *yesterday.* [danced when?]

PLACE: Pat dances *everywhere.* [dances where?]

DEGREE: Pat dances *excessively.* [dances to what extent or degree?]

An adverb phrase or clause can also describe *why:* Pat dances *to keep in condition.* (Sections 21–22, pages 70–73, explain phrases and clauses.)

Some adverbs can modify an adjective or another adverb. Such adverbs are called **adverbs of degree** (or **intensifiers** or **qualifiers**):

Pat dances *quite* gracefully. [gracefully to what degree? how gracefully?] Pat prefers *very* fast music.

For **conjunctive adverbs,** see section 39B, page 131.

7. Words That Connect

A. **Conjunctions.** A conjunction joins other words or word groups. There are two kinds of conjunctions:

(1) A coordinating conjunction (*and, but, or, nor, for, yet, so*) joins words or word groups of the same kind and same importance:

WORDS: Eleanor *and* Franklin

WORD GROUPS (PHRASES): after their marriage *but* before his illness

WORD GROUPS (CLAUSES): Franklin stayed often at his Hyde Park estate, *but* Eleanor preferred her smaller house at Valkill.

Note: *And, but, or,* or *nor* may be used with other words to form a **correlative conjunction**—*not only . . . but also; (n)either . . . (n)or; both . . . and:*

Both Eleanor *and* Franklin disliked the senator.

Neither Eleanor *nor* Franklin spoke to him.

*(2) A **subordinating conjunction** (if, because, although, when, unless,* etc.) joins a dependent (subordinate) clause to an independent (main) clause. The subordinating conjunction begins the dependent clause: ***if** the heat continues;* ***because** repair crews arrived late and with insufficient equipment:*

The road may buckle *if the heat continues.*

If the heat continues, the road may buckle.

Traffic was delayed across much of the South Side *because repair crews arrived late and with insufficient equipment.*

Because repair crews arrived late and with insufficient equipment, traffic was delayed across much of the South Side.

Do not write a subordinate clause alone as if it were a sentence:

WRONG: The road may buckle. If the heat continues.

Section 26A, pages 90–91, discusses this serious error (a *fragment*).

Other common subordinating conjunctions are *after, as, as if, as soon as, as though, before, in order that, provided, since, so that, than, though, until, whenever, where, whereas, wherever, whether, while.* See section 22B(2), page 72.

Note: Other kinds of words that join clauses are **relative pronouns** (such as *who* or *which*—see section 18B(2), page 62) and **conjunctive adverbs** (such as *therefore* or *however*—see section 37B, page 127).

B. Prepositions. A preposition is a connecting word such as *in, on, of, for,* or *into* that shows how a noun is related to the sentence containing it:

The plane flew *over* the clouds.

The plane flew *into* the clouds.

The plane flew *through* the clouds.

Each preposition above shows a different relation between the noun *clouds* and the action of the sentence. Other common prepositions are:

about	beneath	instead of	since
above	beside	in addition to	through(out)
against	besides	in front of	to
among	between	like	toward
as	by	near	under
as well as	despite	next to	underneath
at	down	off	until
because of	during	onto	up
before	except	out (of)	upon
behind	from	outside	within
below	inside	past	without

The word group beginning with the preposition and ending with the noun is called a **prepositional phrase.** The noun (or pronoun) is called the **object of the preposition:**

[preposition in **bold**; object of preposition in *italics*]

behind her cheery *facade* **of** his *memories* **with** *us*

FLASH FOCUS

ESL *Prepositions of Time, Place, and Travel:*

	at	on	in
Time	a specific time: *at* 9:45, *at* noon	a day or date: *on* Monday, *on* May 5	a longer time: *in* a week, *in* two months, *in* 2005
Place	a particular spot: *at* home, *at* work, *at* the store, *at* 5th and Main, *at* the end	the top or surface of: *on* Main Street, *on* Mackinac Island	within an area: *in* jail, *in* her office, *in* Iowa, *in* China, *in* bed
Means of Travel		*on* a bike, *on* a bus, *on* a ship, *on* a plane	*in* a car, *in* a carriage, *in* a canoe

8. Words That Express Emotion: Interjections

Unlike the other kinds of words, the interjection has little or no grammatical connection with the rest of the sentence:

MILD INTERJECTION (punctuated with comma): *Oh,* I don't care. *Well,* Dr. Lopez might know.

STRONG INTERJECTION (punctuated with exclamation point): *Rats!* He's cheated us. *Wow!* It's snowing.

9. Words as More than One Part of Speech

The way a word is used in a particular sentence determines its part of speech in that sentence. To determine the part of speech of a word in a particular sentence, examine its grammatical use (**syntax**) in that sentence: If it names something, it is a noun; if it describes a noun, it is an adjective; and so forth:

NOUN: We could see the first *light* of dawn.

VERB: They would *light* signal fires that night.

ADJECTIVE: Wearing *light* colors enhances visibility.

Note: You can often determine a word's part of speech by its position or its ending. For example, a word following a limiting adjective (*a, my, this,* etc.) is likely to be a noun: *my* **brother,** *this* **test** (another adjective may intervene: *this* impossible **test**). A word following an auxiliary verb is likely to be a verb: *has* **grown,** *might have been* **saved** (an adverb may intervene: *has* hardly **grown**). Most words with an *-ly* ending are adverbs: *slowly, awkwardly;* words ending in *-tion, -ity, -ness, -ment, -hood,* or *-cy* are usually nouns; words ending in *-ify* or *-ize* are probably verbs; words ending in *-al, -ous, -ful,* or *-less* are probably adjectives.

FLASH TEST

PART 1

Write the **part of speech** of each boldfaced word (use the abbreviations in parentheses):

noun	adjective (adj)	preposition (prep)
pronoun (pro)	adverb (adv)	conjunction (conj)
verb		interjection (inter)

EXAMPLE: Shaw wrote many **plays**   **noun**

1. *Moby Dick* is a **novel**. — noun ①
2. You must **replace** the alternator. — verb ②
3. **She** anticipated the vote. — pro ③
4. The new law affected **all**. — pro ④
5. Robert felt **tired**. — ADJ ⑤
6. She was **here** a moment ago. — ADV ⑥
7. The **primary** goal is to reduce spending. — ADJ ⑦
8. The test was hard **but** fair. — conj ⑧
9. Do you want fries **with** that? — prep ⑨
10. **This** book is mine. — ADJ ⑩
11. **This** is the car to buy. *demonstrative* — pro ⑪
12. She lives **across** the street. — prep ⑫
13. Is this **your** book? — ADJ ⑬
14. The book is **mine**. — pronoun ⑭
15. He wants an **education**. *noun* — noun ⑮
16. **Wow**, what a shot that was! — Inter ⑯
17. He agreed to proceed **slowly**. — ADVERB ⑰
18. They **were sleeping** soundly at noon. — VERB ⑱
19. The candidate selected a **charismatic** running mate. *noun* — ADJ ⑲
20. She is **unusually** talented. — ADV ⑳

FLASH TEST

PART 2

In the first blank in each sentence, write a word of your own that **sounds right** and **makes sense**. Then, in the blank at the right, tell what **part of speech** your word is (use the abbreviations in parentheses):

noun	adjective (adj)	preposition (prep)
pronoun (pro)	adverb (adv)	conjunction (conj)
verb		interjection (inter)

EXAMPLE: The singer wore a <u>gaudy</u> jacket.   **adj**

1. The letter should arrive _soon_ .   1. _____

2. May I ___see___ you Friday?   **2.** _verb_

3. Every night, ___ugly___ monsters filled his dreams.   **3.** _adjective_

4. The weather was gray ___and___ miserable.   **4.** _conjunction_

5. Is ___this___ your locker?   **5.** _pronoun_

6. The _____ was deathly quiet.   **6.** _____

7. ___My___ vacation proved quite hazardous.   **7.** _adjective_

8. ___Damn___! I dropped my keys down the sewer.   **8.** _interjection_

9. Many _____ trees are threatened by acid rain.   **9.** _____

10. This plane goes ___to___ Cleveland.   **10.** _prep_

11. He is a real ___jerk___.   **11.** _noun_

12. ___Sit___ now.   **12.** _verb_

13. They put the motion to a vote, but ___it___ failed.   **13.** _pronoun_

14. Ms. Kostas ___is___ a registered pharmacist.   **14.** _verb_

15. The senator would ___gladly___ accept a bribe.   **15.** _adv_

16. Approach that pit bull dog ___very___ carefully.   **16.** _adv_

17. Arles is in France, ___but___ Aachen is in Germany.   **17.** _conjunction_

18. The jury found that she was _____.   **18.** _____

19. ___After___ he won the lottery, he was envied.   **19.** _conjunction_

20. ___Some___ of the runners collapsed from the heat.   **20.** _____

FLASH TEST

PART 3

In each blank, write the **correct** preposition: **at, in,** or **on.**
(In some blanks, either of two prepositions may be correct.)

EXAMPLE: Franko lives <u>in</u> an apartment <u>on</u> Broadway.

Fran Bradley, a retired banker, lived _on_ a pleasant street _in_ a small town _in_ the Midwest. Most mornings she awakened promptly _at_ six, except _on_ Sundays, when she slept until eight. Then she would ride to worship _in_ her 1987 Ford or _on_ her old three-speed bicycle. Often she was the first one _at_ her house of worship.

Answers to Exercises for: The Parts of Speech

Part 1

1. noun	**6.** adv	**11.** pro	**16.** inter
2. verb	**7.** adj	**12.** prep	**17.** adv
3. pro	**8.** conj	**13.** adj	**18.** verb
4. pro	**9.** prep	**14.** pro	**19.** adj
5. adj	**10.** adj	**15.** noun	**20.** adv

Part 2

(Words are samples)

1.	shortly	adv	11.	loser	noun
2.	call	verb	12.	begin	verb
3.	frightful	adj	13.	it	pro
4.	and	conj	14.	was	verb
5.	that	pro	15.	eagerly	adv
6.	house	noun	16.	very	adv
7.	my	adj	17.	but	conj
8.	rats!	inter	18.	guilty	adj
9.	deciduous	adj	19.	after	conj
10.	to	prep	20.	several [*or* four]	pronoun noun

Part 3

line 1   on . . . in . . . in . . .

line 2   at . . . on . . .

line 3   in . . . on . . .

line 4   at [*or* in] . . .

10–11 Using Nouns

FLASH SUMMARY

Recall that nouns name persons, places, or things.

10. The Kinds of Nouns

Nouns are classified in several ways:

A. **Singular or Plural.** A **singular** noun names one person, place, or thing: *woman, city, house, chair.* A **plural** noun names two or more persons, places, or things: *women, cities, houses, chairs.* Most singular nouns become plural by the addition of *-s.* See section 67, pages 169–170, for rules on the formation of plurals.

B. **Common or Proper.** A **common** noun names one or more members of a class of things: *woman, women, mice, city, chair, auditorium.* A **proper** noun names a specific person, place, or thing: *Maria Hernandez, Mickey Mouse, Singapore, Mormon Tabernacle.*

C. **Concrete or Abstract.** A **concrete** noun names an object that can be perceived by the senses: *woman, Maria Hernandez, mice, cheese.* An **abstract** noun names a quality or **idea:** *liberty, sadness, ambition, love, tragedy, height.*

D. **Collective.** A **collective** noun names a group of things: *jury, team, flock, committee, army.*

E. **Count or Noncount.** See section 16E(2), page 57.

11. The Main Uses of Nouns

Recall the basic sentence pattern: S V (C) (C). That is, each sentence has a subject, a verb, and possibly one or two complements. The subject and the complements are usually nouns.

A. Subject of a Sentence. Pattern: **S** V (C) (C). The **subject** tells *who* or *what* if placed before the verb:

The *judge* imposed a heavy fine. [Who imposed?]

Both *projects* were abandoned. [What were abandoned?]

Duff and *Fong* began the project. [Who began? (compound subject)]

B. Complement. A **complement** is a word in the complete predicate that completes the meaning of the verb. There are four kinds of complements:

(1) A *direct object* is a noun (or pronoun) that tells *whom* or *what* after an action verb. Usual pattern: S V **C**:

Duff assembled the *equipment.* [assembled what?]

Fong is training *workers.* [training whom?]

(2) An *indirect object* is a noun (or pronoun) that appears after certain action verbs, telling *to* or *for whom,* or *to* or *for what,* the action of the verb is done. Pattern: S V **C** (ind. obj.) C (dir. obj.):

The mayor sent her *aide* a gift. [sent to whom?]

The aide had done the *mayor* a favor. [done for whom?]

(3) A *subjective complement* (also called a *predicate nominative*) is a noun (or pronoun) that follows a linking verb and renames or explains the subject. Pattern: S V (link) **C**:

Felicia Gray is the head *programmer.* [*Programmer* gives another name or title for *Felicia Gray.*]

A kumquat is a *fruit.*
[*Fruit* explains what *kumquat* is.]

Note: An adjective can also be a subjective complement: Ms. Gray is highly *competent.*

For a full list of linking verbs, see section 13C, page 38.

(4) An *objective complement* is a noun that follows a direct object and renames or explains it. Pattern: S V C (dir. obj.) **C** (obj. comp.):

Everyone considers Ms. Gray an *expert.* [*Expert* gives another name or title for *Ms. Gray.*]

The director called her appointment a *godsend.*

The objective complement occurs most commonly with such verbs as *call, name, designate, elect, consider, appoint, think.*

Note: An adjective can also be an objective complement—The director called her appointment *fortunate.*

C. An Object of a Preposition is a noun (or pronoun) that ends a prepositional phrase and answers the question *whom* or *what* after the preposition:

Ms. Roy met with her *publisher.* [with whom?]

Stores in *town* struggle against new *malls.* [in what? against what?]

D. An Appositive is a noun that closely follows another noun and renames or further identifies that other noun:

Ms. Gray, the head *programmer,* knows the language. [*Programmer* is another name or title for *Ms. Gray.* It is an appositive (or *in apposition*) to *Ms. Gray.*]

They hoped the new year, *1939,* would bring peace.

E. **Direct Address.** A noun (or pronoun) in **direct address** names the person being spoken to:

NOUN: *Carlo,* the manager wants to see you.

PRONOUN: Get over here, *you!*

FLASH TEST

PART 1

In the blank, tell how the boldfaced word in each sentence is **used** (use the abbreviations in parentheses):

subject **(subj)**	indirect object **(ind obj)**	appositive **(app)**
subject complement **(subj comp)**	objective complement **(obj comp)**	direct address **(dir add)**
direct object **(dir obj)**	object of preposition **(obj prep)**	

EXAMPLE: The passenger gave the **driver** a tip.   **ind obj**

1. The **Braves** were defeated.   1. _____
2. The delegates gathered for the **vote.**   2. _____
3. The **judges** declared Kimiko the winner.   3. _____
4. The judges declared **Kimiko** the winner.   4. _____
5. The judges declared Kimiko the **winner.**   5. _____
6. Kimiko will be a **contestant** at the national level.   6. _____
7. The contractors paved the **driveway.**   7. _____
8. **Ladies** and gentlemen, here is the star of tonight's show.   8. _____
9. Ladies and gentlemen, here is the **star** of tonight's show.   9. _____
10. The young star, **Leslie Mahoud,** appeared nervous.   10. _____
11. Antilock brakes give the **driver** more control.   11. _____
12. These brakes have become a **source** of controversy.   12. _____
13. These brakes have become a source of **controversy.**   13. _____
14. Misapplication of these brakes has caused some **accidents.**   14. _____
15. Which **company** will get the contract?   15. _____
16. Which company will get the **contract?**   16. _____
17. Everyone was bored by the speaker's **redundancy.**   17. _____
18. Redundancy, needless **repetition,** can put an audience to sleep. 18. _____
19. Marie, make that **customer** an offer she cannot refuse.   19. _____
20. **Marie,** make that customer an offer she cannot refuse.   20. _____

FLASH TEST

PART 2

In each sentence, fill in the blank with a noun of your own that **makes sense.** Then in the blank at the right, tell how that noun is **used** (use the abbreviations in parentheses):

subject **(subj)**	indirect object **(ind obj)**	appositive **(app)**

subject complement (subj comp)	objective complement (obj comp)	direct address (dir add)
direct object (dir obj)	object of preposition (obj prep)	

EXAMPLE: We sang songs far into the **night**.   <u>obj prep</u>
(Collaborative option: Students work in pairs, alternating; one writes the word, the other names its use.)

1. First prize was a brand-new _____.   **1.** _____

2. _____, please make more coffee.   **2.** _____

3. The new _____ in town should expect a warm welcome.   **3.** _____

4. Every autumn the region's trees, mostly _____, delight touring leaf-peepers.   **4.** _____

5. Brad's CD collection contains mostly songs by _____.   **5.** _____

6. Before the examination Professor Ferrano gave us a(n) _____.   **6.** _____

7. Paula's attitude made her a(n) _____ to many classmates.   **7.** _____

8. Warmhearted Pat gave the _____ a hug.   **8.** _____

FLASH TEST

PART 3

In the blank, tell how each boldfaced complement is **used** (use the abbreviations in parentheses). If any complement is an adjective, **circle** it.

subjective complement (subj comp)	objective complement (obj comp)
direct object (dir obj)	indirect object (ind obj)

EXAMPLES: The ambassador delivered the **ultimatum**.   <u>dir obj</u>
            The queen became furious.   <u>subj comp</u>

1. He has been an **environmentalist** for thirty years.   **1.** _____
2. We gave the **car** a shove.   **2.** _____
3. The logging industry has lost **jobs** to international competitors.   **3.** _____
4. Alaska made Juneau its **capital.**   **4.** _____
5. She lent me a **map** of Warsaw.   **5.** _____
6. Give **me** your solemn promise.   **6.** _____
7. The student conducted an **experiment**.   **7.** _____
8. She sounds **happier** every day.   **8.** _____
9. **Whom** did you meet yesterday?   **9.** _____
10. Will the company give **John** another offer?   **10.** _____
11. Politicians will promise **us** anything.   **11.** _____
12. The group had been studying **anthropology** for three semesters.   **12.** _____
13. Her former employer gave **her** the idea for the small business.   **13.** _____
14. I named him my **beneficiary.**   **14.** _____
15. She is an **instructor** at the community college.   **15.** _____
16. She became an **administrator.**   **16.** _____
17. I found the **dictionary** under the bed.   **17.** _____

18. He considered her **brilliant.**

19. Select whatever **medium** you like for your art project.

20. The company made her **manager** of the branch office.

18. _____

19. _____

20. _____

Answers to Exercises for: The Main Uses of Nouns

Part 1

1. subj	**6.** subj comp	**11.** ind obj	**16.** dir obj
2. obj prep	**7.** dir obj	**12.** subj comp	**17.** obj prep
3. subj	**8.** dir add	**13.** obj prep	**18.** app
4. dir obj	**9.** subj	**14.** dir obj	**19.** ind obj
5. obj comp	**10.** app	**15.** subj	**20.** dir add

Part 2
(Words are samples.)

1. computer	subj comp		**5.** Garth Brooks	obj prep
2. Charles	dir add		**6.** review	dir obj
3. sheriff	subj		**7.** confidante	obj comp
4. maples	app		**8.** dog	ind obj

Part 3

1. subj comp	**6.** ind obj	**11.** ind obj	**16.** subj comp
2. ind obj	**7.** dir obj	**12.** dir obj	**17.** dir obj
3. dir obj	**8.** subj comp [circled]	**13.** ind obj	**18.** obj comp [circled]
4. obj comp	**9.** dir obj	**14.** obj comp	**19.** dir obj
5. dir obj	**10.** ind obj	**15.** subj comp	**20.** obj comp

12–15 Using Verbs

FLASH SUMMARY

A verb is the core of every sentence. Without a verb, a group of words is only a fragment of a sentence instead of a complete sentence. Even if a sentence contains only one word, that word must be a verb: *Run! Wait.* (Every verb must have a subject, expressed or understood. In sentences such as *Run!* and *Wait,* the subject is understood to be *you.*) The function of a verb is to assert something about its subject—that is, to tell what the subject *does* (*did, will do*) or that the subject *is* (*was, will be*) something (in interrogative sentences the verb will *ask,* and in imperative sentences it will *command* or *request*):

The storm *raged.*

Emergency vehicles *were racing* through the streets.

Power *was* out for hours in several areas of the city.

Where *were* the emergency vehicles *going*?

[You] *Prepare* for a long, cold night.

12. Identifying the Verb

There is a simple way to identify the verb in a sentence. The verb is the word that will usually change its form if you change the time of the sentence:

> This week they *plan* the budget. Last week they *planned* the budget. Next week they *will plan* the budget. For the last five years they *have planned* the budget.

13. The Kinds of Verbs

A verb is classified according to the kind of complement (if any) that follows it. In addition, there is a special kind of verb called an **auxiliary** (or helping) verb that may accompany a main verb.

A. **A Transitive Verb** is one that needs a direct object to complete its meaning. That is, it expresses an action that passes across (transits) from a "doer" (the subject—the person or thing that does the action) to a "receiver" (the direct object—the person or thing upon whom the action is done).

> Dr. Hourani *removed* the tumor. [*Dr. Hourani* did the action, removing; *tumor* (direct object) received the action.]

> Red lights *stop* traffic. [*Lights* do the action; *traffic* receives the action.]

B. **An Intransitive Verb** is one that does not need a direct object to complete its meaning. It expresses an action that does not have a receiver:

> The meeting *adjourned.*

> The chairperson *stayed* after the meeting. [*After the meeting* is a prepositional phrase, telling when. It is not a direct object.]

> Pollutants *act* insidiously. [*Insidiously* is an adverb, telling how. It is not a direct object.]

Note: Many verbs can be transitive in some uses and intransitive in others. Dictionaries label each meaning of a verb as *v.t.* (*verb, transitive*) or *v.i.* (*verb, intransitive*).

C. **A Linking (State-of-Being, Copulative) Verb** expresses no action at all. It merely expresses state of being; it indicates a link of identity or description between the subject and the subjective complement following the verb:

> Borneo *is* an island. [*Borneo = island.*]

> The Amish *have been* industrious. [*Industrious* describes *Amish.*]

> Her cousin *became* a minister. [*Cousin = minister.*]

The chief linking verb is *be.* Its parts are:

am	is	are	was	were	being	been

Other linking verbs are those roughly like *be* in meaning—

seem	appear	remain	prove	become	grow	turn

—and the verbs of the five senses:

look	sound	feel	smell	taste

Some verbs may be linking verbs in one sense and action verbs in another:

Linking	*Action*
I *looked* disheveled.	I *looked* out the window.
Mitsuko *grew* pensive.	Mitsuko *grew* cabbages.

D. Auxiliary (Helping) Verbs. A verb may contain more than one word, as in *could have helped.* The last word in the verb is the **main verb.** The others are called auxiliary verbs, or simply **auxiliaries.** They convey some condition of the main verb, such as tense or mood.

Only a few verbs can be auxiliaries:

have	shall	might
be (am, is, . . .)	should	must
do	can	have to
will	could	ought (to)
would	may	need (to)

All except *have, be,* and *do* are called **modal auxiliaries,** or just **modals.** Generally, modals work like *will* and *would* (see section 14B(3), (6), (7), pages 42–44.): He *will* go. He *might* go. He *ought to* go. He *might have* gone. He *could have been* going.

After *be,* the main verb uses its present participle (*-ing* form): *is flying.* After *have,* the main verb uses its past participle (*-ed* or irregular form): *has departed, had gone* (for more on participles, see section 14A below; section 14D(2), pages 44–45, and section 15D, pages 46–47):

> The plane ***is** flying* here nonstop.
>
> The plane ***will be** landing* soon.
>
> The plane ***had** departed* from Hawaii.
>
> The plane ***did** arrive* on time.
>
> The plane ***should** arrive* on time.
>
> The plane ***must*** certainly ***have** landed* by now. [Note that other words may come between parts of the verb.]
>
> ***Would*** any of the planes ***have** landed* sooner?

Note: Verbs of more than one word are sometimes called **verb phrases.**

14. Using Verbs Correctly

A. Know the Three Principal Parts of Verbs. The **principal parts** are the parts you need to know to form all of a verb's tenses (time forms):

FLASH FOCUS

ESL

Principal Part	Present Tense	Past Tense	Past Participle
Regular verb	walk	walked	walked
Irregular verb	see	saw	seen

Regular verbs form their past tense and past participle by adding *-ed* to the present (with some minor spelling changes, as in *stopped, cried*). Irregular verbs form these parts in various ways, such as *broken, thought, sung, made, swum.* See section 15D, pages 46–47, for forms of many irregular verbs. Consult your dictionary when in doubt about others, because you cannot safely take one irregular verb as a model for another; consider *make (made, made)* and *take (took, taken).*

Note: Some texts and dictionaries list a fourth principal part, the **present participle,** formed with *-ing* added to the present form: *seeing, playing.* It is always regular, except for some minor spelling changes *(stopping, loving).*

B. Use the Correct Verb Tense and Form. *Tense* refers to time; verbs use different tense forms when expressing different times. Among all its tenses, English has only three common verb endings: *-s* (sometimes *-es*), *-ed* (sometimes *-d*), and *-ing.* Proofread your writing very carefully to be sure you never omit these endings.

Note: Verb forms are often listed by **person.** In grammar, there are three persons: the *first person* means the person(s) doing the speaking: *I* or *we.* The *second person* means the person(s) being spoken to: *you.* The *third person* means the person(s) or thing(s) being spoken about: *he, she, it, they,* or any noun, such as *house, athletes, Horace.* For the meaning of *singular* and *plural,* see section 10A, page 33.

(1) The present tense

✓ **The basic present tense form** (using the first principal part). Note where the *-s* ending occurs:

FLASH FOCUS

	Singular	**Plural**
First person	I walk	we walk
Second person	you walk	you walk
Third person	he/she/it walks	they walk

Use this form for an action that happens regularly or always: I usually *watch* the late news. Beth *drives* a minivan. The sun *sets* in the west. Use this form also usually with *be, have,* and verbs of mental action, emotion, and the senses—such as *see, hear, think, understand, mean, feel, know*—for something happening at the present moment (I *am* ready. They *have* coffee. I *hear* a plane. She *understands* it. They *know* the way.)

✓ **The present progressive form.** Note the *-ing* ending:

FLASH FOCUS

	Singular	**Plural**
First person	I am walk**ing**	we are walk**ing**
Second person	you are walk**ing**	you are walk**ing**
Third person	he/she/it is walk**ing**	they are walk**ing**

With most verbs, use this form to stress that something is in progress at the present moment: Right now I *am* (or I'm) *exercising.* She *is* (or She's) *traveling* today. Use the progressive also in questions (and their answers) and negatives as follows: *Are* you *walking? Is* she *walking? Are* the Smiths *coming?* I *am* (or I'm) not *walking.* She *is* (or She's) not *walking.* The Smiths *are* not (or *aren't*) *coming.*

✓ The present emphatic form:

FLASH FOCUS

	Singular	**Plural**
First person	I do walk	we do walk
Second person	you do walk	you do walk
Third person	he/she/it do**es** walk	they do walk

Use this form in almost all other questions (and their answers) and negatives: *Do* you *walk* regularly? Yes, I *do* (*walk*). *Does* she *care* for him? Yes, she *does* (*care*). *Do* the students *like* Dr. Fossle? They *do* (*like* him). I *do* not (*don't*) *walk*. She *does* not (*doesn't*) *care* for him. The students *do* not (*don't*) *like* Dr. Fossle. Use this form also when you want to emphasize the verb: You never remember my birthday. Yes, I *do remember* it.

(2) The past tense

✓ **The basic past form** (using the second principal part). Note the *-ed* ending (on regular verbs only):

FLASH FOCUS

	Singular	**Plural**
First person	I walk**ed** [regular], I saw [irregular]	we walk**ed,** saw
Second person	you walk**ed,** saw	you walk**ed,** saw
Third person	he/she/it walk**ed,** saw	they walk**ed,** saw

Use this form for an action that was completed at a definite time in the past, or done regularly and completed in the past: I *walked* two miles yesterday. I *attended* college for two years.

✓ **The past progressive form:**

FLASH FOCUS

	Singular	**Plural**
First person	I was walk**ing**	we were walk**ing**
Second person	you were walk**ing**	you were walk**ing**
Third person	he/she/it was walk**ing**	they were walk**ing**

Use this form to stress that something was in progress at a time in the past: I *was walking* last night. She *was studying* when I called her. Use the past progressive also in questions (and their answers) and negatives as follows: *Were* you *walking*? *Was* she *walking*? *Were* the Smiths *coming*? I *was* not (*wasn't*) *walking*. She *was* not (*wasn't*) *walking*. The Smiths *were* not (*weren't*) *coming*.

✓ **The past emphatic form:**

FLASH FOCUS

	Singular	Plural
First person	I did walk	we did walk
Second person	you did walk	you did walk
Third person	he/she/it did walk	they did walk

Use this form in most other questions (and their answers) and to emphasize an action: *Did* you *walk* [yesterday or regularly]? Yes, I *did* (*walk*). *Did* she *care* for him? Yes, she *did* (*care*). *Did* the students *like* Dr. Fossle? They *did* (*like* him). I *did* not (*didn't*) *walk*. She *did* not (*didn't*) *care* for him. The students *did* not (*didn't*) *like* Dr. Fossle. Yes, I *did remember* your birthday.

(3) The future tense

✓ **The basic form** (*shall* or *will* + the first principal part):

FLASH FOCUS

Note: In the United States, *I shall* and *we shall* are considered very formal. *Shall,* everywhere, in all persons, also conveys determination or command: We *shall overcome.* They *shall* not *pass.*

	Singular	Plural
First person	I will/shall walk	we will/shall walk
Second person	you will walk	you will walk
Third person	he/she/it will walk	they will walk

Use this form for future happenings: I *will* (*shall*) *walk* tomorrow. She *will study* just before the test. The Smiths *will come. Will* you *walk* tomorrow? I *will* (*walk*). I'll *walk.*

✓ **The future progressive form:**

FLASH FOCUS

	Singular	Plural
First person	I will/shall be walking	we will/shall be walking
Second person	you will be walking	you will be walking
Third person	he/she/it will be walking	they will be walking

Use this form to stress that something will be in progress: I *will* (I'll) *be leaving* soon. She *will* (She'll) *be studying* when you call. *Will* she *be studying*? No, she *will* not (*won't*) *be studying.*

There is no emphatic form for the future or any of the following tenses.

(4) The present perfect tense

 ✓ **The basic form** (*have* or *has* + the third principal part):

**FLASH FOCUS**

	Singular	Plural
First person	I have walk**ed,** I have seen	we have walk**ed,** seen
Second person	you have walk**ed,** seen	you have walk**ed,** seen
Third person	he/she/it has walk**ed,** seen	they have walk**ed,** seen

Use this form generally when something happened in the past but has some connection with the present, or was completed at some indefinite time in the past: I *have* (I've) *walked* for hours. She *has* (She's) *studied* since midnight. Ms. Stein *has lived* here forty years [lived here in the past, still lives here]. He *has received* constant death threats [began in the past, may still be going on]. They *have signed* a contract [at some indefinite time in the past].

 ✓ **The progressive present perfect:** I *have been walking,* she *has been walking,* and so forth. Use this form to stress that something has been and still is in progress: I *have* (I've) *been walking* since noon. *Have* you *been walking?* I *have* not (haven't) *been walking.*

(5) The past perfect tense

 ✓ **The basic past perfect form** (*had* + the third principal part):

FLASH FOCUS

	Singular	Plural
First person	I had walk**ed**	we had walk**ed**
Second person	you had walk**ed**	you had walk**ed**
Third person	he/she/it had walk**ed**	they had walk**ed**

Use this form for something completed earlier than, or up to the time of, something else in the past: I *had walked* for hours before help came. Until I arrived with the car, she *had walked.* The witness said [yesterday] that she *had seen* the accident [last month]. She *had lived* there forty years when the building collapsed.

 ✓ **The progressive past perfect form:** I *had been walking,* she *had been walking,* and so forth. Use this form to stress that something was in progress earlier than, or up to the time of, something else in the past: I *had been investing* heavily when the market collapsed. She *had been acting* depressed before her suicide.

(6) The future perfect tense

 ✓ **The basic future perfect form** (*shall* or *will have* + the third principal part):

FLASH FOCUS

	Singular	Plural
First person	I will/shall have walk**ed**	we will/shall have walk**ed**
Second person	you will have walk**ed**	you will have walk**ed**
Third person	he/she/it will have walk**ed**	they will have walk**ed**

Use this form for something that will already be completed at a certain future time: I *shall/will have walked* five miles by the time I get home. They *will have left* when you reach their home. By March [future time] Stark *will* already *have left* office [completed action]. When I reach Phoenix [future], she *will have found* my letter [completed action]. (Note that future event, *reach*, uses the present tense.)

✓ **The progressive future perfect form:** I *shall/will have been walking*, she *will have been walking*, and so forth. Use this form to stress that something will have been in progress: By midnight she *will have been studying* for fifteen hours non-stop. Next Monday he *will have been working* here a month.

Note: Sometimes there seems little difference in meaning between the basic and progressive perfect forms, and either will do—I *have waited* here since noon. I *have been waiting* here since noon.

(7) The conditional forms. Use the conditional forms (I *would walk*, you *would walk*, and so forth; I *would have walked*, you *would have walked*, he *would have walked*, and so forth) when something depends on some less-than-probable condition. Use *would* for a future condition: If the stock market rose [in the future], bond prices *would fall*. (Note that the other verb, *rose*, uses the past tense.) Use *would have* for a past condition that did not actually happen: If the stock market had risen [it did not], bond prices *would have fallen*. (Note that the other verb, *had risen*, uses the past perfect tense.)

Do not use *would* in both clauses:

WRONG: If the stock market *would have risen*, bond prices *would have fallen*.

RIGHT: If the stock market *had risen*, bond prices *would have fallen*.

Do not use *have* as an auxiliary in both verbs:

WRONG: They *would have liked* to *have seen* Paris.

RIGHT: They *would have liked* [in the past] to *see* Paris. They *would like* [now] to *have seen* Paris [in the past]. They *would like* [now] to *see* Paris [in the future].

(8) Other modals (can, could, may, might, must, should). See section 13D, page 39.

C. **Make the Verb Agree in Person and Number with the Subject.** Sections 23–24, pages 81–84, deal with the very important topic of agreement.

D. **Distinguish a Verbal from a Verb.** A **verbal** is a form derived from a verb. It is used not as a verb but as a noun, adjective, or adverb. There are three kinds of verbals: **infinitives, participles,** and **gerunds.**

(1) Infinitive (*to* + verb), used as

✓ Noun:

To act is her ambition. [subject]

She desires *to act.* [direct object]

Her ambition is *to act.* [subjective complement]

✓ Adjective:

Hers is an ambition *to admire.* [modifies *ambition*]

✓ Adverb:

Her goal is not easy *to attain.* [modifies *easy*]

She came here *to study.* [modifies *came*]

(2) Participle, used as adjective:

✓ Present participle (verb + -*ing*):

The *cheering* crowd stormed the stage. [modifies *crowd*]

The crowd, *cheering* wildly, stormed the stage. [modifies *crowd*]

✓ Past participle (third principal part of verb: for regular verbs, verb + -ed; for irregular verbs, no set form but often ends in -en):

Confused freshmen wandered the campus. [modifies *freshmen*]

Completely *confused,* freshmen wandered the campus. [modifies *freshmen*]

The economy, *driven* by consumer demand, kept expanding. [modifies *economy*]

Use the *present participle* with a person or thing that is doing something: a *devastating* flood (the flood is doing the devastating). Use the *past participle* with a person or thing to which something has been done: the *devastated* land (the land has had devastation done to it).

(3) Gerund (verb + -ing), used as noun:

Seeing [subject] is *believing* [subjective complement].

The prisoners considered *escaping* [direct object] by *tunneling* [object of preposition].

See section 38C, page 130, for possessives with gerunds.

Note: An *-ing* verbal may be either a gerund or a participle, depending on its use in a particular sentence:

Swimming is excellent exercise. [gerund: used as subject noun]

The *swimming* child reached the raft. [participle: used as adjective, modifying *child*]

Infinitives, participles, and gerunds also have a *have* form for events already past: *To have worked* so hard exhausted him [infinitive]. *Having worked* hard for years, he was glad to retire [participle]. He was praised for *having worked* so hard [gerund].

15. Avoiding Verb Errors

A. Do Not Shift Tense Without Reason.

WRONG: In the film she *becomes* pregnant but *refused* to name the father.

RIGHT: In the film she *becomes* pregnant but *refuses* to name the father.

RIGHT: In the film she *became* pregnant but *refused* to name the father.

B. Do Not Overuse the Passive Voice.
Transitive verbs have two voices. In the **active voice,** the more common one, the subject does the action (it is the "doer"): A million citizens rousingly *cheered* the queen. (The subject, *citizens*, did the cheering.) In the **passive voice,** the subject "receives" the action (it is being acted upon, having the action done to it), and the doer is put inside a *by* phrase or not mentioned at all: The queen *was cheered* rousingly by a million citizens. The queen *was cheered* rousingly.

The passive voice uses *be* (*am, is, was* . . .) + the past participle: *was cheered, is held, might have been told, will be shot.* In general, the active voice, which stresses the doer of an action, is more forceful than the passive, which stresses the receiver. To make a passive sentence active, ask "Who is doing the action?" Make the answer your subject. In the sentences below, Alice Walker is doing the action—reading:

PASSIVE: The poem *will be read* by **Alice Walker.**

ACTIVE: **Alice Walker** *will read* the poem.

But do use the passive when

✓ The doer is unimportant: The package *will be delivered* soon. [The deliverer's name is unimportant.]

✓ Your emphasis is on the receiver: The senator *has been punched* by an irate taxpayer. [The focus is on the senator, not the puncher.]

✓ The doer is unknown: Their car *was stolen* from the driveway.

✓ You want to de-emphasize or conceal the doer: Yes, an error *has been made* at this office. [The person who committed the error is not named.]

Avoid needless shifting between active and passive. See section 27D(3), page 94.

C. Do Not Shift Mood without Reason. The mood of a verb indicates how the idea of a sentence is to be regarded. Sentences that state facts or ask questions are in the **indicative** mood:

Kinshasa *is* the capital of Zaire.

Is Kinshasa the capital of Zaire?

Requests and commands are in the **imperative mood:**

Take Flight 715 for Kinshasa. [*You* is the understood subject.]

The **subjunctive mood** expresses doubt, uncertainty, wish, or supposition or signals a condition contrary to fact. In the subjunctive mood, *am, is,* and *are* become *be; was* becomes *were; has* becomes *have;* and *-s* endings are dropped from other verbs:

WISH: God *be* with you. Long *live* the queen. Far *be* it from me [that is, *May it be far from me*] to interfere in his life.

DOUBT OR UNCERTAINTY: If I *were* to tell him, he might tell everyone.

CONDITION CONTRARY TO FACT: If I *were* you, I would tell.

Use the subjunctive also in a *that* clause when the main clause expresses a demand, command, recommendation, request, or parliamentary motion:

They demanded that the management *refund* their money.

The board recommends that the treasurer *resign* at once.

I move that the meeting *be* adjourned.

Do not shift moods illogically:

WRONG: First *press* the ESC key; then you *should exit* from the program. [*Press* is imperative in mood; *should exit,* indicative.]

RIGHT: First *press* the ESC key; then *exit* from the program.

D. Do Not Misuse Irregular Verb Forms. Here are the standard principal parts of some common troublesome verbs. Asterisked verbs (∗) are further treated in section 73, pages 183–192.

FLASH FOCUS
ESL

Present Tense	Past Tense	Past Participle
[be] am, is, are	was, were	been
begin	began	begun
blow	blew	blown
*break	broke	broken

Present Tense	Past Tense	Past Participle
*bring	brought	brought
choose	chose	chosen
(be)come	(be)came	(be)come
cost	cost	cost
do	did	done
drink	drank	drunk
drive	drove	driven
fall	fell	fallen
fly	flew	flown
forbid	forbade, forbad	forbidden
freeze	froze	frozen
give	gave	given
go	went	gone
grow	grew	grown
know	knew	known
*lay [to put]	laid	laid
*lead	led	led
*lie [to rest]	lay	lain
*lose	lost	lost
mean	meant	meant
pay	paid	paid
read [say "reed"]	read [say "red"]	read [say "red"]
ride	rode	ridden
ring	rang	rung
*(a)rise	(a)rose	(a)risen
run	ran	run
say	said	said
see	saw	seen
seek	sought	sought
shake	shook	shaken
shine [to give off light]	shone	shone
[Shine—to polish—is a different verb. It is regular.]		
show	showed	shown, showed
sink	sank	sunk
speak	spoke	spoken
steal	stole	stolen
swear	swore	sworn
swim	swam	swum
swing	swung	swung
*take	took	taken
tear	tore	torn
think	thought	thought
throw	threw	thrown
(a)wake	(a)woke, (a)waked	(a)waked, (a)woke(n)
[Awaken is a different verb. It is regular.]		
wear	wore	worn
*write	wrote	written

E. **Do Not Confuse Verbs Similar in Meaning or Spelling.** Sometimes mentally substituting a synonym for the verb that is puzzling you (such as *rest* for *lie* and *put* for *lay*) helps solve your puzzle. Many sets of troublesome verbs, such as *lie/lay* and *affect/effect* are explained in section 73, pages 183–192.

FLASH TEST

PART 1

Identify the tense or other form of the boldfaced verb (use the abbreviations in parentheses):

present (**pres**)	past perfect (**past perf**)
past	future perfect (**fut perf**)
future (**fut**)	conditional (**cond**)
present perfect (**pres perf**)	past conditional (**past cond**)

EXAMPLE: They **spoke** too fast for us.   _____ past _____

1. The sun **sets** in the west.   1. _____
2. He **will** surely **write** us soon.   2. _____
3. Next summer, we **shall have lived** in this house for ten years.   3. _____
4. The Allens **have planted** a vegetable garden.   4. _____
5. By noon he **will have finished** the whole job.   5. _____
6. If the study were flawed, it **would be rejected.**   6. _____
7. **Shall** we **reserve** a copy for you?   7. _____
8. The widow's savings **melted** away.   8. _____
9. I **had** not **expected** to see her.   9. _____
10. If the study had been flawed, it **would have been rejected.**   10. _____
11. The company **guaranteed** that the package would arrive in the morning.   11. _____
12. Dylan **will begin** cello lessons in the spring.   12. _____
13. The children **have created** a snow castle in the front yard.   13. _____
14. **Have** you an extra set of car keys?   14. _____
15. They **would have passed** if they had studied harder.   15. _____
16. I **wrote** a review of the school play.   16. _____
17. The family **has planned** a vacation.   17. _____
18. The comic **laughed** at his own jokes.   18. _____
19. In one week the flu **hit** five staff members.   19. _____
20. This Friday **would have been** my grandmother's hundredth birthday.   20. _____

FLASH TEST

PART 2

In each blank, write the needed **ending: ed**(or **d**), **s**(or **es**), or **ing**. If no ending is needed, leave the blank empty.

EXAMPLE: Every day the sun rise_s_ later, and I wake _____ up later.

Today the brown cliffs rise _____ directly from the sea; no beach separate _____ the cliffs from the water. The waves have pound _____ the granite base of that cliff for ages but have fail _____ to wear it away. Now, as always, great white gulls are swoop _____ just above the foam; they are seek _____ fish that are destine _____ to become their dinner. Years ago, when my friend Jan and I first gather _____ the courage to approach the cliff's sheer edge and peer over, we imagine _____ what it would be like if we tumble _____ over and fell into that seething surf far below. At that time, the thought fill ___ me with terror.

Today, ten years later, as my friend and I stand _____ atop the cliffs, Jan speak _____ of how she felt then. I can tell that she is try _____ to relive that experience of our youth. We are not feel _____ the same terror now, and we will never feel _____ it again. Still, nothing would make _____ us go closer to the edge. When a man or woman reach _____ age thirty, he or she often attempt _____ to recapture the excitement of youth but rarely succeed _____. In a few moments, Jan and I will walk _____ back to where our cars are park _____. We have been pretend _____ to be youngsters again, but now each of us know _____ that we can never repeat the past. Jan look _____ at me with a smile.

FLASH TEST

PART 3

Write **T** if the verb is **transitive.**

Write **I** if it is **intransitive.**

Write **L** if it is **linking.**

EXAMPLE: The house **looked** decrepit.   L

1. Jenny **kissed** me when we met.   1. _____
2. His laughter **sounded** bitter.   2. _____
3. **Lay** your wet coat by the furnace.   3. _____
4. The window **opened** onto the bay.   4. _____
5. The island **lies** not far off the mainland.   5. _____
6. The last express **has** already **left.**   6. _____
7. **Place** the keys on my dresser.   7. _____
8. The childhood playmates **remained** friends for life.   8. _____
9. In early autumn children **prepare** for Halloween.   9. _____
10. The plane **arrived** ten minutes late.   10. _____
11. The snow **piled** up into tall, crusty drifts.   11. _____
12. The boys **created** valentines for their teachers, friends, and family. 12. _____
13. My friend **seemed** nervous.   13. _____
14. The new class **ended** abruptly.   14. _____
15. Women **have been** instrumental in maintaining the social structure of the   15. _____
    American Protestant churches.

FLASH TEST

PART 4

Rewrite each boldfaced verb in the tense or form given in parentheses.

EXAMPLE: Now we **live** in Hamilton Hall. (present perfect) <u>For the past year we</u>
<u>have lived in Hamilton Hall</u>.

1. Packing material from the box **clutters** the floor. (past)

   _____

   _____

2. The CIA **appointed** Choi its chief agent in Asia. (present perfect)

   _____

   _____

3. The CIA **appointed** Choi its chief agent in Asia. (past perfect)

_____

_____

4. The Red Sox **will win** the pennant by next fall. (future perfect)

_____

_____

5. The Everglades **will die** without relief from pollution. (conditional)

_____

_____

6. The Everglades **will die** without relief from pollution. (past conditional)

_____

_____

7. The Piffle Company **seeks** a new vice-president. (present progressive)

_____

_____

8. The Piffle Company **seeks** a new vice-president. (past emphatic)

_____

_____

9. The Piffle Company **seeks** a new vice-president. (present perfect)

_____

_____

10. The Piffle Company **seeks** a new vice-president. (present perfect progressive)

_____

_____

FLASH TEST

PART 5

First write **A** if the boldfaced verb is in the **active voice** or **P** if it is in the **passive voice**. Then **rewrite** the sentence in the opposite voice (if it was active, make it passive; if it was passive, make it active). If necessary, supply your own subject.

EXAMPLES: A car **struck** the lamppost.
<u>The lamppost was struck by a car.</u>   <u>   A   </u>

   The door **was left** open.
<u>Someone left the door open.</u>   <u>   P   </u>

1. One name **was** inadvertently **omitted** from the list.   1. _____

_____

_____

2. The negotiator **carried** a special agreement to the union meeting.   2. _____

_____

_____

3. The media **bashed** the incumbent's speech.

3. _____

_____

4. The meeting **was called** to order.

4. _____

_____

5. The ancient city **was** totally **destroyed** by a volcanic eruption.

5. _____

_____

6. An accounting error **was discovered.**

6. _____

_____

7. Younger voters **have selected** a presidential candidate.

7. _____

_____

8. The prosecutor **subjected** the witness to a vigorous cross-examination.

8. _____

_____

9. By dawn the police **will have barricaded** every road.

9. _____

_____

10. The status report **will be submitted** next week.

10. _____

_____

11. The left fielder **threw out** the runner.

11. _____

_____

12. Environmental activists **have begun** a nationwide antipollution campaign.

12. _____

_____

FLASH TEST

PART 6

Rewrite each sentence in the **subjunctive** mood.

EXAMPLE: Today the sky is sunny.
          I wish the sky <u>were</u> sunny today.

 1. Benito is on time.

   I wish Benito _____ on time.

 2. I am a scuba diver; I search for sunken ships.

   If I _____ a scuba diver, I would search for sunken ships.

3. The customers insisted; their money was returned.

The customers insisted that their money _____ returned.

FLASH TEST

PART 7

Identify each boldfaced verbal by writing:

inf for infinitive	**pres part** for present participle
ger for gerund	**past part** for past participle

EXAMPLE: The **outnumbered** soldiers surrendered.   _____past part_____

1. Do you like **to watch** football?   1. _____

2. Our car just missed the **leaping** deer.   2. _____

3. The President's first job was **to restore** the economy for all Americans.   3. _____

4. Our **laughing** distracted him.   4. _____

5. I submitted a **typed** application.   5. _____

6. **Encouraged** by their initial weight loss, Cecilia and Roy continued their diets.   6. _____

7. He was eager **to start** an exercise program.   7. _____

8. By **surveying** the chapter, he knew what he needed to learn.   8. _____

9. **Seeing** us, she smiled.   9. _____

10. She enjoys **driving** sports cars.   10. _____

11. The movie *Titanic*, **seen** on a small TV screen, is much less impressive.   11. _____

12. **Examining** the report, the consumer decided not to invest.   12. _____

13. **Frightened,** he became cautious.   13. _____

14. The purpose of the cookbook is **to reduce** the threat of cancer through a   14. _____
healthful diet.

15. **Reducing** carbon dioxide emissions was a top priority in a recent bill.   15. _____

FLASH TEST

PART 8

Complete each sentence with a verbal or verbal phrase of your own. Then, in the blank at the right, tell how it is **used** (use the abbreviations in parentheses):

subject (**subj**)	object of preposition (**obj prep**)
subject complement (**subj comp**)	adjective (**adj**)
direct object (**dir obj**)	adverb (**adv**)

EXAMPLES: <u>Faced with the evidence</u>, the suspect admitted the crime.   _____adj_____
          The suspect was accused of <u>absconding with company funds.</u>   ___obj prep___

(Collaborative option: Students work in pairs, alternating—one writes the word or phrase, the other identifies its use.)

1. _____ is no way to greet the day.   1. _____

2. Binoy likes _____.   2. _____

3. The _____ crowd rose to its feet.   3. _____

4. The driver got out and opened the hood [for what purpose?]   4. _____

5. Professor Zullo's obsession is _____   5. _____

6. I earned an *A* in her course by _____   6. _____

7. The huge motor home, _____, lumbered up the mountain road.   7. _____

8. As a last resort the officials tried _____   8. _____

9. My ambition since childhood has been _____   9. _____

10. Oddly, _____ has never been one of my goals.   10. _____

FLASH TEST

PART 9

In each blank, write the **correct form** of the verb in parentheses (some answers may require more than one word).

EXAMPLES: (prefer) We have always <u>preferred</u> vanilla.
                 (see) Yesterday all of us <u>saw</u> the rainbow.

1. (use) The young man had never _____ a microwave.

2. (begin) He found the instruction book and _____ to read it.

3. (cross) They were _____ the busy street in the wrong place.

4. (blow) Trees of all sizes were _____ down in the storm.

5. (try) If I had found the courage, I would _____ _____ skydiving.

6. (drink) Drivers who had _____ alcoholic beverages were detained by the police.

7. (fly) By the time I reach Hawaii, I shall _____ _____ for thirteen hours nonstop.

8. (freeze) If they had not brought heavy clothing, they would _____ _____ on the hike.

9. (possess) The Tsar's court felt that Rasputin _____ a strange power over them.

10. (choose) The district has always _____ a Republican for Congress.

FLASH TEST

PART 10

Write **C** if the boldfaced verb is used **correctly**. Write **X** if it is used **incorrectly**.

EXAMPLES: In chapter 1 Greg goes to war, and in chapter 10 he **died**.   X
                 The lake **was frozen** overnight by the sudden winter storm.   C

1. I **payed** the news carrier.   1. _____

2. We **have flown** home to Wyoming four times this year.   2. _____

3. In the summer, we **swam** in the creek behind our home.   3. _____

4. The bell in Clark Tower **has rang** every evening at 6:00 p.m. for the past fifty years.   4. _____

5. My hat **was stole** when I left it at the restaurant.   5. _____

6. We **have ridden** the train to Chicago many times.   6. _____

7. The little child **tore** open the present wrapped in bright yellow paper.   7. _____

8. The student **sunk** into his chair to avoid being called on by the professor.   8. _____

9. We **have gone** to the county fair every year since we moved to San Antonio.   9. _____

10. We **should have known** that Robert would be late for the meeting.   10. _____

Answers to Exercises for: Using Verbs

Part 1

1. pres	6. cond	11. past	16. past
2. fut	7. fut	12. fut	17. pres perf
3. fut perf	8. past	13. pres perf	18. past
4. pres perf	9. past perf	14. pres	19. past
5. fut perf	10. past cond	15. past cond	20. past cond

Part 2

line 1   rise . . . separates . . .

line 2   pounded . . . failed . . .

line 3   swooping . . . seeking . . . destined . . .

line 4   gathered . . .

line 5   imagined . . . tumbled . . .

line 6   filled . . .

line 7   stand . . . speaks . . .

line 8   trying . . . feeling . . .

line 9   feel . . . make . . . reaches . . .

line 10   attempts . . . succeeds . . .

line 11   walk . . . parked . . . pretending . . .

line 12   knows . . . looks . . .

Part 3

1. T	6. I	11. I
2. L	7. T	12. T
3. T	8. L	13. L
4. I	9. I	14. I
5. I	10. I	15. L

Part 4

1. cluttered	**6.** would have died
2. has appointed	**7.** is seeking
3. had appointed	**8.** did seek
4. will have won	**9.** has sought
5. would die	**10.** has been seeking

Part 5
(Some wording may vary.)

1. P   The typist inadvertently omitted one name from the list.

2. A   A special agreement was carried to the union meeting.

3. A   The incumbent's speech was bashed by the media.

4. P   The chair called the meeting to order.

5. P   A volcanic eruption totally destroyed the ancient city.

6. P The auditor discovered an accounting error.

7. A A presidential candidate has been selected by younger voters.

8. A The witness was subjected to a vigorous cross-examination by the prosecutor.

9. A By dawn every road will have been barricaded by the police.

10. P The vice-president will submit the status report next week.

11. A The runner was thrown out by the left fielder.

12. A A nationwide antipollution campaign has been begun by environmental activists.

Part 6

1. were

2. were

3. be

Part 7

1. inf	**6.** past part	**11.** past part
2. pres part	**7.** inf	**12.** pres part
3. inf	**8.** ger	**13.** past part
4. ger	**9.** pres part	**14.** inf
5. past part	**10.** ger	**15.** ger

Part 8
(Words or phrases are samples.)

1.	Grumbling about breakfast	subj
2.	to discuss religion	dir obj
3.	amazed	adj
4.	to check the fan belt	adv
5.	playing Scrabble	subj comp
6.	writing a paper on Cather	obj prep
7.	towing a 25-foot boat	adj
8.	phoning everyone on the list	dir obj
9.	to be a published writer	subj comp
10.	marrying	subj

Part 9

1. used	**6.** drunk
2. began	**7.** have flown
3. crossing	**8.** have frozen
4. blown	**9.** possessed
5. have tried	**10.** chosen

Part 10

1. X	**3.** C	**5.** X	**7.** C	**9.** C
2. C	**4.** X	**6.** C	**8.** X	**10.** C

FLASH SUMMARY

Recall that an adjective modifies (describes or limits) a noun or occasionally a pronoun, and that an adverb modifies a verb or sometimes another modifier (adjective or adverb):

> ADJECTIVES: [descriptive] a *red* barn, a *swift* ride, a *happy* woman; [limiting] *this* isle, *seven* clowns, *some* cookies.

> ADVERBS: The horse ran *swiftly*. [modifying a verb, *ran*]
> The horse was *very* swift. [modifying an adjective, *swift*]
> The horse ran *very* swiftly. [modifying an adverb, *swiftly*]

Many adverbs are formed by the addition of *-ly* to adjectives:

> smooth ➔ smoothly   regrettable ➔ regrettably

> delightful ➔ delightfully   easy ➔ easily

An *-ly* ending thus usually signals an adverb—but not always, because *friendly, womanly,* and *saintly* are adjectives. A few common adverbs have the same form as their corresponding adjectives: *late, early, fast.* Some adverbs have two forms: *slow(ly), quick(ly).* The sure way to tell an adjective from an adverb is to determine the word that is modified: You drive too *fast* [drive how? *fast:* adverb]. You are in the *fast* lane [which lane? *fast:* adjective].

The word *not* is an adverb.

16. Using Adjectives and Adverbs Correctly

A. Use an Adverb, Not an Adjective.

(1) *To modify an action verb:*

> WRONG: The team played *careless* today.

> RIGHT: The team played *carelessly* today.

(2) *To modify an adjective:*

> WRONG: This was a *real* good clambake.

> RIGHT: This was a *really* good clambake.

(3) *To modify another adverb:*

> WRONG: Tamara tries *awful* hard.

> RIGHT: Tamara tries *awfully* (better, *extremely*) hard.

B. Use an Adjective (as Subjective Complement) After a Linking Verb.

> The weather was *dismal.* [*Dismal* describes *weather.*]

> Our tiny room smelled *damp.* [*Damp* describes *room.*]

See section 13C, page 38, for an explanation and full list of linking verbs and an example of the same verb as both linking and action.

C. Use *Good* and *Well, Bad* and *Badly* Correctly. Use *good* and *bad* (adjectives) as complements after a linking verb: This is *good.* I feel *good.* This fish tastes *bad.*

Use *well* and *badly* (adverbs) to modify an action verb: She sings *well.* I have failed *badly.*

Note: *Well* can be an adjective in the limited sense of "in good health": I am feeling *well*. She is not a *well* woman. *I feel good,* on the other hand, refers to any kind of good feeling.

D. Use Comparative and Superlative Forms Correctly.

(1) Most adjectives and adverbs have three degrees. Notice how the *-er* and *-est* endings change the degree:

POSITIVE (MODIFYING ONE THING OR ACTION): The Toyonda is a *sleek* car that can accelerate *fast.*

COMPARATIVE (COMPARING TWO): The Chrysillac is the *sleeker* of the two cars, and it can accelerate *faster.*

SUPERLATIVE (COMPARING THREE OR MORE): The Lexmobile is the *sleekest* car on the road, and it can accelerate (the) *fastest* of all.

Most long adjectives and most adverbs use *more* and *most* instead of *-er* and *-est: fanciful, more fanciful, most fanciful; smoothly, more smoothly, most smoothly.* Some adjectives and adverbs use either form: *costlier, costliest* or *more costly, most costly.* (To express the opposite of *more* and *most,* use *less* and *least: less smoothly, least smoothly.*)

(2) A few adjectives and adverbs have irregular forms of comparison:

good/well, better, best   many/much, more, most

bad/badly, worse, worst   little, less, least

(3) Use the comparative (not the superlative) when comparing two things:

WRONG: Lee is the *smallest* of the twins.

RIGHT: Lee is the *smaller* of the twins.

(ESL) E. Use Articles and Determiners Correctly.

(1) A and an. Before a vowel sound (*a, e, i, o, u,* sometimes *y*) use *an: an* accident, *an* image, *an* honest person (*h* is silent), *an* uncle, *an* FBI (eff-bee-eye) agent, *an* $80 (eighty-dollar) check. Before a consonant (any nonvowel) sound, use *a: a* car, *a* mystery, *a* university (*u* pronounced as consonant *yu*), a *D* (dee), a $70 (seventy-dollar) check.

(2) Count and noncount nouns. A **count noun** is one that can be counted, such as *car:* one car, two cars, three cars, several cars . . .; one reason, two reasons, many reasons. . . . A **noncount noun** cannot be counted: *health* (we do not say *one health, two healths, many healths*), *courage, gold.* Noncount nouns include concepts and qualities *(truth, honesty),* emotions *(sadness),* activities *(swimming),* substances *(methane, milk),* school subjects *(chemistry),* and other noncountables *(baggage, underwear).* Certain nouns are sometimes noncount (I felt *joy*) and sometimes count (the *joys* of youth).

A **familiar term** is one that we already know; the writer may have mentioned it already or may explain it immediately, or it may be in our prior knowledge (such as your campus gym). An **unfamiliar** term is the opposite: the writer has not previously mentioned it or does not immediately explain it, nor is it in our prior knowledge (a faraway gym, any gym).

Use articles *(a, an, the)* as follows:

Before—	Use—	Example
COUNT NOUNS Unfamiliar singular	*a* or *an*	*An* [any] accident *victim* needs *a* [any] good *lawyer*. *A* bus has skidded into *a* tree. [Reader has not known about the bus or tree before.]
Unfamiliar plural	[no article]	*Fires* broke out in Florida. [Reader has not known of these before.] *Victims* [any victims] need *lawyers* promptly.
Familiar (singular or plural)	*the*	[Victim and lawyer mentioned in previous sentence.] *The victim* should see *the lawyer* promptly. *The war* is over. *The stars* are out.

Before—	Use—	Example
NONCOUNT NOUNS	[usually no article]	*Peace* is near. She prefers *wine*. They fought with *honor*.

Other uses of articles

SUPERLATIVES	*the*	*the most fearful child, the highest ratings*
PROPER NOUNS singular	[mostly no article]	*Australia, Lake Erie, Bard College, Queen Victoria* BUT: *the Titanic, the Nile, the Red Sea, the Senate, the Sphinx*
plural	*the*	*the Great Lakes, the Smiths, the Dodgers*

Use limiting adjectives (determiners) as follows:

Before—	Use (with example)—
COUNT NOUNS singular	*one* day, *every* way, *each* new clerk, *either* person, *another* problem
plural	*many* flights, *most* days, *(a) few* new ideas, *all* (the) cars, *other* people, *such* hats, *both* nations, *enough* apples, *some* players, *more* people
NONCOUNT NOUNS	*most* rain, *all* traffic, *other* equipment, *such* joy, *more* noise, *enough* trouble, *(a) little* time, *some* sugar

For more on determiners, see section 6A, page 28.

    (3) Order of adjectives. Before a noun, place adjectives in this order, from the beginning:

1. Articles, determiners, and possessive nouns or pronouns: *the, some, my, Janet's* (my friends)

2. Numbers: *five, fifth* (my five friends)

3. Descriptive adjectives: *enormous, round, old, silver, cranky* (my five old friends)

4. Nouns used as adjectives: *car* wheels, *bank* loans, *elephant* tusks (my five old college friends)

17. Avoiding Adjective and Adverb Errors

A. Do Not Use Both Forms of the Comparative (*-er* and *More*) or of the Superlative (*-est* and *Most*) Together. One form is enough:

WRONG: This beam is *more stronger* than the other.

RIGHT: This beam is *stronger* than the other.

WRONG: She is the *most unlikeliest* of heroes.

RIGHT: She is the *unlikeliest* (or the *most unlikely*) of heroes.

B. Do Not Compare Adjectives That Cannot Logically Be Compared, such as *unique, fatal, impossible, square, empty.* A task is either possible or impossible; it cannot be more (or less) impossible. Instead, say *more nearly impossible.*

WRONG: Newman's diagram is *more square* than Lombardo's. [A *square* must have four 90° angles; *more or less* square is not possible.]

RIGHT: Newman's diagram is *more nearly square* than Lombardo's.

 **FLASH TEST**

PART 1

If the boldfaced adjective or adverb is used **correctly,** leave the blank empty.

If the boldfaced adjective or adverb is used **incorrectly,** write the correct word(s) in the blank.

EXAMPLES: Her performance was truly **impressive.** _____
The Yankees are playing **good** this year. | **Well**

1. The sun feels **good.** 1. _____
2. The team shouldn't feel **badly** about losing that game. 2. _____
3. She was the **most** talented member of the dance couple. 3. _____
4. He keeps in **good** condition always. 4. _____
5. He was very **frank** in his evaluation of his work. 5. _____
6. My father spoke very **frankly** with us. 6. _____
7. Of the two students, she is the **smartest.** 7. _____
8. My leg aches **bad.** 8. _____
9. The student looked **cheerful.** 9. _____
10. The student looked **wearily** at the computer monitor. 10. _____
11. I comb my hair **different** now. 11. _____
12. Was the deer hurt **bad**? 12. _____
13. He seemed **real** sad. 13. _____
14. The learning assistant tried **awful** hard to keep the residence hall quiet during finals week. 14. _____
15. Reading Eudora Welty's work is a **real** pleasure. 15. _____
16. The teaching assistant glanced **nervously** at the class. 16. _____
17. The bus driver seemed **nervous.** 17. _____
18. The campus will look **differently** when the new buildings are completed. 18. _____
19. Yours is the **clearest** of the two explanations. 19. _____
20. The book is in **good** condition. 20. _____

 **FLASH TEST**

PART 2

In each blank, write the **correct** article: **a, an,** or **the;** or leave the blank empty if **no** article is needed.
(In some blanks, either of two answers is correct.)

EXAMPLE: When the moon and a planet come close to each other in the sky, an exciting sight awaits _____ viewers.

_____ exciting play occurred yesterday in _____ big-league baseball game at _____ Dodger Stadium. _____ Dodger player dropped _____ ball in the glare of _____ sun. When _____ ball fell to _____ ground, three Dodger players ran after it; thus _____ nobody was guarding the bases for _____ Dodgers. _____ crowd groaned with _____ disappointment. _____ batter from _____ other team ran around _____ bases with _____ determination. _____ Dodger player retrieved _____ ball and made _____ accurate throw that reached home plate ahead of the runner, who was called "Out!" _____ cheers burst from the crowd. The Dodgers won the game and celebrated with _____ champagne from _____ France. This was _____ biggest Dodger victory of the year.

 **FLASH TEST**

PART 3

For each blank, choose from the list any determiner (limiting adjective) that **sounds right**, and write it in. Try not to use any word on the list more than once.

every	many	other	more	some
each	most	such	(a) little	
either	(a) few	both	much	
another	all	enough	any	

EXAMPLE: They needed another person to help lift the car.

1. _____ country that voted for the United Nations resolution was praised.

2. _____ countries that voted against it were criticized.

3. _____ discussions took place before the vote.

4. _____ of the neutral countries tried to postpone the vote.

5. But _____ pressure was put on these countries to vote.

6. _____ effort to influence the neutral countries' vote was rebuffed.

7. Delegates from _____ countries wanted to get the voting finished.

8–9._____ delegates had _____ patience.

10. Finally, the Secretary General declared that _____ voting would take place the next day.

Answers to Exercises for: Using Adjectives and Adverbs

Part 1

1. –	5. –	9. –	13. really	17. –
2. bad	6. –	10. –	14. awfully [*or* very]	18. different
3. more	7. smarter	11. differently	15. –	19. clearer
4. –	8. badly	12. badly	16. –	20. –

Part 2

An . . . a [*or* the] . . . — . . A . . .

a . . . the . . . the . . . the . . .

— . . . the . . . The . . . — . . .

The . . . the . . . the . . . — . . . The [*or* A] . . .

the . . . an . . .

— . . . — . . . — . . . the . . .

Part 3

1. Every [*or* Any, Each]

2. All [*or* Most, Both, Some, A few, Other, Many]

3. Many [*or* Some, A few, Enough]

4. Some [*or* A few, Most, Each, Many, All, Both, Either]

5. much [*or* enough, every, a little]

6. Another [*or* All, Any, Every, Such]

7. other [*or* many, most, some, such, both, enough, all]

8. Most [*or* Some, Both, All, Many, Few]

9. little [*or* any, enough, more]

10. all [*or* any, some, most, more]

18–20 Using Pronouns

FLASH SUMMARY

A pronoun substitutes for a noun, so that instead of saying *The song was so popular for the song's witty lyrics that the song sold ten million copies,* we can say *The song was so popular for **its** witty lyrics that **it** sold ten million copies.* The noun that the pronoun substitutes for (stands for) is called its **antecedent.** In the sentence above, *song* is the antecedent of *its* and *it.* (Not all kinds of pronouns have expressed antecedents.)

Pronouns share almost all the uses of nouns. (To review those uses, see section 11, page 34.)

18. The Kinds of Pronouns

A. The Personal Pronouns. These designate one or more particular persons or things:

FLASH FOCUS

Person	Singular	Plural
FIRST [person(s) speaking]	I, my, mine, me	we, our, ours, us
SECOND [person(s) spoken to]	you, your, yours	you, your, yours
THIRD [any other person(s) or thing(s)]	he, his, him, she, her, hers, it, its	they, their, theirs, them

B. The Interrogative and Relative Pronouns

(1) The interrogative pronouns are *who (whose, whom), which, what.* They ask questions:

Who broke the silence? *Whose* voice was heard? *What* was said? *Which* of the members spoke? To *whom* was the remark directed?

(2) The relative pronouns are the same as the interrogative, plus *that* and the *-ever* forms: *whoever (whomever), whichever, whatever.* Relative pronouns introduce certain kinds of dependent clauses (sometimes called **relative clauses**):

The diplomat *who spied* was arrested.

VCRs, *which are quite complex,* puzzle me.

The President will veto *whatever reaches his desk.*

Use *who* for persons, *which* for things, and *that* for either:

PERSON: Students *who* (or *that*) use the dining hall must have meal cards.

THING: Tonight's meal is fajitas, *which* I enjoy. A meal *that* I enjoy is fajitas.

Note: When *of which* sounds awkward, you may use *whose* with things: Venice is a city *whose* traffic jams are confined to waterways.

C. The Demonstrative Pronouns are *this* (plural: *these*) and *that* (plural: *those*). They point out:

This is the page. Take any one of *these.*

That is her office. *Those* are the elevators.

D. The Indefinite Pronouns refer to no particular person or thing:

 FLASH FOCUS

Number	Indefinite Pronouns
Singular	another, anybody, anyone, anything, each, either, everybody, everyone, everything, neither, nobody, no one, nothing, one, somebody, someone, something
Plural	both, few, many, others, several
Singular or Plural	all, any, more, most, none, some, such

Many will complain, but *few* will act; *most* will do *nothing.*

Someone must do *something,* but *no one* wants to do *anything.*

Note: Closely related to the indefinite pronouns are the two **reciprocal** pronouns, *each other* and *one another.* See section 73, page 187.

E. The Reflexive and Intensive Pronouns are the *-self* forms of personal pronouns: *myself, yourself, yourselves, himself, herself, itself, ourselves, themselves.*

(1) They are called reflexive when used as objects or as subjective complements:

The computer will reboot *itself* after a shutdown [direct object]. The seniors produced the yearbook by *themselves* [object of preposition].

The dean is not *herself* today [subjective complement].

(2) *They are called intensive when used as appositives, for emphasis:*

I *myself* am to blame. Only they *themselves* are to blame.

Do not use a *-self* pronoun where a personal pronoun suffices:

WRONG: The message was for Pat and *myself.*

RIGHT: The message was for Pat and *me.*

Note: There are no such words in standard English as *hisself, ourselfs, theirself, theirselves, yourselfs, themself, themselfs.*

19. Using the Right Case

The case of a pronoun is the form it takes in a particular use in a sentence (subject, direct object, etc.). English has three cases: **nominative, possessive,** and **objective.**

 **FLASH FOCUS**

	Nominative Case (subject forms)	**Possessive Case** (possessive forms)	**Objective Case** (object forms)
Singular	I	my, mine	me
	he, she, it	his, her, hers, its	him, her, it
Plural	we	our, ours	us
	they	their, theirs	them
Singular and Plural	you	your, yours	you
	who	whose	whom

The pronouns with different nominative and objective forms cause the most confusion: *I/me, he/him, she/her, we/us, they/them, who/whom.*

A. Nominative Case. Use the distinctive nominative (subject) forms—*I, he, she, we, they, who*—for

(1) *Subject:* *I* know it. *He* and *I* know it. *Who* knows it? *They* know it.

(2) *Subjective complement* (after linking verbs): The only one invited was *she.*

Note: Although *It was her* or *It wasn't me* is common in informal usage, most writers and speakers adhere to the nominative in formal usage: It was *she.* It was not *I.* If a sentence such as *The only one invited was she* sounds awkward, you can recast it: *She was the only one invited.* See C(4) note below for pronoun case with the infinitive *to be.*

B. Objective Case. Use the distinctive object(ive) forms—*me, him, her, us, them, whom*—for any kind of object:

DIRECT OBJECT: The environmentalists castigated *him.*

INDIRECT OBJECT: He told *her* and *me* the details.

OBJECT OF PREPOSITION: He told the details to *us.*

C. Special Problems with Nominative and Objective Cases. (For *who* and *whom,* see D and E below on pages 64–65.)

(1) *A **pronoun in a compound*** (with *and, or, but*) takes the same case as it would if not compounded:

> WRONG: *Him* and *me* can go. [Would you say *Him* can go or *Me* can go?]

> RIGHT: *He* and *I* can go. [*He* can go. *I* can go.]

> WRONG: Awards went to Luis and *I*. [to *I*?]

> RIGHT: Awards went to Luis and *me*. [to *me*]

Note: *Luis and myself* is also wrong. See section 18E(2), page 63.

> WRONG: Between you and *I* there should be no secrets.

> RIGHT: Between you and *me* there should be no secrets.

(2) *A **pronoun followed by a noun appositive*** takes the same case as it would without the noun:

> WRONG: Only *us* Bostonians know. [*us* know?]

> RIGHT: Only *we* Bostonians know. [*we* know]

> RIGHT: It is known only to *us* Bostonians. [to *us*]

For definition of *appositive*, see section 11D, pages 34–35.

(3) *A **pronoun appositive*** takes the same case as the word to which it is in apposition:

> Two *students*, *you* and *she*, will share the prize.

> Professor Hunt told *us*—Len and *me*—to leave.

> Let's [Let *us*] *you* and *me* try the bookstore.

(4) *A **pronoun in an incomplete comparison*** takes the same case as if the comparison were complete:

> RIGHT: She liked Pat more than *I* [did].

> RIGHT: She liked Pat more than [she liked] *me*.

Note: A pronoun between a verb and an infinitive (called the **subject of the infinitive**) takes the objective case: They urged *her* to run. She asked *them* to reconsider. In a sentence such as the following, a pronoun following *to be* takes the same case as the subject of the sentence (nominative): *The winner was thought to be she.*

D. *Who* and *Whom* as Interrogative Pronouns. *Who* is nominative case; *whom* is objective:

> *Who* voted against the child-support law? [subject]

> *Whom* can the people blame? → The people can blame *whom*? [direct object]

> *Whom* can people appeal to? → To *whom* can people appeal? [object of preposition]

Note: When in doubt about using *who* or *whom*, try substituting *he* or *him*. If *he* sounds right, use *who*; if *him* sounds right, use *whom*:

> (Who/Whom) rang the bell? → *He* rang the bell. *Who* rang the bell?

> (Who/Whom) did you see? → You did see *him*. → You did see *whom*? → *Whom* did you see?

Although *Who did you see?* and *Who did you go with?* are common in informal usage, *whom* is expected in formal usage. Directly after a preposition, always use *whom*: With *whom* did you go? (Exception—when the subject of a noun clause follows the preposition: The United States sent arms to *whoever fought Hitler* [not *whomever*—see E below]).

E. **Who and Whom as Relative Pronouns.** The case of a relative pronoun is determined by its use *within* its clause:

> Liu is the one **who** *arranged the affair.* [*Who* = subject of *arranged.*]
>
> Liu is the one **whom** *we should thank.* [→ *we should thank whom. Whom* = direct object of *should thank.*]
>
> We should also thank **whoever** *helped her.* [*Whoever* = subject of *helped.*]
>
> We should inform **whomever** *we see.* [→ *we see whomever. Whomever* = direct object of *see.*]
>
> Send a note to **whoever** *participated in the affair.* [*Whoever* = subject of *participated.*]

Do not be misled by other intervening clauses, such as *I think, it seems,* or *we are convinced:*

> Liu is the one **who** ⬚I think⬚ *arranged the affair.*
>
> Liu is the one **whom** ⬚it seems⬚ *we should thank.*

F. **Possessive Case**

   (1) Use the apostrophe ['] to form the possessive case of indefinite and reciprocal pronouns: someone's, everybody's, no one's, each other's, etc.

   (2) Use the possessive case before a gerund:

   WRONG: We resented *him* leaving.

   RIGHT: We resented *his* leaving.

   (3) Do not use the apostrophe in the possessive case of personal pronouns (his, hers, its, ours, yours, theirs) or of who (whose): Whose book is this? Is it ours or theirs? It can't be hers. It is a common error to confuse the possessives *its, whose, their,* and *your* with the contractions *it's, who's, they're,* and *you're.*

Possessive Pronouns (never take apostrophe)	Contractions (always take apostrophe)
its	it's (it is)
their	they're (they are)
your	you're (you are)
whose	who's (who is)

   The store lost *its* license. *Whose* fault was that?

   The stores lost *their* licenses. Was *your* store included?

Note: To tell which form you need, mentally substitute the uncontracted form (*it is,* etc.). If it sounds right, you need the contraction:

> (*Its/It's*) a fine day. → *It is* a fine day. → *It's* a fine day.
>
> The tree shed (*its/it's*) leaves. → The tree shed *it is* leaves? → No. The tree shed *its* leaves.

20. Avoiding Faulty Reference

Be sure that each pronoun refers unmistakably only to its antecedent—the noun it stands for.

A. **Ambiguous Reference** occurs when a pronoun may refer to more than one noun. Clarify such ambiguity by rephrasing the sentence:

   AMBIGUOUS: This program will not work on a model 5X computer because *it* is too old. [Does *it* refer to the program or the computer?]

CLEAR: This program will not work on a model 5X computer, *which* is too old.

CLEAR: This program, *which* is too old, will not work on a model 5X computer.

B. Vague Reference occurs when a pronoun has no easily identifiable antecedent. Clarify the sentence by supplying the needed noun:

VAGUE: In Japan *they* name *their* years after animals. [*They* and *their* have no antecedent. Who are *they*?]

CLEAR: The *Japanese* name their years after animals.

Avoid using *which, it, this,* or *that* to refer to a whole clause or sentence in a unclear way:

VAGUE: The treaty was approved by Congress, *which* raised hopes for world peace. [Can you find a clear antecedent for *which? Congress?* The *treaty?* Actually, neither. It is the *approval.*]

CLEAR: The treaty's *approval* by Congress raised hopes for world peace.

VAGUE: Acid rain is still a problem in the Northeast, thus increasing support for a stronger antipollution law in Congress. What will happen because of *this* is uncertain.

CLEAR: . . .What will happen because of *this new support* is uncertain.

CLEAR: . . .What will happen because of *this continued pollution* is uncertain.

Note: A possessive noun cannot logically be the antecedent of a nominative or objective pronoun:

WRONG: Princess *Diana's* death stunned the world, for *she* had been loved by millions. [*She* cannot have a possessive, *Diana's,* as antecedent.]

RIGHT: Diana's death stunned the world, for the *princess* had been loved by millions.

It is acceptable in *It is raining, It is a fine day,* and so on.

FLASH TEST

PART 1

Classify each boldfaced pronoun (use the abbreviations in parentheses):

personal pronoun (**pers**)	indefinite pronoun (**indef**)
interrogative pronoun (**inter**)	reflexive pronoun (**ref**)
relative pronoun (**rel**)	intensive pronoun (**intens**)
demonstrative pronoun (**dem**)	

EXAMPLE: **Who** is your partner?   _____inter_____

1. I made him an offer that **he** could not refuse.   1. _____
2. **No one** believed Albert's latest reason for missing work.   2. _____
3. **This** supports the importance of proper rest when studying for finals.   3. _____
4. He has only **himself** to blame for his predicament.   4. _____
5. **Which** of the city newspapers do you read?   5. _____
6. She is the executive **who** makes the key decisions in this company.   6. _____
7. I **myself** have no desire to explore the rough terrain of mountainous regions.   7. _____
8. **Everyone** promised to be on time for the staff meeting.   8. _____
9. They chose three charities and gave a thousand dollars to each of **them.**   9. _____

10. A small motor vehicle **that** can travel on rough woodland trails is called an all-terrain vehicle.

10. _____

11. Be sure that you take care of **yourself** on the expedition.

11. _____

12. These are my biology notes; **those** must be yours.

12. _____

13. **Who** do you think will win the poetry contest?

13. _____

14. It is they **themselves** who are the victims.

14. _____

15. **Neither** of the organizations worked on increasing membership.

15. _____

FLASH TEST

PART 2

Write the number of the **correct** pronoun.

EXAMPLE: The message was for Desmond and (1)**I** (2)**me**.

_____2_____

1. Three of (1)**we** (2)**us** jury members voted for acquittal.

1. _____

2. Although I tried to be careful around the cat, I still stepped on (1)**its** (2)**it's** tail three times.

2. _____

3. May we—John and (1)**I** (2)**me**—join you for the meeting?

3. _____

4. Between you and (1)**I** (2)**me**, I feel quite uneasy about the outcome of the expedition.

4. _____

5. Were you surprised that the book was written by Jake and (1)**he** (2)**him?**

5. _____

6. It must have been (1)**he** (2)**him** who wrote the article about plant safety for the company newsletter.

6. _____

7. Why not support (1)**we** (2)**us** students in our efforts to have a new student union?

7. _____

8. No one except (1)**she** (2)**her** could figure out the copier machine.

8. _____

9. He is much more talented in dramatics than (1)**she** (2)**her**.

9. _____

10. The audience cheered (1)**whoever** (2)**whomever** made fun of the mayor and his city council.

10. _____

FLASH TEST

PART 3

In the first blank, write the **number** of the **correct** pronoun.

In the second blank, write the **reason** for your choice (use the abbreviations in parentheses):

subject (**subj**)   indirect object (**ind obj**)
subjective complement (**subj comp**)   object of preposition (**obj prep**)
direct object (**dir obj**)

EXAMPLE: The tickets were for Jo and (1)**I** (2)**me**.

____2____   __obj prep__

1. Do you think it was (1)**she** (2)**her** who poisoned the cocoa?

1. _____ _____

2. Were you and (1)**he** (2)**him** ever in Montana?

2. _____ _____

3. Fourteen of (1)**we** (2)**us** students signed a petition to reverse the ruling.

3. _____ _____

4. The assignment gave (1)**she** (2)**her** no further trouble after it was explained.

4. _____ _____

5. Sam Lewis preferred to be remembered as the person (1)**who** (2)**whom** invented the jalapeño-flavored lollipop.

   5. _____ _____

6. I invited (1)**he** (2)**him** to the senior dance.

   6. _____ _____

7. Speakers like (1)**she** (2)**her** are both entertaining and informative.

   7. _____ _____

8. I was very much surprised when I saw (1)**he** (2)**him** at the art exhibit.

   8. _____ _____

9. Have you and (1)**he** (2)**him** completed your research on the origins of American rodeos?

   9. _____ _____

10. We asked Joan and (1)**he** (2)**him** about the playground activities.

   10. _____ _____

11. The leader of the student group asked, "(1)**Who** (2)**Whom** do you think can afford the 10 percent increase in tuition?"

   11. _____ _____

12. All of (1)**we** (2)**us** tourists spent the entire afternoon in a roadside museum.

   12. _____ _____

13. It was (1)**he** (2)**him** who made all the arrangements for the dance.

   13. _____ _____

14. Television network executives seem to think that ratings go to (1)**whoever** (2)**whomever** broadcasts the sexiest shows.

   14. _____ _____

15. My two friends and (1)**I** (2)**me** decided to visit Window Rock, Arizona, headquarters of the Navajo nation.

   15. _____ _____

FLASH TEST

PART 4

Write **C** if the boldfaced word is used **correctly**.

Write **X** if it is used **incorrectly**.

EXAMPLE: Gulliver agreed with his master that **he** was a Yahoo.

   _____ **X** _____

1. David won the lottery and quit his job. **This** was unexpected.

   1. _____

2. Jane told Monisha that **she** wasn't ready for the chemistry test.

   2. _____

3. Daniel decided to drop out of college. He later regretted **that** decision.

   3. _____

4. On the white card, list the classes **that** you plan to take.

   4. _____

5. The veteran football player practiced with the rookie because **he** wanted to review the new plays.

   5. _____

6. In Buffalo, **they** eat chicken wings served with blue cheese dressing and celery.

   6. _____

7. I was late filing my report, **which** greatly embarrassed me.

   7. _____

8. In the United States, **they** mail approximately 166 billion letters and packages each year.

   8. _____

9. She was able to complete college after earning a research assistantship. We greatly admire her for **that.**

   9. _____

10. The physician's speech focused on the country's inattention to the AIDS epidemic; the country was greatly surprised by **it.**

   10. _____

11. President Nixon's resignation stunned the nation, for **he** was the first President ever to step down from office.

   11. _____

12. They planned to climb sheer Mount Maguffey, a feat **that** no one had ever accomplished.

   12. _____

13. Pat always wanted to be a television newscaster; thus she majored in **it** in college.

   13. _____

14. The average American child watches over thirty hours of television each week, **which** is why we are no longer a nation of readers.

   14. _____

15. **It** was well past midnight when the phone rang.

15. _____

Answers to Exercises for: Using Pronouns

Part 1

1. pers	**4.** ref	**7.** intens	**10.** rel	**13.** inter
2. indef	**5.** inter	**8.** indef	**11.** ref	**14.** intens
3. dem	**6.** rel	**9.** pers	**12.** dem	**15.** indef

Part 2

1. 2	**3.** 1	**5.** 2	**7.** 2	**9.** 1
2. 1	**4.** 2	**6.** 1	**8.** 2	**10.** 1

Part 3

1. 1 subj comp
2. 1 subj
3. 2 obj prep
4. 2 ind obj
5. 1 subj
6. 2 dir obj
7. 2 obj prep
8. 2 dir obj
9. 1 subj
10. 2 dir obj
11. 1 subj
12. 2 obj prep
13. 1 subj comp [or subj—It _is actually an expletive._]
14. 1 subj
15. 1 subj

Part 4

1. X	**4.** C	**7.** X	**10.** X	**13.** X
2. X	**5.** X	**8.** X	**11.** X	**14.** X
3. C	**6.** X	**9.** X	**12.** C	**15.** C

21–22 Recognizing Phrases and Clauses

FLASH SUMMARY

Being able to recognize phrases and clauses helps you avoid agreement errors, fragments, comma splices, fused sentences, and misplaced or dangling modifiers.

21. Phrases

A **phrase** is a group of related words that is less than a sentence because it lacks subject + verb. (Some phrases contain a part of a verb—a verbal.) A phrase usually functions as if it were a single word: noun, adjective, or adverb. For this reason it is important to think of and recognize phrases as units. There are two main kinds of phrases.

A. The Prepositional Phrase is used chiefly as an adjective or adverb. It consists of preposition + object (and possible modifiers of that object):

> AS ADJECTIVE: The CD player *with the best sound* is lowest in price. [tells which player]

> AS ADVERB: I bought it *at a discount store.* [tells where]
> I bought it *for a birthday gift.* [tells why]

See section 7B, page 29, for a list of prepositions.

B. The Verbal Phrase. There are three kinds: infinitive, participial, and gerund. (See section 14D, pages 44–45, for explanation of these terms).

(1) An infinitive phrase (infinitive + complement or modifiers or both):

> AS NOUN: *To become governor* is her aim. [subject]
> She wants *to become governor.* [direct object]

> AS ADJECTIVE: I have a plan *to suggest to you.* [modifies *plan*]

> AS ADVERB: We sued the company *to obtain justice.* [modifies *sued*]
> Darryl is eager *to leave soon.* [modifies *eager*]

(2) A participial phrase (present or past participle + complement or modifiers or both). It is always used as an adjective:

> A computer *using a modem* can access the Internet. [modifies *computer*]

> *Equipped with a modem,* a computer can access the Internet. [modifies *computer*]

Another kind of phrase using a participle is the **absolute phrase** (subject + participle + possible complement or modifiers or both), so called because it is grammatically independent of the sentence (although logically connected to it):

> *Her heart pounding,* Karen rose to speak.

> Karen rose to speak, *her heart pounding.*

(3) A gerund phrase (*-ing* form + complement or modifiers or both). It is always used as a noun:

> *Saving the environment* will take worldwide effort. [subject]

> The speaker stressed *saving the environment.* [direct object]

> What can we do about *saving the environment?* [object of preposition]

> Her chief concern is *saving the environment.* [subjective complement]

For avoidance of dangling or misplaced phrases, see section 27A(2), (3), B, pages 92–94.

Note: Some authorities use the term **noun phrase** to refer to a noun and its modifiers (*the five old men in their wheelchairs*), and **verb phrase** for a main verb and its auxiliaries (*might have been drinking*).

22. Clauses

A **clause** is a group of related words containing subject + verb. There are two kinds: **independent (main)** and **dependent (subordinate).**

A. Kinds of Clauses

(1) *An independent clause* sounds complete and makes sense when it stands alone. Every simple sentence is an independent clause; however, the term *clause* usually refers to such a word group as part of a larger sentence:

[clauses in *italics*]

The virus began to spread, and *doctors grew alarmed.*

Independent clauses are normally connected by *and, but, yet, or, nor, for,* or *so* (coordinating conjunctions) or a semicolon (;). The conjunction is not considered part of either clause.

(2) *A dependent clause,* although it contains subject + verb, cannot stand alone grammatically. What makes a clause dependent is a connecting word that forces the clause to be linked to an independent clause:

[dependent clause in *italics;* connecting word in **bold**]

You may graduate ***when*** *you pay your library fines.*

*The topic **that*** *Elva chose was controversial.*

In dependent clauses (unlike independent clauses) the connecting word is considered part of the clause.

B. Kinds of Dependent Clauses

(1) *An adjective clause* is used as an adjective, modifying a preceding noun or pronoun. It is introduced and connected to the independent clause by the relative pronoun *who (whose, whom), which,* or *that,* or sometimes by *when, where,* or *why:*

Nations *that reduce tariffs* often prosper. [modifies *Nations*]

It frightened everyone *who saw it.* [modifies *everyone*]

Osgood's, *which is downtown,* sells CDs. [modifies *Osgood's*]

That was a time *when peace prevailed.* [modifies *time*]

Sometimes you may omit the relative pronoun: The people [*that/whom*] we met were friendly. But such omission may sometimes damage clarity or tone. It is better to keep the pronoun in most formal writing situations.

Adjective clauses are either **restrictive** or **nonrestrictive,** depending on their necessity in the sentence. See section 28F(1), pages 117–118, for explanation and punctuation.

(2) *An adverb clause* is used as an adverb, modifying a verb, adjective, or other adverb. It tells *how, when, where, why, with what result, under* or *despite what condition,* or *to what degree.* It is introduced and connected to the independent clause by a subordinating conjunction, such as the ones listed below:

Adverb Clause Telling	Introduced by Subordinating Conjunction	Example
Time [*when?*]	when(ever), while, after, before, since, as, as soon as, until	They kept dancing *after the music stopped.*
Place [*where?*]	where, wherever	We went *where the land was fertile.*
Manner [*how?*]	as, as if, as though	He walks *as if he's dazed.*
Cause [*why?*]	because, since	I left *because I was angry.*
Purpose [*why?*]	(so) that, in order that	She came *so that she might help.*
Concession [*despite what condition?*]	(al)though, even though	They played, *although they were tired.*
Condition [*under what condition?*]	if, unless, whether, provided	You may go *if you leave early.*
Result [*that what resulted?*]	that	He ran so fast *that he was exhausted.*
Comparison [*to what degree?*]	as, than	She is taller *than I [am].*

You can shift most adverb clauses to the beginning of the sentence for variety, emphasis, or clarity of sequence:

Although they were tired, they played.

If you leave early, you may go.

(3) *A noun clause* is used as a noun. It is introduced and connected to the independent clause by the relative pronoun *who(ever), which(ever), what(ever),* or *that* or by *when, where, why, how,* or *whether:*

What they knew frightened him. [subject]

I understand *that you need help.* [direct object]

She gave *whoever passed by* a brochure. [indirect object]

She gave a brochure to *whoever passed by.* [object of preposition]

As with adjective clauses, you may sometimes omit *that* (I understand [*that*] you need help), but in formal writing it is usually better to keep it.

C. Clauses in Sentences. Sentences can be classified according to their structure—that is, the number and kind(s) of clauses they have. There are four kinds of sentences:

(1) *The simple sentence* (one independent clause):

Management made a new offer.

(2) *The compound sentence* (two or more independent clauses):

Management made a new offer, and *the union agreed.*

Management made a new offer, the union agreed, and *the workers ended their strike.*

(3) *The complex sentence* (one independent clause + one or more dependent clauses):

[dependent clause in **bold**]
When management made a new offer, the union agreed.

(4) The compound–complex sentence (a compound sentence + one or more dependent clauses):

When management made a new offer, the union agreed, and the workers ended their strike.

FLASH TEST

PART 1

In the first blank, write the number of the **one** set of words that is a prepositional phrase.

In the second blank, write **adj** if the phrase is used as an adjective or **adv** if it is used as an adverb.

EXAMPLE: The starting pitcher for the Dodgers is a left-hander.	_2_	_adj_

1. When we came downstairs, a cab was awaiting us at the curb.   1. _____ _____
2. The red-brick building erected in the last century collapsed last week without warning.   2. _____ _____
3. The lady wearing the fur stole has been dating an animal activist from Oregon.   3. _____ _____
4. What they saw before the door closed shocked them beyond belief.   4. _____ _____
5. The most frequently used word in the English language is the word *the*.   5. _____ _____
6. The need for adequate child care was not considered when the President addressed the convention.   6. _____ _____
7. The observation that men and women have different courtship rituals seems debatable in a modern postindustrial society.   7. _____ _____
8. At our yard sale, I found out that people will buy almost anything if the price is right.   8. _____ _____
9. Until ten thousand years ago, all humans relied on food gathering and hunting to maintain their existence.   9. _____ _____
10. Although skateboarding is a relatively new sport, there have been world championships staged since 1966.   10. _____ _____

FLASH TEST

PART 2

Some of the boldfaced expressions are verbal phrases; others are parts of verbs (followed by modifiers or complements). In the blank, **identify** each phrase (use the abbreviations in parentheses):

verbal phrase used as adjective (**adj**)

verbal phrase used as adverb (**adv**)

verbal phrase used as noun (**noun**)

part of verb (with modifiers or complements)(**verb**)

EXAMPLES: **Singing in the rain** can give one a cold.	_noun_
Gene is **singing in the rain** despite his cold.	_verb_

1. **Taking portrait photographs of pets** is her means of earning a living.   1. _____
2. Now she is **taking portrait photographs of pets** as her means of earning a living.   2. _____

3. **To prepare his income taxes,** Sam spent several hours sorting through the shoe boxes filled with receipts.

3. _____

4. By age 30, many women begin **sensing a natural maternal need.**

4. _____

5. Both lawyers, **having presented their closing arguments,** nervously awaited the jury's verdict.

5. _____

6. The Clementes were **having the Robertsons to dinner that evening.**

6. _____

7. His idea of a thrill is **driving in stock-car races.**

7. _____

8. **Driving in stock-car races,** he not only gets his thrills but also earns prize money.

8. _____

9. The minister is **attempting to collect money for a special project.**

9. _____

10. He would like **to build his own home someday.**

10. _____

 FLASH TEST

PART 3

In each sentence, find a verbal phrase. **Circle** it, and in the small blank at the right, tell how it is used: as adjective (write **adj**), adverb (write **adv**), or **noun.**

EXAMPLE: A study conducted by the Yale Medical School found that smoking is addictive.

_____**adj**_____

1. Seeing the traffic worsen, Adam chose an alternate route.

1. _____

2. Losing their tickets to the Pacers' game made their day one of gloom.

2. _____

3. Public awareness is a crucial step in protecting our lakes and rivers.

3. _____

4. Hopelessly in love, June neglected to go to her science class.

4. _____

5. Realizing the importance of financial planning, David contacted an expert.

5. _____

6. To provide safe neighborhoods, the police have begun intensified night-time patrols.

6. _____

7. I can't help liking her even though she isn't interested in my favorite sport, hockey.

7. _____

8. Disappointed with her grades, Sabrina made an appointment with her counselor.

8. _____

9. I appreciate your helping us at the craft fair.

9. _____

10. Our lacrosse team, beaten in the playoffs, congratulated the winners.

10. _____

11. After I received a huge car repair bill, I promised myself to change the oil more often.

11. _____

12. The speaker frowned at us as we tried to ask more questions.

12. _____

13. Rock climbing is a sport demanding endurance.

13. _____

14. I passed chemistry by studying past midnight all last week.

14. _____

15. The hunter put down his gun, realizing that the ducks had flown out of range.

15. _____

 FLASH TEST

PART 4

Complete each sentence with a verbal phrase of your own. Then, in the small blank at the right, tell how you used it: **adj, adv,** or **noun.**

1. To take the test without _____ was not wise at all.   1. _____

2. Alison organized a group of senior citizens [hint: for what purpose?] _____   2. _____
   _____

3. Worried about her children, the young mother decided _____   3. _____
   _____

4. _____ may be linked to increased risk of rectal and blad-   4. _____
   der cancer.

5. She tried to obtain the information without _____   5. _____

6. The student _____ is here to select a major.   6. _____

7. The best book _____ is one that helps you escape daily   7. _____
   tension.

8. _____, he found an article that was easy to understand.   8 _____

9. Physicians recommend that patients _____ donate their   9. _____
   own blood.

10. _____ has been the cause of too many fires.   10. _____

FLASH TEST

PART 5

Classify each boldfaced phrase (use the abbreviations in parentheses):

   prepositional phrase (**prep**)   gerund phrase (**ger**)

   infinitive phrase (**inf**)   absolute phrase (**abs**)

   participial phrase (**part**)

EXAMPLE: The economies **of Asian countries** grew shaky.   _____prep_____

1. The woman standing **between the delegates** is an interpreter.   1. _____

2. The woman **standing between the delegates** is an interpreter.   2. _____

3. The first televisions had small round screens encased **in large wooden cabi-** 3. _____
   nets.

4. **His insisting that he was right** made him unpopular with his associates.   4. _____

5. The committee voted **to adjourn immediately.**   5. _____

6. **Because of the storm,** the excursion around the lake had to be postponed.   6. _____

7. **To stay awake in Smedley's class** required dedication and plenty of black cof- 7. _____
   fee.

8. **During early television programming,** many commercials were five minutes   8. _____
   long.

9. **Flying a jet at supersonic speeds** has been Sally's dream since childhood.   9. _____

10. The agent **wearing an official badge** is the one to see about tickets.   10. _____

11. **Realizing that his back injury would get worse,** the star player retired from 11. _____
    professional basketball.

12. **To pay for their dream vacation,** Harry and Sue both took on extra jobs.   12. _____

13. The children were successful in **developing their own lawn-mowing com-**   13. _____
    pany.

14. **The semester completed,** students were packing up to go home.   14. _____

15. The distinguished-looking man **in the blue suit** is the head of the company. 15. _____

 **FLASH TEST**

PART 6

Classify each boldfaced clause (use the abbreviations in parentheses):

    independent [main] clause (**ind**)

    dependent [subordinate] clause: adjective clause (**adj**)

    adverb clause (**adv**)

    noun clause (**noun**)

EXAMPLE: The program will work **when the disk is inserted.**   _____**adv**_____

1. Day-care employees complain **because there is no economic incentive to stay in the field.**   1. _____

2. The governor considered the latest proposal, **which called for local police units to work more closely with school districts.**   2. _____

3. Late-night television viewers know **how the comedian begins his monologue.**   3. _____

4. The student **who made the top grade in the history quiz** is my roommate.   4. _____

5. **Whether I am able to go to college** depends on whether I can find employment.   5. _____

6. **After Judd had written a paper for his English class,** he watched television.   6. _____

7. Canada celebrates Thanksgiving in October; **the United States celebrates it in November.**   7. _____

8. The career center offers seminars to anyone **who needs help writing a resume.**   8. _____

9. There is much excitement **whenever election results are announced.**   9. _____

10. The detective listened carefully to the suspect's answers, but **she couldn't find a reason to charge the suspect.**   10. _____

FLASH TEST

PART 7

Underline the dependent clause in each item. Then, in the blank, **classify** it as an adjective (**adj**), adverb (**adv**), or **noun.**

EXAMPLE: The textbook explained fully <u>what the instructor had outlined</u>.   _____**noun**_____

1. Although most Americans want better city services, over fifty percent complain about high taxes.   1. _____

2. The children of the war-torn city search each day for a place where the gunfire won't reach them.   2. _____

3. The early bicycles weren't comfortable, because they had wooden wheels and wooden seats.   3. _____

4. The student who complained about the food was given another dessert.   4. _____

5. Whether Camille dyes her hair remains a mystery.   5. _____

6. After Jonathan had read the morning paper, he threw up his hands in despair.   6. _____

7. Whoever predicted today's widespread use of computers was truly a prophet.   7. _____

8. Professor George gave extra help to anyone who asked for it.   8. _____

9. There is always much anxiety whenever final exams are held.   9. _____

10. The coach decided that I was not going to play that year.   10. _____

FLASH TEST

PART 8

Combine each of the following pairs of sentences into one sentence. Do this by reducing one of the pair to a noun or adjective clause.

EXAMPLES: Something puzzled the police. What did the note mean?
<u>What the note meant puzzled the police.</u>

The X-Files became immensely popular in the late 1990s. It appeared on the Fox TV network.
<u>*The X-Files,* which appeared on the Fox TV network, became immensely popular in the late 1990s.</u>

1. One thing remained unsolved. Who was the more accomplished chef? [Hint: try a noun clause.]

_____

_____

2. The programmer retired at twenty. She had written the new computer game. [Hint: try an adjective clause.]

_____

_____

3. I do not see how anyone could object to that. The senator said it.

_____

_____

4. The laboratory assistant gave the disk to Janine. He had helped Janine learn the word-processing software.

_____

_____

5. They planned something for the scavenger hunt. It seemed really bizarre.

_____

_____

FLASH TEST

PART 9

Combine each of the following pairs of sentences into one sentence. Do this by reducing one of the pair to the kind of adverb clause mentioned in brackets.

EXAMPLES: The sun set. Then the lovers headed home. [time]
<u>When the sun set, the lovers headed home.</u>

Students must score 1400 on their College Boards. Otherwise they will not be admitted. [condition]

<u>Students will not be admitted unless they score 1400 on their College Boards.</u>

1. [cause] Four hundred thousand Americans each year get skin cancer. Therefore, many parents are teaching their children to avoid overexposure to sunlight.

_____

_____

2. [place] The candidate was willing to speak anywhere. But she had to find an audience there.

_____

_____

3. [manner] Carl ran the race. He seemed to think his life depended on it.

_____

_____

4. [comparison] Her brother has always been able to read fast. She has always been able to read faster.

_____

_____

5. [purpose] This species of tree has poisonous leaves. That way, insects will not destroy it.

_____

_____

FLASH TEST

PART 10

Classify each sentence (use the abbreviations in parentheses):

    simple (**sim**)   complex (**cx**)

    compound (**cd**)   compound-complex (**cdcx**)

EXAMPLE: Hank opened the throttle, and the boat sped off.   _____**cd**_____

1. Mr. Taylor still insisted that he was an excellent driver.   **1.** _____

2. The comedienne, who has a popular television series, is starring in a movie.   **2.** _____

3. Completion of the new library will be delayed unless funds become available.   **3.** _____

4. Consider the matter carefully before you decide; your decision will be final.   **4.** _____

5. This year, either medical companies or discount store chains are a good investment for the small investor.   **5.** _____

6. The play, which was written and produced by a colleague, was well received by the audience.   **6.** _____

7. The storm, which had caused much damage, subsided; we then continued on our hike.   **7.** _____

8. We waited until all the spectators had left the gymnasium.   **8.** _____

9. The site for the theater having been selected, construction was begun.   **9.** _____

10. The prescription was supposed to cure my hives; instead it made my condition worse.   **10.** _____

Answers to Exercises for: Recognizing Phrases and Clauses

Part 1

1.	4	adj	**6.** 2	adj
2.	4	adv	**7.** 4	adv
3.	5	adj	**8.** 1	adv
4.	4	adv	**9.** 1	adv
5.	2	adj	**10.** 4	adv

Part 2

1. noun	**3.** adv	**5.** adj	**7.** noun	**9.** verb
2. verb	**4.** noun	**6.** verb	**8.** adj	**10.** noun

Part 3

1. Seeing the traffic worsen	adj
2. Losing their tickets to the Pacers' game	noun
3. protecting our lakes and rivers	noun
4. to go to her science class	noun
5. Realizing . . . financial planning	adj
6. To provide safe neighborhoods	adv
7. liking her	noun
8. Disappointed with her grades	adj
9. (your) helping us (at the craft fair)	noun
10. beaten in the playoffs	adj
11. to change the oil more often	noun
12. to ask more questions	noun
13. demanding endurance	adj
14. studying past midnight all last week	noun
15. realizing that the ducks . . . range	adj

Part 4

(Phrases are samples.)

1. studying for it	noun
2. to watch out for one another	adv
3. to quit her job and spend more time with them	noun
4. Drinking contaminated water	noun
5. being caught	noun
6. waiting in the office	adj
7. to read in the evening	adj
8. Browsing through the magazine racks	adj
9. preparing for surgery	adj
10. Being careless with campfires	noun

Part 5

1. prep	**4.** ger	**7.** inf	**10.** part	**13.** ger
2. part	**5.** inf	**8.** prep	**11.** part	**14.** abs
3. prep	**6.** prep	**9.** ger	**12.** inf	**15.** prep

Part 6

1. adv	**3.** noun	**5.** noun	**7.** ind	**9.** adv
2. adj	**4.** adj	**6.** adv	**8.** adj	**11.** ind

Part 7

1. Although . . . services	adv
2. Where . . . them	adj
3. because . . . seats	adv
4. who . . . food	adj
5. Whether . . . hair	noun
6. After . . . paper	adv
7. Whoever . . . computers	noun
8. who asked for it	adj
9. Whenever . . . held	adv
10. that I . . . year	noun

Part 8
(Some items have other possible answers.)

1. Who was the more accomplished chef remained unresolved.

2. The programmer who had written the new computer game retired at twenty.

3. I do not see how anyone could object to what the senator said.

4. The laboratory assistant, who had helped Janine learn . . . software, gave the disk to her.

5. What they planned for the scavenger hunt seemed really bizarre.
   [*or* For the scavenger hunt, they planned something that seemed really bizarre.]

Part 9
(Some items have other possible answers.)

1. Because 400,000 Americans get skin cancer each year, many parents are . . .

2. The candidate was willing to speak wherever she could find an audience.

3. Carl ran the race as if his life depended on it.

4. She has always been able to read faster than her brother [can].

5. This species of tree has poisonous leaves so that insects will not destroy it.

Part 10

1. cx	**3.** cx	**5.** sim	**7.** cdcx	**9.** sim
2. cx	**4.** cdcx	**6.** cx	**8.** cx	**10.** cd

FLASH SUMMARY

In sentences, subjects and verbs have matching forms to show their grammatical relation. So do pronouns and their antecedents. This relation is called **agreement.**

23. Subject–Verb Agreement

A. **Agreement in Person.** Use the verb form that matches the person of the subject. (See section 14B, page 40, for explanation of *person.*) For most verbs, only the third person present tense singular, with the ending *-s,* causes a problem. *I run, we run,* and *you run,* but *he/she/it runs.* The verb *be* is special. The first person is *I am, we are* (past tense: *I was, we were*); the second person is *you are* (past tense: *you were*); the third person is *he/she/it is, they are* (past tense: *he/she/it was, they were*):

WRONG: *You is* late.   RIGHT: *You **are*** late.

Note: When two or more subjects in different persons are joined by *or,* the verb agrees with the subject nearer to it: Either she or I *am* going. In a dependent clause with *who* or *that* as subject, the verb agrees with the antecedent of *who* or *that:* It is I who *am* right. [Antecedent of *who* is *I.*]

B. **Agreement in Number. Singular** number refers to one thing, and **plural** number refers to more than one. Singular subjects must take singular verbs; plural subjects must take plural verbs. Except for *be* (see A above), only the third person singular in the present causes a problem, because of its *-s* ending:

WRONG: A *bear like* honey, but *it don't* [*do* not] like bees.

RIGHT: A *bear **likes*** honey, but *it **does**n't* [***does*** not] like bees.

WRONG: Only one rock *concert have* been scheduled here.

RIGHT: Only one rock *concert **has*** been scheduled here.

C. **Intervening Word Groups.** Make subject and verb agree regardless of phrases or clauses between them:

PHRASE: Their *performance* |on all tests| ***is*** impressive.

CLAUSE: *Trees* |that get the disease| ***are*** cut down.

Parenthetical phrases introduced by *(together) with, like, as well as, including, in addition to,* and so on do not affect the number of the actual subject:

The *city,* |as well as the suburbs|, ***votes*** Democratic.

Ted, |in addition to the twins|, ***has*** accepted.

D. **Two or More Subjects**

(1) *Joined by* **and:** Use a plural verb:

A *book and* a *pencil **are*** all I need.

Are *chemistry and history* required?

However, if both subjects refer to the same single person or thing, use a singular verb:

Her *mentor and friend **was*** at her side during the ordeal. [One person is both mentor and friend.]

*Ham and eggs **is*** on the menu. [one dish]

Use a singular verb when *each* or *every* precedes the subjects:

> *Every dog and cat is* tested for rabies.

(2) *Joined by* nor *or* or: Make the verb agree with the nearer subject:
Renee or Kareem is volunteering.

> The *Garcias* and the *Jacksons are* volunteering.

> *Neither Renee nor* the *Jacksons are* inexperienced.

> *Neither* the *Jacksons nor Renee is* inexperienced.

E. **Singular Pronouns.** Use a singular verb when the subject is a singular indefinite pronoun, such as *one, each, either, neither, everyone, everybody, anyone, anybody, someone, somebody, no one,* or *nobody.* Do not be misled by intervening phrases or clauses:

> *Each* | of the blouses in the shipments | *has* a tiny defect.

> *Everyone* | who has ever seen any of her plays | *is* calling this her best.

After *all, any, most, none, some,* or *such,* use either a singular or a plural verb, depending on whether the pronoun refers to something singular or plural:

> The milk was left in the sun; *all* of it *has* turned sour.

> The guests became bored; *all have* left.

> *Such were* the joys of youth. *Such is* the way of the world.

F. **Collective Nouns.** In U.S. usage, use a singular verb when thinking of the group as a unit:

> The *audience was* the largest this season.

Use a plural verb when thinking of the group members as individuals:

> The *audience were* leaving, one or two at a time.

G. **Linking Verbs.** Make a linking verb agree with its subject, not with its subjective complement:

> His *problem was* wild pitches. Wild *pitches were* his problem.

H. **Singular Nouns in Plural Form.** Such nouns as *news, billiards, whereabouts, athletics, measles, mumps, mathematics,* and *economics* are logically singular. Use a singular verb:

> Muller is discovering that *economics requires* much study.

> *Mumps leaves* some children with impaired hearing.

However, use a plural verb with two-part things such as *trousers, pants, pliers, scissors, tweezers:*
The *tweezers are* not useful here; perhaps the *pliers are.*

I. ***It* and *There* as Expletives** (words with no meaning in a sentence):

(1) *There* is *never the subject.* In sentences beginning with *there is (was)* or *there are (were),* look *after* the verb for the subject, and make the verb agree with the subject:

> There *is* a *taxi* at the curb. [A *taxi is* at the curb.]

> There *are* two *taxis* at the curb. [Two *taxis are* at the curb.]

> There *are* a *taxi* and a *limousine* at the curb.

(2) *It, on the other hand, is always singular:*

> *It was* my fax machine that malfunctioned.

> *It was* our fax machines that malfunctioned.

J. **Literary Titles and Words Considered as Words** are always singular:

Chaucer's *Canterbury Tales* **depicts** life in medieval England.

Zeroes **is** spelled with either *-oes* or *-os*.

K. **Sums of Money and Measurements.** When considering a sum as a single unit, use a singular verb:

Six hundred dollars **was** too much for a guitar.

Seven miles uphill **is** quite a grueling run.

When considering individual dollars, gallons, miles, and so on, use a plural verb:

The *dollars* **were** neatly arranged in stacks.

All those *miles* **take** a toll on a runner's stamina.

In an arithmetic problem, you may use either:

Six and four **is [makes]** ten. *Six and four* **are [make]** ten.

Note: *The number* takes a singular verb; *a number,* plural: *The number* of crimes **is** down. *A number* of crimes **are** unsolved.

L. **Relative Pronouns.** Use a singular verb if the antecedent of *who, which,* or *that* is singular; use a plural verb if the antecedent is plural:

He is the only *one* of the chimps *that* **comprehends.** [Antecedent of *that* is *one.* Only one comprehends.]

He is one of the *chimps that* **comprehend.** [Antecedent of *that* is *chimps.* Several chimps comprehend.]

24. Pronoun–Antecedent Agreement

Every pronoun must agree with its antecedent in person and number.

A. **Illogical Shifts to *You*.** Avoid them:

WRONG: *Students* like English 302 because it exposes *you* to classic films.

RIGHT: *Students* like English 302 because it exposes ***them*** to classic films. *I* like English 302 because it exposes ***me*** to classic films.

B. **Singular Pronouns.** Generally, use a singular pronoun when referring to antecedents such as *person, woman, man, one, anyone, anybody, someone, somebody, each, either, neither, everyone, everybody:*

Neither of the nations would yield on ***its*** position.

Has *anyone* lost ***her*** bracelet?

Everyone in the fraternity pledged ***his*** loyalty.

A *person* should know what ***he*** wants in life. [or *what **she** wants in life.*]

For a mixed group of men and women, should you use *they* with a singular pronoun (*Everyone* lost *their* money)? In formal English, no. For discussion of this important, thorny problem, see section 72A(1), pages 182–183.

C. **Antecedents Joined by *And, Or,* or *Nor*.** Follow the same principles as for subject-verb agreement (see section 23D, pages 81–82).

(1) ***With antecedents joined by* and,** use a plural pronoun:

Michigan and *Ohio* may regain ***their*** industries.

(2) With antecedents joined by or or nor, make the pronoun agree with the nearer antecedent:

Either *Michigan* or *Ohio* may regain *its* industries.

Neither the *Carolinas* nor *Georgia* should see *its* wealth decline.

D. Collective Nouns. Follow the same principle as for subject–verb agreement (see section 23F, page 82); let the meaning of the noun determine the number of the pronoun:

Tonight's *audience* has angered the performers by *its* rudeness.

One by one, the *audience* are leaving *their* seats.

E. Demonstrative Pronouns Used as Adjectives. Make *this, that, these,* or *those* agree with the noun it modifies:

WRONG: I like *these kind* of fish. [*These* is plural; *kind,* singular.]

RIGHT: I like *this* kind of fish. I like *these* kinds of fish.

F. One of the . . . After *one of the,* use a plural noun.

WRONG: Burlington is *one of the* most livable *city* in America.

RIGHT: Burlington is *one of the* most livable **cities** in America.

 **FLASH TEST**

PART 1

Write the number of the **correct** choice.

EXAMPLE: One of the network's best programs (1)**was** (2)**were** canceled.   ___1___

1. Neither the researcher nor the subject (1)**has** (2)**have** any idea which is the placebo.   1. _____

2. Economics (1)**is** (2)**are** what the students are most interested in.   2. _____

3. Working a second job to pay off my debts (1)**has** (2)**have** become a priority.   3. _____

4. Not one of the nominees (1)**has** (2)**have** impressed me.   4. _____

5. (1)**Does** (2)**Do** each of the questions count the same number of points?   5. _____

6. The number of jobs lost in California's Silicon Valley (1)**has** (2)**have** increased significantly in the past two years.   6. _____

7. *Ninety-nine* (1)**is** (2)**are** hyphenated because it is a compound number.   7. _____

8. The college president, along with five vice-presidents, (1)**was** (2)**were** ready for the meeting.   8. _____

9. Both the secretary and the treasurer (1)**was** (2)**were** asked to submit reports.   9. _____

10. Everyone in the audience (1)**was** (2)**were** surprised by the mayor's remarks.   10. _____

11. *Women* (1)**is** (2)**are** spelled with an *o* but pronounced with an *i* sound.   11. _____

12. Every junior and senior (1)**was** (2)**were** expected to report to the gymnasium.   12. _____

13. There (1)**is** (2)**are** a professor, several students, and a teaching assistant meeting to discuss the course reading list.   13. _____

14. Ten dollars (1)**is** (2)**are** too much to pay for that book.   14. _____

15. (1)**Is** (2)**Are** there any computers available in the lab this morning?   15. _____

16. Neither the neighbors nor the police officer (1)**was** (2)**were** surprised by the violent crime.   16. _____

17. Each of the crises actually (1)**needs** (2)**need** the President's immediate attention.　17. _____

18. (1)**Is** (2)**Are** your father and brother coming to see you graduate tomorrow?　18. _____

19. A good book and some chocolate donuts (1)**was** (2)**were** all she needed to relax.　19. _____

20. There (1)**is** (2)**are** one coat and two hats in the hallway.　20. _____

FLASH TEST

PART 2

Write the number of the **correct** choice.

EXAMPLE:　One of the women fell from (1)**her** (2)**their** horse.　_____1_____

1. Agatha Christie is the kind of writer who loves to keep (1)**her** (2)**their** readers guessing until the last page.　1. _____

2. Many tourists traveling in the West enjoy stopping at roadside attractions because (1)**you** (2)**they** never know what to expect.　2. _____

3. If anyone on the football team has found my wallet in the locker room, would (1)**he** (2)**they** please return it.　3. _____

4. He majored in mathematics because (1)**it** (2)**they** had always been of interest to him.　4. _____

5. Lucy edited the news because (1)**it was** (2)**they were** often full of inaccuracies.　5. _____

6. He assumed that all of his students had done (1)**his** (2)**their** best to complete the test.　6. _____

7. Both Ed and Luis decided to stretch (1)**his** (2)**their** legs when the bus reached Houston.　7. _____

8. Ironically, neither woman had considered how to make (1)**her** (2)**their** job easier.　8. _____

9. Each of the researchers presented (1)**a** (2)**their** theory about the age of the solar system.　9. _____

10. He buys his books at the campus bookstore because (1)**it has** (2)**they have** low prices.　10. _____

11. Neither the president nor the members of the community advisory committee were willing to ignore (1)**her** (2)**their** personal opinions to find a solution to the city's budgetary problems.　11. _____

12. Every member of the men's basketball team received (1)**his** (2)**their** individual trophy.　12. _____

13. All in the class voted to have (1)**its** (2)**their** term papers due a week earlier.　13. _____

14. I like swimming because it develops (1)**one's** (2)**your** muscles without straining the joints.　14. _____

15. Neither Aaron nor Marzell has declared (1)**his** (2)**their** major.　15. _____

16. Citizens who still do not recycle (1)**your** (2)**their** garbage need to read this news article.　16. _____

17. The Zoomation Company has just introduced (1)**its** (2)**their** new 95-gigabyte computer.　17. _____

18. Neither the guide nor the hikers seemed aware of (1)**her** (2)**their** danger on the trail.　18. _____

19. The faculty has already selected (1)**its** (2)**their** final candidates.　19. _____

20. Critics argue that (1)**those kind** (2)**those kinds** of movies may promote violent tendencies in children.　20. _____

FLASH TEST

PART 3

Write **C** if the sentence is **correct.**

Write **X** if it is **incorrect.**

EXAMPLE: Nobody in the first two rows were singing.   _____ **X** _____

1. The deep blue of the waters seem to reflect the sky.   1. _____

2. All of the fish swim upstream in spring.   2. _____

3. All of the fish tastes good if you grill it properly.   3. _____

4. The strength of these new space-age materials have been demonstrated many times.   4. _____

5. All these experiences, along with the special love and care that my daughter needs, have taught me the value of caring.   5. _____

6. Evan's pants are ripped beyond repair.   6. _____

7. Does the six-thirty bus and the eight-o'clock train arrive in Detroit before midnight?   7. _____

8. According to a recent survey, almost every American feels that their self-esteem is important.   8. _____

9. The management now realizes that a bigger budget is needed; they plan to ask for federal assistance.   9. _____

10. When an older student senses that an institution understands nontraditional students, she generally works to her academic potential.   10. _____

11. I found that the thrill of attending college soon leaves when you have to visit the bursar's office.   11. _____

12. Everyone who read the letter stated that they were surprised by the contents.   12. _____

13. You should hire one of those experts who solves problems with computers.   13. _____

14. Two hundred miles was too much for a day trip.   14. _____

15. At school, there are constant noise and confusion at lunch.   15. _____

16. Cleveland or Cincinnati are planning to host the statewide contests.   16. _____

17. Bacon and eggs are no longer considered a healthy breakfast.   17. _____

18. Probably everybody in the computer center, except Colleen and Aaron, know how to run the scanner.   18. _____

19. Neither Chuck nor Arnold are as blessed with talent as Sylvester.   19. _____

20. *The Avengers* was a popular British television show in the 1960s.   20. _____

Answers to Exercises for: Agreement

Part 1

1. 1	**5.** 1	**9.** 2	**13.** 2	**17.** 1
2. 1	**6.** 1	**10.** 1	**14.** 1	**18.** 2
3. 1	**7.** 1	**11.** 1	**15.** 2	**19.** 2
4. 1	**8.** 1	**12.** 1	**16.** 1	**20.** 2

Part 2

1. 1	5. 1	9. 1	13. 2	17. 1
2. 2	6. 2	10. 1	14. 1	18. 2
3. 1	7. 2	11. 2	15. 1	19. 1
4. 1	8. 1	12. 1	16. 2	20. 2

Part 3

1. X	5. C	9. X	13. X	17. X
2. C	6. C	10. C	14. C	18. X
3. C	7. X	11. X	15. C	19. X
4. X	8. X	12. X	16. X	20. C

25–27 Effective Sentences

FLASH SUMMARY

Effective sentences are more than just correct. Good writers edit each sentence to gain precision, clarity, economy, originality, and harmony with the rest of the paragraph.

25. Creating Effective Sentences

A. Vary Your Sentences. Sentences that plod dully along one after another, unvaried in length or structure, bore your readers and sap their attention. One short, simple sentence *(Then the net broke)* can be forceful. But a string of short sentences usually gives a choppy, juvenile effect:

The book is titled *Ethan Frome.* Edith Wharton wrote it. It is set on a New England farm.

Strings of clauses joined by *and* or *and so* are little better:

The book is entitled *Ethan Frome* and Edith Wharton wrote it, and. . . .

At the other extreme, a series of long, complex sentences can also stupefy. Like a good baseball pitcher, vary what you serve up. See sections B through G below.

Vary your sentence beginnings too, where appropriate. You need not always start with the subject; try moving an adjective or adverb construction to the beginning, or shift word order for emphasis:

To attain these goals, the council met frequently.

Straining to comprehend, the family said nothing.

Such chaos they had never seen.

Caution: Do not vary just for variety's sake; you may weaken your paper, for example, by switching from active voice to passive merely for variety or by moving a modifier to an unnatural position. Judging when and how to vary becomes easier with experience.

B. Use Coordination. You can regard related simple sentences as independent clauses and join them with a coordinating conjunction (preceded by a comma) to form a compound sentence:

CHOPPY: The South's army was small. The North hesitated to attack.

BETTER: The South's army was small, **but** the North hesitated to attack. [The conjunction *but* shows the contrast between the two statements.]

CHOPPY: The store closed. Its clientele had moved.

BETTER: The store closed, *for* its clientele had moved. [The conjunction *for* shows that one fact caused the other.]

CHOPPY: French class met at noon. Art met at two.

BETTER: French class met at noon, *and* art met at two. [The *and*, although it has little effect on meaning, shows that the two ideas are connected and makes a smoother-reading sentence.]

See section 7A, pages 28–29, for more on coordinating conjunctions. Avoid overuse of coordination, especially with *and* or *so*.

C. **Use Compounding.** Combine simple sentences that have the same subjects or verbs so that you have only one sentence, with a compound subject, verb, or other part:

WEAK: The Acme Company has been producing slim laptops. The Brigham Company has also been producing them.

STRONGER: [*Both*] the *Acme* **and** the *Brigham* companies have been producing slim laptops.

WEAK: Acme plans to distribute the laptops it makes. It will sell them too.

STRONGER: Acme plans to *distribute* **and** *sell* the laptops it makes.

D. **Use Subordination.** In combining simple sentences, you can emphasize one by subordinating the other—reducing it to a dependent clause. By doing so, you often express the relation between ideas more clearly than by coordination or compounding. Subordinating is one of the most important skills in good writing. You may subordinate with adjective clauses, adverb clauses, or noun clauses (see section 22B, page 71).

(1) **Adjective clauses** (beginning with *who, [whose, whom], which, that, when, where*) let you show which of two ideas you consider more important. Reduce the *less* important idea to an adjective clause:

WEAK: They signed the treaty. This treaty banned war.

WEAK: They signed the treaty, and it banned war.

Strengthened by adjective-clause subordination:

They signed the treaty, **which** *banned war*. [stresses the act of signing]

The treaty **that** *they signed* banned war. [stresses the banning of war]

(2) **Adverb clauses** (beginning with *when, if, because, although*. . . . See section 22B(2), pages 71–72, for full list) let you show that two ideas are related by time, cause, condition, and so on:

WEAK: The lecture grew dull. Several seniors dozed off.

Strengthened by adverb clause subordination:

When the lecture grew dull, several seniors dozed off. [*When* stresses the time relation between the two facts.]

Several seniors dozed off **because** *the lecture had grown dull*. [*Because* stresses the causal relation between the two facts.]

(3) **Noun clauses** (beginning with *who, that, what, whatever*. . . . See section 22B(3), page 72, for full list) provide smoothness, conciseness, and clarity:

WEAK: Tickets were selling poorly. The play's backers were never told this.

WEAK: Some children are underachievers. Karp's research discovered the reasons for this problem.

Strengthened by noun-clause subordination:

> The play's backers were never told ***that*** *tickets were selling poorly.*

> Karp's research discovered ***why*** *some children are underachievers.*

With subordination, compounding, and coordination, you can smoothly integrate three or even more ideas:

> **WEAK:** Jerome Robbins revolutionized American ballet. He introduced vigorous male dancers. They roughhoused as sailors in *Fancy Free*. They also fought as street toughs in *West Side Story*.

> **SUBORDINATED AND COORDINATED:** Jerome Robbins revolutionized American ballet **when** he introduced vigorous male dancers **who** roughhoused as sailors in *Fancy Free* **and** fought as street toughs in *West Side Story*.

Subordination can be even more effective when combined with **reduction,** explained in section E below.

Caution: Do not overdo subordination; five or six clauses inexpertly combined in a sentence can bewilder readers. And never subordinate your main idea—the one you would mention if you could mention only one. See section G below.

E. **Use Reduction.** Wherever possible, eliminate needless words by reducing clauses to phrases and phrases to single words:

> **WORDY (CLAUSE):** *Because she was discouraged about writing stories,* Erika decided to try nonfiction.

> **TIGHTER (PHRASE):** *Discouraged about writing stories,* Erika decided to try nonfiction.

> **WORDY (CLAUSE):** The person *who is holding the pistol* is the starter.

> **TIGHTER (PHRASE):** The person *holding the pistol* is the starter.

> **WORDY (PHRASE):** She is a child *possessed of talent.*

> **TIGHTER (WORD):** She is a *talented* child.

Here is the last example from section **D** above, further tightened by reduction:

> Jerome Robbins revolutionized American ballet by **introducing** vigorous male dancers **roughhousing** as sailors in *Fancy Free* and **fighting** as street toughs in *West Side Story.*

F. **Use Parallel Structure** (the same grammatical form) with two or more coordinate expressions, in comparisons, and with correlative conjunctions:

WRONG—NOT PARALLEL:

Tourists come	*to see the city's museums,* [infinitive phrase]
	its skyscrapers, [noun]
and	*to hear its opera company.* [infinitive phrase]

RIGHT—PARALLEL:

Tourists come to the city for its	*museums,* [noun]
	skyscrapers, [noun]
and	*opera company.* [noun]

ALSO PARALLEL:

Tourists come	*to see the city's museums,*
	(to) gawk at its skyscrapers,
and	*(to) hear its opera company.* [all infinitive phrases]

WRONG:	The study **not only**	*examined men*
		[verb + noun]
	but also	*women.* [noun]
RIGHT:	The study examined **not only**	*men* [noun]
	but also	*women.* [noun]

WRONG: Campers learn *scuba diving* and *to kayak.*

RIGHT: Campers learn *scuba diving* and *kayaking.*

RIGHT: Campers learn *to scuba dive* and [*to*] *kayak.*

WRONG: The study was more *critical* than *it offered solutions.*

RIGHT: The study offered more *criticism* than *solutions.*

Be sure your items are parallel logically as well as grammatically:

ILLOGICAL: The city has three museums, a concert hall, an opera house, and two hundred garbage trucks. [Garbage trucks do not belong with the other items, which are cultural attractions. Avoid such illogic, unless you intend humor or irony.]

Parallelism is one of the most powerful ways to express a complex series of facts or ideas clearly.

G. **Position Main Ideas Prominently.** Do not bury your main point in the middle of your sentence or in a phrase or subordinate clause:

POOR—INTENDED MAIN IDEA (the death of the dinosaurs) LOST IN MIDSENTENCE, in a subordinate clause: Millions of years ago a huge meteorite, *which obliterated the dinosaurs,* spread a deadly cloud over the earth.

Put your main idea at the beginning or, for even more emphasis and a sense of climax, at the end.

BETTER—MAIN POINT UP FRONT: *The dinosaurs were obliterated* millions of years ago by a huge meteorite that spread a deadly cloud over the earth.

BETTER AND CLIMACTIC—MAIN POINT AT END: Millions of years ago a huge meteorite, spreading a deadly cloud over the earth, *obliterated the dinosaurs.*

26. Conquering the "Big Three" Sentence Errors

Fragments, comma splices, and fused sentences are by far the most common, and often the most obvious, of major sentence structure errors. Make it a priority to rid your papers of these faults.

A. **Fragments.** A **fragment** is a part of a sentence, such as a phrase or dependent clause, erroneously punctuated as if it were a complete sentence. When you discover a fragment in your writing, either (1) attach the fragment to an independent clause or (2) rewrite the fragment to form a sentence by itself. Even a statement with a subject and a predicate can be a fragment if it follows a subordinating conjunction, such as *if, when,* or *because,* or begins with a relative pronoun—*who(m), which, that.* In the incorrect examples below, the fragments are in *italics:*

WRONG: Garbage collections decreased. *Because recycling took effect.*

RIGHT: Garbage collections decreased *because recycling took effect.* [fragment attached to independent clause]

WRONG: Audrey Buller's painting *Morning Glory* shows in its foreground an orderly swirl of bright blossoms. *Which contrasts with a pile of dried leaves beneath, representing death.*

RIGHT: Audrey Buller's painting *Morning Glory* shows in its foreground an orderly swirl of bright blossoms, *which contrasts with a pile of dried leaves beneath, representing death.* [fragment attached to independent clause]

WRONG: *An island that shimmers in the sun.*

RIGHT: *The island shimmers in the sun.* [fragment rewritten as a sentence by itself]

Be alert also for omitted verbs and for participial or other phrases mistakenly written as sentences:

WRONG: *Her mother a maid in a rich family's house, and her father a sailor on an oil tanker.*

RIGHT: Her mother *was* a maid in a rich family's house, and her father *was* a sailor on an oil tanker. [verbs added to make a sentence]

WRONG: Security was particularly tight at Kennedy Airport. *Being a main entry point for smugglers.* Or *It being a main entry point for smugglers.* Or *A main entry point for smugglers.*

RIGHT: Security was particularly tight at Kennedy Airport, *a main entry point for smugglers.*

B. Comma Splices and Fused Sentences. A **comma splice** is the erroneous joining of independent clauses with a comma rather than with a conjunction or semicolon:

WRONG: Running relieves stress, it can prolong life.

WRONG: In recent years adults have been smoking fewer cigarettes, teenagers have been smoking more.

A **fused sentence** is the erroneous joining of independent clauses with no conjunction or punctuation at all:

WRONG: Running relieves stress it can prolong life.

WRONG: In recent years adults have been smoking fewer cigarettes teenagers have been smoking more.

To avoid such errors (both also called **run-ons**), first be sure that you can recognize an independent clause. Review section 22A(1), pages 70-71, if necessary. Next, learn these four ways to correct run-ons; choose the way that best fits your purpose and your paragraph.

(1) Separate the clauses into two sentences:

RIGHT: Running relieves stress. It can prolong life.

This is the simplest but rarely the best way, because too many short sentences make your writing sound choppy and immature. Moreover, you fail to specify a relation between the ideas in the clauses.

(2) Join the clauses with a coordinating conjunction:

RIGHT: Running relieves stress, *and* it can prolong life.

This is often a better way than making separate sentences, but you must not overuse this either. *And,* especially, shows only a very general relation between ideas.

(3) Join the clauses with a semicolon:

RIGHT: Running relieves stress; it can prolong life.

A semicolon can give your writing a formal tone; it is often effective in balanced sentences, such as *Today was delightful; yesterday was dreadful.*

(4) Join the clauses by making one of them a dependent (subordinate) clause. Join them with subordinating conjunctions, such as *because, if, when, since, after,*

although, and *unless,* or with relative pronouns: *who(m), which, that.* Subordinating is often the best way to eliminate run-ons, since subordinating conjunctions and relative pronouns show the precise relation between ideas:

RIGHT: Running, which relieves stress, can prolong life.

RIGHT: Because running relieves stress, it can prolong life.

For more on subordination, see section 22, page 70 and section 25D, pages 88–89. Here are more corrected comma splices:

WRONG: In recent years adults have been smoking fewer cigarettes, however teenagers have been smoking more.

RIGHT: In recent years adults have been smoking fewer cigarettes; teenagers, however, have been smoking more. [clauses joined by semicolon—see section 37B, page 27]

RIGHT: Although adults have been smoking fewer cigarettes in recent years, teenagers have been smoking more. [first clause subordinated]

WRONG: Cole's study (1996) concluded that pupils with more stable home environments had higher reading scores, this finding corroborated Lynch's 1987 study.

RIGHT: . . . higher reading scores, a finding that corroborated Lynch's 1987 study. [last clause subordinated]

RIGHT: . . . higher reading scores. This finding corroborated Lynch's 1987 study. [last clause made separate sentence]

27. Avoiding Other Sentence Faults

A. Needless Separation of Related Sentence Parts

(1) *Do not needlessly separate subject and verb or verb and complement:*

AWKWARD: *She,* filled with dreams of happiness, *married* him.

SMOOTH: Filled with dreams of happiness, *she married* him.

AWKWARD: They *bought,* by emptying their bank accounts and cashing in their bonds, a large *house.*

SMOOTH: By emptying their bank accounts and cashing in their bonds, they *bought* a large *house.*

(2) *Place modifying words, phrases, and clauses as close as possible to the words they modify:*

✓ **Adverb:**

WRONG: It was sad that the cousins *almost* **lost** all their savings in the swindle. [*Almost lost* means that they came close to losing but lost nothing.]

RIGHT: It was sad that the cousins lost *almost* **all** their savings in the swindle.

This same caution applies to *only, nearly, scarcely, hardly, just,* and *even:* Only **Sara** heard the loon, Sara *only* **heard** the loon, and Sara heard *only* the **loon** all have different meanings.

✓ **Phrase:**

WRONG: *Buried a thousand feet under Yucatan,* **geologists** have found traces of a huge crater.

RIGHT: Geologists have found traces of a huge **crater** *buried a thousand feet under Yucatan.*

Note: Sometimes you can correctly separate a phrase from the word it modifies, but be especially careful that no misreading is possible—that no other noun could sensibly be modified:

> UNCLEAR: We left the outdoor party in Marty's old Volkswagen, *covered with confetti from the celebration.* [Who is covered—*we* or *Volkswagen?*]
>
> CLEAR: We left the outdoor party in an upbeat mood, *covered with confetti from the celebration.* [The phrase can sensibly refer only to *we.*]

✓ **Clause:**

> WRONG: Pat left the model in the **subway** *that she had built.*
>
> RIGHT: Pat left in the subway the **model** *that she* had built.

(3) Avoid "squinting" modifiers. A squinter comes between two verbs so that the reader cannot tell to which verb it refers:

> WRONG: The Democrats **vowed** *after the primaries* to **unite.**
>
> RIGHT: *After the primaries* the Democrats **vowed** to unite.
>
> RIGHT: The Democrats vowed to **unite** *after the primaries.*

(4) Avoid awkward splitting of infinitives. The two parts of an infinitive belong together; avoid putting words between them (unless your sentence would otherwise be unclear or sound odd):

> WRONG: He wanted *to* every now and then *call* her.
>
> RIGHT: He wanted *to call* her every now and then.

It is quite all right, however, to place an appropriate adverb within the infinitive: They decided *to quickly replace* the dog that had died.

(5) What about ending a sentence with a preposition? (They saw the house he had lived *in.*) It is now more widely accepted than in the past, but follow this rule of thumb in formal writing: Try recasting the sentence using *which;* if the result sounds smooth, not awkward, use it: They saw the house *in which* he had lived.

> INFORMAL: Nicaragua is another country that baseball has become popular *in.*
>
> FORMAL: Nicaragua is another country *in which* baseball has become popular.

Note: Some verbs contain a *particle*—a word that looks like a preposition but is actually part of the meaning of the verb—e.g., *call up, find out, give up, turn into* (become), *put up with.* It is perfectly all right—sometimes necessary—to end a formal sentence with a particle: He promised to *call* her *up.*

B. **Dangling Modifiers.** A modifier (usually a phrase) "dangles" when there is no word in the sentence to which it can logically or grammatically refer. Correct a dangler in any of the ways shown below.

(1) Dangling participle:

> WRONG: *Sweeping to victory in the September primary,* **election** in November seemed assured. [The nearest noun to the phrase should name the person who swept.]
>
> RIGHT: *Sweeping to victory in the September primary,* **Bates** felt assured of his election in November. [person who swept, *Bates,* put nearest to phrase]
>
> RIGHT: *When* **Bates swept** *to victory in the September primary,* his election in November seemed assured. [phrase expanded into clause naming the person who swept]

Note: Possessives do not count as the "nearest noun":

> WRONG: *Sweeping to victory in the primary,* Bates's **election** in November seemed assured.

> RIGHT: See above.

(2) *Dangling gerund:*

> WRONG: *After harvesting the crops,* a **truck** hauled them to market. [Did the truck harvest the crops?]

> RIGHT: *After harvesting the crops,* the **farmer** trucked them to market.

> RIGHT: *After the **farmer harvested** the crops,* a truck hauled them to market.

(3) *Dangling Infinitive:*

> WRONG: *To access the map program,* a floppy **disk** must be inserted. [Who is doing the accessing? Not the disk.]

> RIGHT: *To access the map program,* **you** must insert a floppy disk. [You are doing the accessing.]

(4) *Dangling elliptical clause.* An elliptical clause is one from which the subject and all or part of the verb have been dropped as understood, e.g., *while* [I was] *skiing in Utah:*

> WRONG: *While on the wrestling team,* Leo's **dog** came along to practices. [Was the dog on the team?]

> RIGHT: *While on the wrestling team,* **Leo** took his dog along to practices.

> RIGHT: *While **Leo was** on the wrestling team,* his dog came along to practices.

Ellipsis makes sense only when the subject of both clauses is the same, as in the first correct example above (*Leo* is the understood subject of the elliptical clause).

C. Incomplete Comparisons or Expressions of Degree

> WRONG: The test was *so easy.*

> RIGHT: The test was *so easy that everyone passed.*

> WRONG: Prices of some train tickets are higher *than* planes. [illogically compares prices with planes]

> RIGHT: Prices of some train tickets are higher *than those of* planes. [compare prices with prices]

D. Needless Shifts

(1) *In number:*

> WRONG: When a *freshman* fails a test, *they* may grow depressed.

> RIGHT: When a *freshman* fails a test, *she* [or *he*] may grow depressed.

> RIGHT: When *freshmen* fail a test, *they* may grow depressed.

This is a matter of agreement; see section 24B, page 83. For the *he/she* problem, see section 72A(1), pages 182–183.

(2) *In person:* See section 24A, page 83.

(3) *In subject or voice of verb:*

> WRONG: As I *flew* over the city, clogged *freeways could be seen.* [*Flew* is active; *could be seen,* passive. Subject shifts from *I* to *freeways.*]

> RIGHT: As I *flew* over the city, I *could see* clogged freeways.

(4) *In tense or mood of verb:* See section 15A, C, pages 45–46.

E. Mixed Construction. When finishing a sentence, keep in mind how you began it. All its parts should match both grammatically and logically. Remember that the subject must be a noun or something serving as a noun (such as a noun clause or a gerund):

WRONG: *By the Republicans' nominating Ochoa* makes the Democrats' task harder. [The adverb phrase cannot logically be the subject. It tells *how*, not *what*.]

RIGHT: The Republicans' *nomination* of Ochoa has made the Democrats' task harder. [the noun *nomination* made subject]

WRONG: She asked *when did they leave*. [direct-question word order in indirect-question form]

RIGHT: She asked *when they left*. [indirect question]

RIGHT: She asked, *"When did they leave?"* [direct question]

See also, in section 70B, pages 177–178, the entry for *reason was because*. For more on indirect questions, see section 31A, page 123.

The verb *be* is like an equal sign (=) in mathematics—what is on one side of *be* must be the same, grammatically and logically, as what is on the other:

WRONG: Her favorite *pastime* was *at the movies*. [Pastime does not = place; a pastime is not a place.]

RIGHT: Her favorite *pastime* was *going to the movies*. [pastime = pastime]

WRONG: *Angioplasty* is *when* [or is *where*] a tiny balloon is inserted into an artery. [*When* and *where* refer to time and place, but angioplasty is a procedure, not a time or place.]

RIGHT: *Angioplasty* [procedure] is the *insertion* [procedure] of a tiny balloon into an artery. [procedure = procedure]

WRONG: *Because the National League has more teams* [adverb clause] does not mean *that it has more talent* [noun clause].

RIGHT: *That the National League has more teams* [noun clause] does not mean *that it has more talent* [noun clause].

RIGHT: *Though the National League has more teams* [adverb clause], it does not have more talent [independent clause].

 **FLASH TEST**

PART 1

Choose the **most effective** way of expressing the given ideas. Write the letter of your choice (**A, B,** or **C**) in the blank.

EXAMPLE: A. The floods came. They washed away the roadway. They also uprooted trees.

 B. The floods came, and they washed away the roadway and uprooted trees.

 C. The floods came, washing away the roadway and uprooting trees.   _____C_____

1. A. There was a company in Minneapolis. It shortened its work week from 40 hours to 36 hours. The company's output increased.   **1.** _____

 B. A company in Minneapolis shortened its work week from 40 hours to 36 hours, and this company found out the company's output increased.

 C. When a Minneapolis company shortened its work week from 40 to 36 hours, its output increased.

2. A. Broadway has been revived by a new band of actors. These new actors are from Hollywood. They find it refreshing and challenging to perform before a live audience.

   B. Broadway has been revived by a new breed of actors—Hollywood stars, who find it refreshing and challenging to perform before a live audience.

   C. Broadway has been revived by this new breed of actors, which has seen actors coming from Hollywood; they have found it refreshing and challenging to perform before a live audience.

2. _____

3. A. Recreational tree climbing has become popular. Ecologists hope that a code of tree-climbing ethics will be developed. Such a code may help to prevent damage to the delicate forest ecosystems.

   B. Recreational tree climbing has become popular and ecologists hope that a code of tree-climbing ethics will be developed, and such a code may help to prevent damage to the delicate forest ecosystems.

   C. Before recreational tree climbing becomes any more popular, ecologists hope that a code of tree-climbing ethics will be developed to prevent permanent damage to delicate forest ecosystems.

3. _____

4. A. Harry Truman, who woke up the next morning to find himself elected President, had gone to bed early on election night.

   B. Harry Truman, who had gone to bed early on election night, woke up the next morning to find himself elected President.

   C. Harry Truman went to bed early on election night, and he woke up the next morning and found himself elected President.

4. _____

5. A. The papers were marked Top Secret. The term *Top Secret* indicates contents of extraordinary value.

   B. The papers were of extraordinary value, and therefore they were marked Top Secret.

   C. The papers were marked Top Secret, indicating their extraordinary value.

5. _____

6. A. The university was noted for its outstanding faculty, its concern for minorities, and the quality of its graduates.

   B. The university was noted for its outstanding faculty, it showed concern for minorities, and how well its graduates did.

   C. The university was known for three things: it had an outstanding faculty, it showed concern for minorities, and the quality of its students.

6. _____

7. A. The Broadway theater, which has survived many changes, is changing rapidly again, the change being that wealthy entertainment corporations, which include, for example, Disney's company, are taking over the big theaters as they bring in huge musicals that have vapid content, high prices, and draw audiences away from more original plays.

   B. The Broadway theater, having survived many changes, is again changing rapidly as wealthy entertainment corporations such as Disney's take over the big theaters with vapid, high-priced musicals, drawing audiences away from more original plays.

   C. The Broadway theater has survived many changes. Once again it is changing rapidly. Wealthy entertainment corporations are taking over the big theaters. One example is Disney. These corporations bring in huge musicals that prove to be vapid as well as high priced. The result is that they draw audiences away from more original plays.

7. _____

8. A. Nick moves to Long Island and rents a house, and it is next to Gatsby's, but he does not know Gatsby. One night he sees a shadowy figure on the lawn, and he concludes that it must be Gatsby himself.

B. Moving to Long Island, Nick rents a house next to Gatsby's. Though he does not know Gatsby, one night he concludes that the shadowy figure he sees on the lawn must be Gatsby himself.

C. Nick, who moves to Long Island, rents a house which is next to Gatsby's, whom he does not know; one night he concludes that the shadowy figure that he sees on the lawn must be Gatsby himself.   8. _____

9. A. A fungus struck one plant and then another until it had killed nearly all of them, but one of them survived.

B. A fungus that killed nearly all the plants spread from one to another, yet only one survived.

C. A fungus spread among the plants, killing all but one.   9. _____

10. A. One family in a heatless building called the welfare office for money to buy an electric heater.

B. One family lived in a building that had no heat, and so they called the welfare office to get money to buy an electric heater.

C. One family, calling the welfare office for money to buy an electric heater, lived in a building that was heatless.   10. _____

FLASH TEST

PART 2

Rewrite each of the following sets of sentences in the **most effective** way. Your result may contain one sentence or more. You may add, drop, or change words, but do not drop any information.

EXAMPLE: The Lions had the ball on the Broncos' ten-yard line, and they attempted four passes, but they could not score, and so they lost the game.

Though the Lions had the ball on the Broncos' ten-yard line, they lost the game because they could not score in four pass attempts.

1. The Washington Monument was closed to the public. This happened in the spring and fall of 1998. The National Park Service had to repair the structure. That was the reason for the closing.

_____

_____

_____

_____

2. One airline charges an unrestricted fare of $1,734 from Boston to Reykjavik. Reykjavik is in Iceland. The same airline will fly you between the same cities for $298.

_____

_____

_____

3. Many college students have a choice. This is what car-leasing companies say. These college students are the ones who do not have much in savings. One choice is that they can drive an old used car. The other is that they can lease a new car.

_____

_____

_____

_____

4. Computers have become less expensive. They have also become easier to use. And you can get free software. With this you can browse the Internet.

_____

_____

_____

_____

5. More bodies were pulled from the floodwaters in central Texas. This happened as storms continued their eastward march across the Southwest. The storms were torrential, and the march was deadly. One man was killed. This was because his home was swept away in the floods.

_____

_____

_____

_____

6. A new report has come out. It says that girls now outnumber boys in secondary schools. This is true in eighteen countries. Most of these countries are in Latin America.

_____

_____

_____

_____

FLASH TEST

PART 3

In each sentence: in the first three blanks, **identify** each of the boldfaced elements (use the abbreviations in parentheses):

gerund or gerund phrase (**ger**)   participle or participial phrase (**part**)

prepositional phrase (**prep**)   infinitive or infinitive phrase (**inf**)

clause (**cl**)   adjective (**adj**)

noun [with or without modifiers] (**noun**)

verb [with or without modifiers or complements] (**verb**)

Then, in the last blank, write **P** if the sentence contains **parallel structure** or **NP** if it does **not**. (If the sentence is parallel, the first three blanks will all have the same answer.)

EXAMPLES: Congress rushed **to pass the tax bill, the Medicare bill, and to adjourn.**	_inf_	_noun_	_inf_	_NP_
Shakespeare was **a poet, a playwright, and an actor.**	_noun_	_noun_	_noun_	_P_

1. The job required some knowledge of **word processing, desktop publishing, and to write.**

1. _____ _____ _____ _____

2. Hector fought with **great skill, epic daring, and superb intelligence.**

2. _____ _____ _____ _____

3. The mosques of ancient Islamic Spain typically contained **ornate stone screens, long hallways, and the columns looked like spindles.**

3. _____ _____ _____ _____

4. The castle, **built on a hill, surrounded by farmland, and commanding a magnificent view,** protected the peasants from invasions by hostile forces.

4. _____ _____ _____ _____

5. A newly discovered primate from the Amazon has **wide-set eyes, a broad nose, and the fur is striped like a zebra.**

6. By nightfall, we were **tired, hungry, and grumpy.**

7. The guerrillas **surrounded the village, set up their mortars, and the shelling began.**

8. Kiesha did not know **where she had come from, why she was there, or the time of her departure.**

9. Her favorite pastimes remain **designing clothes, cooking gourmet meals, and practicing the flute.**

10. Eliot's poetry is **witty, complex, and draws on his vast learning.**

5. _____ _____ _____ _____

6. _____ _____ _____ _____

7. _____ _____ _____ _____

8. _____ _____ _____ _____

9. _____ _____ _____ _____

10. _____ _____ _____ _____

FLASH TEST

PART 4

Rewrite each sentence in parallel structure.

EXAMPLE: The apartment could be rented by the week, the month, or you could pay on a yearly basis.
<u>The apartment could be rented by the week, month, or year</u>.

1. Before 8 a.m., my youngest son had made himself breakfast, a snow fort in the front yard, and tormented his brothers.

_____

_____

_____

2. Our new wood-burning stove should keep us warm, save us money, and should afford us much pleasure.

_____

_____

3. Christopher Columbus has been remembered as an entrepreneur, an explorer, a sailor, and perhaps now for how he exploited native populations.

_____

_____

_____

4. The chief ordered Agent 007 to break into the building, crack the safe, and to steal the plans.

_____

_____

_____

5. A good batter knows how to hit to the opposite field and staring down the pitcher.

_____

_____

_____

6. When kindergartners were asked how the President should behave, they said someone who was fair, who shares, and not a hitter.

_____

_____

_____

FLASH TEST

PART 5

Write **S** after each item that is one or more **complete sentences.**

Write **F** after each item that contains a **fragment.**

EXAMPLE: Luis was offered the job. Having presented the best credentials.   _____ **F** _____

1. When one is interviewing applicants for the nanny position. It is important to review all references.   1. _____

2. Having applied for dozens of jobs and not having had any offers.   2. _____

3. The manuscript having been returned, Johanna sat down to revise it.   3. _____

4. Harrison desperately wanted the part. Because he believed that this was the film that would make him a star.   4. _____

5. The exercise bike was dusty. Sue never seemed to have time to use it.   5. _____

6. He admitted to being a computer nerd. As a matter of fact, he was proud of his computing skills.   6. _____

7. Over 50 percent of Americans surveyed feel guilty about their child-care arrangements.   7. _____

8. I read all of the articles. Then I wrote the first draft of my paper.   8. _____

9. Many Americans prefer indirect business levies rather than direct taxation. Where do you stand on this issue?   9. _____

10. Maurice kept nodding his head as the coach explained the play. Thinking all the time that it would never work.   10. _____

FLASH TEST

PART 6

Write **S** after any item that is **a complete sentence.**

Write **Spl** after any item that is a **comma splice.**

Write **FS** after any item that is a **fused sentence.**

EXAMPLE: The mission was a success, everyone was pleased.   _____ **Spl** _____

1. The critics unanimously agreed the play was terrible it closed after a week.   1. _____

2. The party broke up at one in the morning, Jack lingered for a few final words with Kathy.   2. _____

3. Determined to sweep the southern and western states, the President authorized extra campaign money to be spent there.   3. _____

4. The Moon enters the Earth's shadow, a lunar eclipse occurs, causing the Moon to turn a deep red.   4. _____

5. The ticket agent had sold eighty-one tickets to boarding passengers there were only eleven empty seats on the train.   5. _____

6. Since she was in the mood for a romantic movie, she hired a babysitter and went to see *Shakespeare in Love.*   6. _____

7. Sheer exhaustion having caught up with me, I had no trouble falling asleep.   7. _____

8. The restaurant check almost made me faint, because I had left my wallet home, I couldn't pay for the meal.   8. _____

9. Those of us who lived in off-campus housing ignored the rule, since we were   9. _____
seniors, we never worried about campus regulations.

10. It was a cloudy, sultry afternoon when we sighted our first school of whales,   10. _____
and the cry of "Lower the boats!" rang throughout the ship.

FLASH TEST

PART 7

Rewrite any item that contains a **fragment, comma splice,** or **fused sentence** so that it contains none of these. You may add words or information as needed, but do not drop any information. If an item is already correct, leave the blank empty.

EXAMPLES: When she saw the full moon rising over the hill.
When she saw the full moon rising over the hill, she thought of the night they had met.
When Peary and Henson reached the Pole, they rejoiced.

1. Because pie, ice cream, and candy bars have practically no nutritional value.

_____

_____

_____

2. When the bindings release, the ski comes off.

_____

_____

_____

3. Which promotes tooth decay when not used properly.

_____

_____

_____

4. Lady Bird Johnson and Barbara Bush, first ladies greatly admired.

_____

_____

_____

5. Whereas older cars run on regular gas and lack complex pollution controls.

_____

_____

_____

6. Because she was not prepared for the interviewer's questions and felt she would never get the job.

_____

_____

_____

7. By installing smoke detectors, families may someday save family members from
perishing in a fire.

_____

_____

_____

8. Watching from the seventh floor during the parade.

_____

_____

_____

9. Which could strengthen your immune system.

_____

_____

_____

10. Stay.

_____

_____

_____

 FLASH TEST

PART 8

If the boldfaced words are **in the wrong place,** draw an arrow from them to the place in the sentence where they should be.

If the boldfaced words are **in the right place,** do nothing.

EXAMPLES: Never give a toy to a child **that can be swallowed.**

People who buy cigars **made in Cuba** violate U.S. laws.

1. He ordered a pizza for his friends **covered with pepperoni.**
2. She **only** had enough money to buy two of the three books that she needed.
3. Americans **who consider medical treatment everyone's right** are demanding a national health-care program.
4. After asking a few questions, we decided **quickly** to end the conference call because we weren't interested in what the company had to offer.
5. We saw the plane taxi onto the field **that would soon be leaving for Chicago.**
6. Unfortunately, many Americans are spending **almost** a third of their income on rent.
7. The President attempted to prevent the outbreak of war **in the Oval Office.**
8. Unfortunately, the resale shop was full of **wrinkled** little girls' dresses.
9. We hurriedly bought a picnic table from a clerk **with collapsible legs.**
10. We learned that no one could discard anything at the municipal dump **except people living in the community.**

FLASH TEST

 ## PART 9

If the boldfaced words form a dangling or misplaced modifier, **rewrite** the sentence correctly in the blanks below it.

If the sentence is correct as is, do nothing.

EXAMPLES: **Returning the corrected essays,** most students were disappointed by their marks.
<u>When the instructor returned their corrected essays, most students were disappointed by their marks.</u>

Roosevelt and Churchill, **meeting at sea,** drafted the Four Freedoms.

_____

_____

1. **Announcing his first baseball game in 1939,** the late Red Barber began a broadcasting career that would last over fifty years.

_____

_____

_____

2. **Rowing across the lake,** the moon often disappeared behind the clouds.

_____

_____

3. **Having worked on my paper for three hours,** the network went down and my paper was lost in cyber-space.

_____

_____

4. **While on vacation,** the idea for a new play came to him.

_____

_____

5. **Worried about what books their children are borrowing from libraries,** the library finally agreed to develop an on-line rating system for families.

_____

_____

_____

6. **Upon entering college,** he applied for part-time employment in the library.

_____

_____

7. **Practicing every day for five hours,** Dani's expensive music lessons really paid off.

_____

_____

8. **Sleeping in late,** the house seemed incredibly quiet with the boys still in bed.

_____

_____

9. **After sleeping in until noon,** the day seemed to go by too quickly.

_____

_____

10. **When nine years old,** my father took my sister and me on our first camping trip.

_____

_____

 **FLASH TEST**

PART 10

If an item is **incorrect** or **ineffective** in any of the ways you learned in Sections 25–27, **rewrite** it correctly or more effectively in the blanks below it.

If an item is **correct** and **effective** as is, do nothing.

EXAMPLES: The lakes were empty of fish. Acid rain had caused this.
<u>Acid rain had left the lakes empty of fish.</u>

Working in pairs, the students edited each other's writing.

_____

1. If one drives a car without thinking, you are more than likely to have an accident.

    _____

    _____

2. The entire class was so pleased at learning that Dr. Turner has rescheduled the quiz.

    _____

    _____

3. John planned to carefully and thoughtfully ask Julia to marry him.

    _____

    _____

4. A study revealed that vigorous exercise may add only one or two years to a person's life. This study used Harvard graduates.

    _____

    _____

5. The film director, thinking only about how he could get the shot of the erupting volcano, endangered everyone.

    _____

    _____

6. With her new auditory implant, Audrey heard so much better.

    _____

    _____

7. Watching the star hitter blast a home run over the fence, the ball smashed a windshield of an expensive sports car.

    _____

    _____

8. The owner of the team seems to insult her players and fans and mismanaging the finances.

    _____

    _____

9. The witness walked into the courtroom, and then she wishes she could avoid testifying.

    _____

    _____

10. An increase in energy taxes causes most people to consider carpooling and improving energy conservation practices in their homes.

_____

_____

Answers to Exercises for: Effective Sentences

Part 1

1. C	**3.** C	**5.** C	**7.** B	**9.** C
2. B	**4.** B	**6.** A	**8.** B	**10.** A

Part 2
(Some answers may vary.)

1. In the spring and fall of 1998, the National Park Service had to close the Washington Monument to the public for repairs.

2. One airline's charges for a flight between Boston and Reykjavik, Iceland, vary from $1,734, for unrestricted travel, to $298.

3. Car-leasing companies say that college students without much in savings can choose between driving an old used car and leasing a new car.

4. Computers have become less expensive and easier to use, and offer free software for browsing the Internet.

5. As torrential storms continued their deadly eastward march across the Southwest, more bodies were pulled from flood waters in central Texas. One man died when floods swept away his home.

6. A new report says that in eighteen countries, mostly in Latin America, girls now outnumber boys in secondary schools.

Part 3

1. ger	ger	inf	NP
2. noun	noun	noun	P
3. noun	noun	cl	NP
4. part	part	part	P
5. noun	noun	cl	NP
6. adj	adj	adj	P
7. verb	verb	cl	NP
8. cl	cl	noun	NP
9. ger	ger	ger	P
10. adj	adj	verb	NP

Part 4
(Some items have other possible answers.)

1. made himself breakfast, built a snow fort, and tormented his brothers.

2. keep us warm, save us money, and afford us much pleasure.

3. an entrepreneur, an explorer, a sailor, and perhaps now as one who exploited the native populations. [or . . . an exploiter of native populations.]

4. to break into the building, crack the safe, and steal the plans.

5. to hit to the opposite field and [to] stare down the pitcher.

6. said a President should be fair, [should] share, and [should] not hit.

Part 5

1. F	**3.** S	**5.** S	**7.** S	**9.** S
2. F	**4.** F	**6.** S	**8.** S	**10.** F

Part 6

1. FS	**3.** S	**5.** FS	**7.** S	**9.** Spl
2. Spl	**4.** Spl	**6.** S	**8.** Spl	**10.** S

Part 7
(Some items are samples or have other possible answers.)

1. . . . value, they are abhorred by dieticians.

2. —

3. This mouthwash promotes . . .

4. . . . Barbara Bush are greatly admired first ladies.

5. Newer cars use unleaded fuel and emit fewer pollutants, whereas . . .

6. . . . job, she canceled the interview.

7. —

8. . . . parade, Williams was able to take several panoramic photographs.

9. Such a drug could strengthen . . .

10. —

Part 8
(Some answers may vary.)

1. He ordered a pizza covered with pepperoni for his friends.

2. . . . only two of the three . . .

3. —

4. — . . . we quickly decided . . . [or . . . end the conference call quickly . . .]

5. . . . plane that would soon be leaving . . .

6. —

7. In the Oval Office the President . . .

8. . . . full of little girls' wrinkled dresses.

9. . . . table with collapsible legs . . .

10. . . . no one except people living . . .

Part 9
(Some answers may vary.)

1. —

2. Rowing across the lake, we often watched the moon disappear . . .

3. . . . for three hours, I was horrified to see the network go down and my paper become lost . . .

4. While on vacation, he got the idea for a new play.

5. Because parents are worried about what books . . .

6. —

7. . . . for five hours, Dani made her expensive music lessons really pay off.

8. With the boys still in bed, sleeping in late, the house seemed . . .

9. After we had slept in until noon, the day seemed . . .

10. When I was nine years old, my father . . .

Part 10
(Some answers may vary.)

1. People who drive a car without thinking are more likely . . .

2. . . . quite pleased . . .

3. Carefully and thoughtfully, John planned . . .

4. A study using Harvard graduates revealed . . .

5. —

6. . . . Audrey heard far better [*or* . . . so much better that she could participate fully in conversations.]

7. We watched the star hitter blast . . . fence, the ball smashing a . . .

8. . . . players and fans and [to] mismanage the finances.

9. . . . and then wished . . .

10. —

 FLASH TEST

GRAMMAR AND SENTENCE REVIEW: UNIT I
PART 1

Write **T** for each statement that is **true.**

Write **F** for each statement that is **false.**

EXAMPLE: A **present participle** ends in -*ing* and is used as an adjective.	T
1. Both a **gerund** and a **present participle** end in -*ing*.	1.
2. The greatest number of words ever used in a **verb** is four.	2.
3. **Parallel structure** is used to designate ideas that are not equal in importance.	3.
4. A **dangling participle** may be corrected by being changed into a dependent clause.	4.
5. *It's* is a contraction of *it is; its* is the **possessive** form of the pronoun *it*.	5.
6. The **verb precedes the subject** in a sentence beginning with the expletive *there*.	6.
7. A **preposition** may contain two or more words; *because of* is an example.	7.
8. The **principal parts of a verb** are the *present tense,* the *future tense,* and the *past participle.*	8.
9. A **collective noun** may be followed by either a singular or plural verb.	9.
10. A **prepositional phrase** may be used only as an adjective modifier.	10.
11. A **compound sentence** is one that contains two or more independent clauses.	11.
12. Not all **adverbs** end in -*ly*.	12.
13. The verb **be** is like an equal sign in mathematics.	13.

14. A **noun clause** may be introduced by the subordinating conjunction *although.*   14. _____

15. An **adjective clause** may begin with *when* or *where.*   15. _____

16. Both **verbals** and **verbs** may have modifiers and complements.   16. _____

17. The terminal punctuation of a declarative sentence is the **exclamation point.**   17. _____

18. *Without* is a **subordinating conjunction.**   18. _____

19. A sentence may begin with the word *because.*   19. _____

20. The **predicate** of a sentence can consist of merely a past participle.   20. _____

21. A **subjective complement** may be a noun, a pronoun, or an adverb.   21. _____

22. A **direct object** may be a noun or a pronoun.   22. _____

23. An **indirect object** always follows a direct object.   23. _____

24. An **objective complement** always precedes the direct object.   24. _____

25. Pronouns used as appositives are called **intensive pronouns.**   25. _____

26. The word *scissors* takes a **singular verb.**   26. _____

27. An **antecedent** is the noun for which a pronoun stands.   27. _____

28. A **simple sentence** contains two or more independent clauses.   28. _____

29. Pronouns in the **objective case** always follow forms of the verb *to be.*   29. _____

30. A **complex sentence** contains at least one independent clause and one dependent clause.   30. _____

31. A **sentence fragment** is not considered a legitimate unit of expression; a **nonsentence** is.   31. _____

32. **Adjectives** never stand next to the words they modify.   32. _____

33. Not all words ending in *-ly* are **adverbs.**   33. _____

34. An **indefinite pronoun** designates no particular person.   34. _____

35. The words *have* and *has* identify the **present perfect tense** of a verb.   35. _____

36. A statement with a subject and a verb can be a fragment if it follows a **subordinating conjunction.**   36. _____

37. An **adverb** may modify a noun, an adjective, or another adverb.   37. _____

38. **Verbs** are words that assert an action or a state of being.   38. _____

39. The **indicative mood** of a verb is used to express a command or a request.   39. _____

40. The function of a **subordinating conjunction** is to join a dependent clause to a main clause.   40. _____

41. The **subjunctive mood** expresses doubt, uncertainty, a wish, or a supposition.   41. _____

42. An **adjective** may modify a noun, a pronoun, or an adverb.   42. _____

43. A **gerund** is a verb form ending in *-ing* and used as a noun.   43. _____

44. A **clause** differs from a **phrase** in that a clause always has a subject and a predicate.   44. _____

45. **Adjectives** tell *what kind, how many,* or *which one;* **adverbs** tell *when, where, how,* and *to what degree.*   45. _____

46. A **comma splice** is a grammatical error caused by joining two independent clauses with a comma.   46. _____

47. **Coordinating conjunctions** *(and, but, or, nor, for, yet, so)* join words, phrases, and clauses of equal importance.   47. _____

48. **Pronouns in the objective case** *(him, me,* etc.) should be used as direct objects of verbs and verbals.   48. _____

49. **Mixed construction** occurs when two sections of a sentence that should match in grammatical form do not.

49. _____

50. A **simple short sentence** can be a forceful expression in a passage.

50. _____

PART 2

Write **C** if the item is **correct**.

Write **X** if it is **incorrect**.

EXAMPLE: Was that letter sent to Paul or **I**?

_____X_____

1. **Having been notified to come at once,** there was no opportunity to call you.

1. _____

2. I suspected that his remarks were directed to Larry and **me**.

2. _____

3. He, **thinking that he might find his friends on the second floor of the library,** hurried.

3. _____

4. If a student attends the review session, **they** will do well on the first exam.

4. _____

5. In the cabin of the boat **was** a radio, a set of flares, and a map of the area.

5. _____

6. The Queen, standing beside her husband, children, and grandchildren, **were** waving regally at the crowd.

6. _____

7. She is a person **who** I think is certain to succeed as a social worker.

7. _____

8. **Is** there any other questions you wish to ask regarding the assignment?

8. _____

9. The driver had neglected to fasten his seat belt, **an omission that cost him a month in the hospital.**

9. _____

10. He particularly enjoys **playing softball** and **to run** a mile every morning.

10. _____

11. Forward the complaint to **whoever** you think is in charge.

11. _____

12. Every girl and boy **was** to have an opportunity to try out for the soccer team.

12. _____

13. Neither the bus driver nor the passengers **were** aware of their danger.

13. _____

14. Within the next five years, personal computers will be **not only** smaller **but also** more affordable.

14. _____

15. Not everyone feels that **their** life is better since the 1960s civil rights movement.

15. _____

16. Homemade bread tastes **differently** from bakery bread.

16. _____

17. Not **having had** the chance to consult his lawyer, Larry refused to answer the officer's questions.

17. _____

18. **Is** either of your friends interested in going to Florida over spring break?

18. _____

19. He enrolled in economics because **it** had always been of interest to him.

19. _____

20. Jacob read **steady** for two weeks before he finished the novel.

20. _____

PART 3

On your own paper, **rewrite** each of the following paragraphs so that it is **free of errors** and more **effective.** You may change or reduce wording, combine sentences, and make any other necessary changes. Do not drop any information.

1. Neither the strength nor the wisdom of Clyde Griffiths' parents were sufficient to bring up their family properly. He grew ashamed of his parents, his clothes, and he had to live in ugly surroundings. Clyde grew older, he dreamed of a life of wealth and elegance. Spending most of his money on clothes and luxuries for

himself, his parents were neglected by him. One night when Clyde's uncle invited him to dinner. He met beautiful, wealthy Sondra Finchely. Determined to have her, she was too far above his social position. So Clyde starts going with a factory worker, her name was Roberta, and she became pregnant by him, but it was decided by Clyde that just because of Roberta was no reason he had to give up his pursuit of Sondra.

2. The novel *Slaughterhouse-Five* tells of a man named Billy Pilgrim, who is a prisoner in World War II and later traveled to the planet Tralfamadore. In one particularly amusing episode, the Tralfamadoreans throw Billy into a cage in one of their zoos, along with a sexy Earthling actress named Montana Wildhack. The Tralfamadoreans crowd around the cage to watch the lovemaking between he and her. The less interesting sections of the novel depict the middle-class civilian life of Billy. Who grows wealthy despite having little awareness of what is going on. Billy acquires his wealth by becoming an optometrist, he marries his employer's daughter, and giving lectures on his space travels. I like most of the book because its the most unique novel I have ever read and because it makes you realize the horrors of war and the hollowness of much of American life. However, after reading the entire book, Kurt Vonnegut, Jr., the author, disappointed me because I, enjoying science fiction, wish they had put more about space travel into it.

3. In reading, critical comprehension differs from interpretive comprehension. Critical comprehension adds a new element. That element was judgment. On the interpretive level a student may understand that the author of a poem intends a flower to represent youth, on the critical level they evaluate the author's use of this symbol. The student evaluate the quality of the poem too. For example. On the interpretive level a student would perceive that the theme of a story is "If at first you don't succeed, try, try again"; on the critical level the student judges whether the saying is valid. Critical comprehension includes not only forming opinions about characters in stories but also judgments about them. By learning to comprehend critically, the student's overall reading ability will increase markedly.

4. Studying the woodland ground with my magnifying glass, I grew astonished. First I saw a column of tiny leaves marching along a two-inch-wide road. Peering through the glass, each leaf was being carried like an umbrella in the jaws of an ant far more smaller than the leaf itself. I began to notice other ant trails, all leading to tiny mounds of earth, they looked like miniature volcanoes. Up the mounds and into the craters trod endless parades of ants, each holding aloft its own parasol, which made my spine tingle with excitement. When I heard a faint buzzing made me look around. Above the ant-roads swarmed squadrons of tiny flies. As if on signal they dived straight down to attack the ants. If a person saw this, they would not have believed it. The ants, their jaws clamped upon the giant leaves, had no means of defense. Yet, as if answering air-raid sirens, you could see an army of smaller ants racing toward the leaf-carriers, who they strove to protect.

5. Because the leaf-carrying ants now had some protection did not mean that the attack was over by the flies. As the first attacking fly dived upon a leaf-carrier, the tiny protector ants reached and snapped at the aerial raider with their formidable jaws and they drove it away, but then all along the leaf-carrying column other flies joined the attack. Now I could see that atop each moving leaf a tiny protector ant was riding shotgun through my magnifying glass. Whenever a fly dive-bombed a leaf-carrier was when the shotgun ant on the leaf reached out and bit the fly. One shotgun ant grasped a fly's leg in its jaws and sends the winged enemy spinning to the ground. The ant's comrades swarmed all over the helpless fly, and it was soon reduced to a lifeless shell by them. Similar scenes were taken place all over the miniature battlefield. Finally the squadrons of flies, unable to penetrate the ants' defenses, rised, seemingly in formation, and droned back to their base. Would they mourn their casualties, I wondered. Will their leader have to report the failed attack to an angry insect general?

PART 4 (REVIEW FOR NON-NATIVE ENGLISH SPEAKERS) (ESL)

In each box, write the **correct** preposition: **at, in,** or **on.**

    On each blank line, write the **correct** verb ending: **ed**(or **d**), **s**(or **es**), or **ing.** If no ending is needed, leave the line empty.

    In each set of brackets [ ], write the correct **article: a, an,** or **the.** If no article is needed, leave the brackets empty.

EXAMPLE: [The] newest building [in] our city is [an] apartment house. It was construct__ed__ for senior citizens.

1. Living [ ] [ ] large city requires strong nerves and [ ] outstanding sense of humor. This is especially true [ ] Mondays. When I wait [ ] my corner for [ ] bus that take _____ me to work, I hear [ ] screams of ambulances and fire engine _____ as they speed by. When I am finally [ ] my office building, I am push _____ into [ ] elevator by [ ] crowd. I manage to get off [ ] [ ] twelfth floor. But when I give [ ] cheery "Good morning!" to [ ] first coworker I meet, I am often answer _____ with [ ] grouchy remark. The people at my former job, [ ] 1999, treat _____ me much better. I stay _____ there only a year, but it was [ ] best job I have had since be _____ [ ] America.

2. In [ ] depth of winter [ ] 1925, [ ] [ ] small Alaskan town called Nome, [ ] epidemic of [ ] deadly disease diphtheria start _____. The people were shock _____ to hear that there was no medicine available to stop [ ] disease from spread _____. The ice-locked town was completely block _____ off from the outside world: no boat or plane could reach _____ it, and no roads or rail lines had yet been construct _____ there. Only [ ] dogsleds might possibly rush _____ the medicine to Nome in time. But [ ] nearest supply of medicine was [ ] the city of Anchorage, a thousand miles away. [ ] Nome's tiny telegraph office, the town's doctor transmitt _____ [ ] desperate message: "Nome need _____ diphtheria medicine at once!"

3. Officials in Anchorage round _____ up all the available medicine and had it shipped [ ] [ ] train to the end of the line [ ] Nenana, still 674 miles from Nome. From there relays of dogsled teams took over. The first team's drivers trudge _____ through the white wilderness to [ ] tiny hamlets of Tolovana and Bluff. [ ] Bluff, Gunnar Kaasen's team, headed by the dog Balto, began [ ] next leg of [ ] tiny hamlets of Tolovana and Bluff. Bluff, Gunnar Kaasen's team, headed by the dog Balto, began [ ] next leg of _____
_____
_____ journey. Through raging blizzards, thirty-below-zero cold, and missed relay stations, [ ] Balto led Kaasen's team all the way to Nome. [ ] just 5½ days the dog teams had cover _____ what was normally [ ] month's journey. Nome had been save _____.

PART 5 (REVIEW FOR NON-NATIVE ENGLISH SPEAKERS) **ESL**

For each blank, choose from the list any determiner (limiting adjective) that sounds right, and write it in. Try not to use any word on the list more than once.

every	many	other	more	some	several
each	most	such	(a) little	another	all
(n) either	(a) few	both	much	enough	any

EXAMPLE: They needed __another__ person to help lift the car.

_____ day last week there were _____ alarming stories in the newspapers. _____ of them made _____ sense. One story said that soon there would not be _____ fish left in the oceans or lakes. _____ story warned that global warming would soon drown or boil us all. _____ of these stories gave me nightmares.

Answers to Grammar and Sentence Review for Unit 1

Part 1

1. T	7. T	13. T	19. T	25. T
2. T	8. F	14. F	20. F	26. F
3. F	9. T	15. T	21. F	27. T
4. T	10. F	16. T	22. T	28. F
5. T	11. T	17. F	23. F	29. F
6. T	12. T	18. F	24. F	30. T

31. T	35. T	39. F	43. T	47. T
32. F	36. T	40. T	44. T	48. T
33. T	37. F	41. T	45. T	49. T
34. T	38. T	42. F	46. T	50. T

Part 2

1. X	5. X	9. C	13. C	17. C
2. C	6. X	10. X	14. C	18. C
3. X	7. C	11. C	15. X	19. C
4. X	8. X	12. C	16. X	20. X

Part 3
(Many variations possible.)

1. Clyde Griffiths' parents had neither the strength nor the wisdom to bring up their family properly; consequently, Clyde grew ashamed of his parents, his clothes, and his ugly surroundings. As he grew older, Clyde dreamed of a life of wealth and elegance. Spending most of his money on clothes and luxuries for himself, he neglected his parents. One night, at a dinner to which his uncle had invited him, he met beautiful, wealthy Sondra Finchley and became determined to have her. She was, however, too far above his social position. Clyde then started going with a factory worker named Roberta, whom he made pregnant. Even this complication, Clyde decided, would not make him give up his pursuit of Sondra.

2. The novel *Slaughterhouse-Five* tells of a man named Billy Pilgrim, who is a prisoner in World War II and later travels to the planet Tralfamadore. In one particularly amusing episode, the Tralfamadoreans throw Billy into a cage in one of their zoos, along with a sexy Earthling named Montana Wildhack. The Tralfamadoreans crowd around the cage to watch them making love. The less interesting sections of the novel depict the middle-class civilian life of Billy, who grows wealthy despite having little awareness of what is going on. Billy acquires his wealth by becoming an optometrist, marrying his employer's daughter, and giving lectures on his space travels. I like most of the book because it is the most nearly unique novel I have ever read and because it makes me realize the horrors of war and the hollowness of much of American life. However, after reading the entire book, I was disappointed that the author, Kurt Vonnegut, Jr., had not added more about space travel, since I enjoy science fiction.

3. In reading, critical comprehension differs from interpretive comprehension in adding a new element, judgment. On the interpretive level students may understand that the author of a poem intends a flower to represent youth; on the critical level they evaluate the author's use of this symbol. Students also evaluate the quality of a poem. For example, on the interpretive level a student perceives that the theme of a story is "If at first you don't succeed, try, try again"; on the critical level the student judges whether the saying is valid. Critical comprehension includes not only forming opinions about characters in stories but also making judgments about them. By learning to comprehend critically, students will markedly increase their overall reading ability.

4. Studying the woodland ground with my magnifying glass, I grew astonished. First I saw a column of tiny leaves marching along a two-inch-wide road. Peering through the glass, I saw that each leaf was being carried like an umbrella in the jaws of an ant far smaller than the leaf itself. I began to notice other ant trails, all leading to tiny mounds of earth that looked like miniature volcanoes. Up the mounds and into the craters trod endless parades of ants, each holding aloft its own parasol, a sight which made my spine tingle with excitement. A faint buzzing made me look around. Above the ant-roads swarmed squadrons of tiny flies. As if on signal, they dived straight down to attack the ants. It was an unbelievable sight. The ants, their jaws clamped upon the giant leaves, had no means of defense. Yet, as if they were answering air-raid sirens, an army of smaller ants raced toward the leaf-carriers, whom they strove to protect.

5. Though the leaf-carrying ants now had some protection, the flies' attack was not over. As the first attacking fly dived upon a leaf-carrier, the tiny protector ants reached and snapped at the aerial raider with their formidable jaws, driving it away. But then, all along the leaf-carrying column, other flies joined the attack. Now I could see through my magnifying glass that atop each moving leaf a tiny protector ant was riding shotgun.

Whenever a fly dive-bombed a leaf-carrier, the shotgun ant on the leaf reached out and bit the fly. One shotgun ant grasped a fly's leg in its jaws and sent the winged enemy spinning to the ground. The ant's comrades swarmed all over the helpless fly, soon reducing it to a lifeless shell. Similar scenes were taking place all over the miniature battlefield. Finally the squadrons of flies, unable to penetrate the ants' defenses, rose, seemingly in formation, and droned back to their base. Would they mourn their casualties, I wondered. Would their leader have to report the failed attack to an angry insect general?

Part 4

1. Living [in] [a] large city requires strong nerves and [an] outstanding sense of humor. This is especially true [on] Mondays. When I wait [at/on] my corner for [the/a] bus that takes me to work, I hear [the] screams of ambulances and fire engines as they speed by. When I am finally [in/at] my office building, I am pushed into [an/the] elevator by [the/a] crowd. I manage to get off [at] [the] twelfth floor. But when I give [a] cheery "good morning!" to [the] first coworker I meet, I am often answered with [a] grouchy remark. The people at my former job, [in] 1999, treated me much better. I stayed there only a year, but it was [the] best job I have had since being [in] America.

2. In [the] depth of winter [in] 1925, [in] [a] small Alaskan town called Nome, [an] epidemic of [the] deadly disease diphtheria started. The people were shocked to hear that there was no medicine available to stop [the] disease from spreading. The ice-locked town was completely blocked off from the outside world: no boat or plane could reach __ it, and no roads or rail lines had yet been constructed there. Only [ ] dogsleds might possibly rush __ the medicine to Nome in time. But [the] nearest supply of medicine was [in/at] the city of Anchorage, a thousand miles away. [In/At] Nome's tiny telegraph office, the town's doctor transmitted [a] desperate message: "Nome needs diphtheria medicine at once!"

3. Officials in Anchorage rounded up all the available medicine and had it shipped [on] [a] train to the end of the line [at/in] Nenana, still 674 miles from Nome. From there relays of dogsled teams took over. The first team's drivers trudged through the white wilderness to [the] tiny hamlets of Tolovana and Bluff. [At/In] Bluff, Gunnar Kaasen's team, headed by the dog Balto, began [the] next leg of [the] journey. Through raging blizzards, thirty-below-zero cold, and missed relay stations, [ ] Balto led Kaasen's team all the way to Nome. [In] just 5½ days the dog teams had covered what was normally [a] month's journey. Nome had been saved.

Part 5
(Some answers may vary depending on previous answers.)

Each/Every day last week there were several/some/more/many/a few alarming stories in the newspapers. None/Few of them made any sense/Few of them made much sense. One story said that there would not be any/many/enough fish left in the oceans or lakes. Another story warned that global warming would soon drown or boil us all. Most/ All/Many/Several/Each/A few of these stories gave me nightmares.

FLASH FOCUS

When you complete Unit II, you should be able to:

✓ Understand the various types of punctuation

✓ Understand how punctuation clarifies written material

✓ Write clear, expressive sentences using punctuation

"A kiss can be a comma, a question mark, or an exclamation point."

—Mistinguett

"Writing energy is like anything else: the more you put in, the more you get out."
—Richard Reeves

FLASH TEST

Before you begin studying the sections in Unit II, take the diagnostic test on punctuation to test your knowledge. If you answer eight or more questions incorrectly, be sure to note where you need extra help or explanation and pay close attention to those particular sections in Unit II.

DIAGNOSTIC TEST: PUNCTUATION

In the blank after each sentence,

Write **C** if the punctuation in brackets is **correct;**

Write **X** if it is **incorrect.**

(Use only one letter in each blank.)

EXAMPLE: Regular exercise[,] and sound nutrition are essential for good health. _____ **X**

1. In the late nineteenth century immigrants from many nations crowded into lower Manhattan[;] the area became notorious for vicious fights between ethnic groups.   1. _____

2. "What is the outlook for religion in the twenty-first century[?]" the speaker asked.   2. _____

3. "Why can't a woman be more like a man["?] the chauvinist asked.   3. _____

4. I learned that the newly elected officers were Marzell Brown, president[;] Leroy Jones, vice president[;] Sandra Smith, treasurer[;] and James Chang, secretary.   4. _____

5. The class expected low grades[. T]he test having been long and difficult.   5. _____

6. It[']s hard to imagine life without a VCR, a personal computer, and a microwave oven.   6. _____

7. Eventually, everybody comes to Rick's[;] the best saloon in Casablanca.   7. _____

8. Recognizing that busing places stress on younger students[,] the state officials are restructuring the school transportation system.   8. _____

9. Richard Hernandez was unhappy at his college[,] he missed hearing Spanish and enjoying his favorite foods.   9. _____

10. That is not the Sullivans' boat; at least, I think that it isn't their[']s.　　　10. _____

11. When it rains, I always think of the opening lines of Longfellow's poem "The Rainy Day": "The day is cold, and dark, and dreary [/] It rains, and the wind is never weary."　　　11. _____

12. Inspector Trace asked, "Is that all you remember?["] "[]Are you sure?"　　　12. _____

13. "The report is ready," Chisholm said[,] "I'm sending it to the supervisor today."　　　13. _____

14. Didn't I hear you say, "I especially like blueberry pie"[?]　　　14. _____

15. Joe enrolled in a small college[;] although he had planned originally to join a rock band.　　　15. _____

16. Stanley moved to Minneapolis[,] where he hoped to open a restaurant.　　　16. _____

17. That was a bit too close for comfort[,] wasn't it?　　　17. _____

18. The advertiser received more than two[-]hundred replies on the Internet.　　　18. _____

19. Sarah is asking for a week[']s vacation to visit relatives in Canada.　　　19. _____

20. On February 21, 2005[,] Robin and Sam are getting married.　　　20. _____

Answers to Diagnostic Test on Punctuation

1. X	5. C	9. C	13. C	17. C
2. X	6. C	10. C	14. C	18. X
3. X	7. X	11. C	15. C	19. X
4. X	8. C	12. C	16. X	20. C

FLASH SUMMARY

Punctuation marks are the traffic signals of writing. They assist the reader through the heavy traffic of ideas that a written passage may contain. Some punctuation marks *separate* words or ideas; others *emphasize* them; still others *group* and *keep together* related ideas. In all, punctuation marks clarify written language that would otherwise confuse and perhaps mislead.

28–30 The Comma [,]

FLASH SUMMARY

Misuse of the comma accounts for about half of all punctuation errors. The following guidelines, combined with your attention to oral pauses and stops (although commas in writing do not always match oral pauses), should help you solve most comma problems.

28. Use a Comma to Set Off

A. **Independent (Main) Clauses.** A comma follows the first of two independent clauses that are joined by a coordinating conjunction *(and, but, or, nor, for, yet, so)*:

The government has spent millions on an AIDS cure, *and* prospects for success are improving.

Scientists around the world are experimenting with hundreds of drugs, *but* so far the hoped-for cure has proven elusive.

Do *not* use a comma

✓ Generally, if there is no full clause (subject + verb) after the conjunction:

WRONG: They voted on the bill Monday, *and* adjourned Tuesday.

RIGHT: They voted on the bill Monday *and* adjourned Tuesday.

✓ *After* the conjunction:

WRONG: They voted on the bill Monday *but,* it was defeated.

RIGHT: They voted on the bill Monday, *but* it was defeated.

✓ Between very short independent clauses:

RIGHT: He lies and she cheats.

✓ Between independent clauses not joined by a coordinating conjunction (use a semicolon instead):

WRONG: The starting gun sounded, the crowd roared.

RIGHT: The starting gun sounded; the crowd roared.

This is a common but serious error. See comma splices and fused sentences, section 26B, pages 91–92.

B. Introductory Elements

(1) An introductory adverb clause:

Whenever war threatens in the Middle East, world stock markets become jittery.

Because the ozone layer was thinning, skin cancer incidence began to rise.

Note: Usually you do not need a comma when the independent clause comes first: World stock markets become jittery *whenever war threatens in the Middle East.* (But see F(1), page 118, on *because* clauses.)

(2) A long prepositional phrase or a series of prepositional phrases:

In the aftermath of the scandal, the director resigned.

Note: Unless clarity demands one, you do not need a comma after one short introductory prepositional phrase: *After the scandal* the director resigned.

(3) A verbal phrase:

To prevent hostilities, the UN sent in a peace force.

By sending in a force, the UN prevented hostilities.

Encouraged by peace hopes, stock traders became active.

An infinitive or gerund phrase used as the *subject* of a sentence is not an introductory element. Do not set it off:

To prevent hostilities was the UN's hope.

Sending in a peace force prevented hostilities.

C. Items in a Series. Use commas to separate words, phrases, or clauses in a series of three or more:

WORDS: A newly released CD contains operatic arias by *Verdi, Puccini, Donizetti,* and *Bellini.*

PHRASES: Allied armies pushed *through the French countryside, across the Rhine,* and *into Germany.*

CLAUSES: *Zelda began ballet lessons, Scott wrote fitfully,* and *together they partied regularly.*

Note: Some writers omit the comma before the final *and* or *or* in a series. Including this comma, however, ensures clarity. Use a comma before *etc.* at the end of a series: pork, beans, etc.

Do **not** use a comma

✓ With only two items: She sought *peace* and *quiet*.

✓ If you repeat *and* or *or* between each two items: She sought *peace* and *quiet* and *solitude*.

✓ Before the first item or after the last:

WRONG: She sought, *peace, quiet,* and *solitude*.

RIGHT: She sought *peace, quiet,* and *solitude*.

WRONG: *Peace, quiet,* and *solitude,* proved elusive.

RIGHT: *Peace, quiet,* and *solitude* proved elusive.

D. Coordinate Adjectives. In a series of two or more, use commas to separate adjectives of equal importance. Do not put a comma after the last adjective:

Tall, stately trees lined the roadway.

Too much *salty, fatty,* or *sugary* food may harm one's health.

Note: Certain combinations of adjectives flow naturally together and need no commas: *little red* schoolhouse; *two creaky old* cars; *additional monetary* demands. Determining when to omit commas is tricky, but if the adjectives would sound odd in a different order (*red little* schoolhouse, *old creaky two* cars, *monetary additional* demands), you probably should omit commas.

E. Parenthetical Expressions. These are words or word groups that interrupt the main flow of thought in a sentence but are not necessary to the sentence; they could be removed from the sentence without changing its essential meaning. Think of the pair of commas almost as parentheses:

They were, *in my opinion,* not guilty.

The jury, *on the other hand,* convicted them all.

The judge, *moreover,* smiled at the verdict.

It is unfortunate, *to be sure.* [Note the significant difference in meaning from *It is unfortunate to be sure.*]

Other common parenthetical expressions include *as a matter of fact, to tell the truth, of course, incidentally, namely, in the first place, therefore, thus, consequently, however, nevertheless.*

Note: Not all these expressions are always set off. You may choose not to set off *perhaps, likewise, at least, indeed, therefore, thus,* and certain others in sentences where you feel they do not interrupt your thought flow:

It was, *perhaps,* just an oversight.

It was *perhaps* just an oversight.

F. Nonrestrictive (Nonessential) Elements

(1) Nonrestrictive clauses. A **nonrestrictive** clause (usually beginning with *which* or a form of *who*) is parenthetical. The information it gives is *not* essential to the meaning of the sentence. Thus the clause is set off within commas, like other parenthetical elements:

Crestwood Mall, *which Mr. Pappas owns,* is expanding.

Professor Mikasa, *who was born in Japan,* teaches Asian literature.

Read the above sentences, omitting the italicized clauses. Do we still know *which* mall is expanding and *which* professor teaches Asian literature? Yes. The clauses are thus merely parenthetical, not essential; they need commas.

A **restrictive** clause *is* essential to the meaning of the sentence. It fully or partly identifies the preceding noun; it answers the question "which one?" Such a clause is written without commas:

> The mall *that Mr. Pappas owns* is expanding.

> A professor *who was born in Japan* teaches Asian literature.

Read the above sentences, omitting the italicized clauses. Do we still know *which* mall and *which* professor? No. Without these restrictive clauses the sentences may refer to any mall or any professor. The clauses are therefore essential (restrictive) and take no commas.

One easy way to tell whether a clause is restrictive is to use the *that* test. Adjective clauses beginning with *that* are always restrictive; so are clauses beginning with *who* or *which* that can be changed to *that* and still sound right:

> RESTRICTIVE: A professor *who* [or *that*] *was born in Japan* teaches Asian literature. [*That* sounds right.]

> NONRESTRICTIVE: Professor Mikasa, *who* [but not *that*] *was born in* Japan, teaches Asian literature. [*That* would sound wrong.]

Note: In U.S. usage, *that* is generally preferred over *which* to begin a restrictive clause: The team *that* (rather than *which*) finishes fifth will miss the playoffs.

Note: A *because* clause containing your main point is restrictive:

> Dewey lost the 1948 election because he was overconfident. [You assume your reader already knows that Dewey lost; you are stressing the reason he lost.]

A *because* clause giving merely incidental information is nonrestrictive:

> Classes are being canceled today, because a water main has broken. [The canceling is the main point—your reader did not previously know this; the cause is merely incidental.]

(2) **Nonrestrictive (nonessential) phrases.** Follow the principle for nonrestrictive clauses (see (1) above):

> NONRESTRICTIVE: The governor, *waving the state flag,* led the parade.

> RESTRICTIVE: A woman *waving the state flag* led the parade.

> NONRESTRICTIVE: Significantly more progress was made by the control group, *composed of five-year-olds.*

> RESTRICTIVE: Significantly more progress was made by the group *composed of five-year-olds.*

(3) **Nonrestrictive appositives:**

> The male lead of *Titanic, Leonardo DiCaprio,* became an instant teenage idol.

> Cobb wrote to his daughter, *Ella.* [The comma shows that the appositive, Ella, is not identifying *which* daughter; thus Cobb must have only one daughter.]

Restrictive appositives take no commas:

> The actor *Leonardo DiCaprio* became an instant teenage idol.

> Cobb wrote to his daughter *Ella.* [one of two or more daughters]

G. **Absolute Phrases** (see section 21B(2) page 70, for definition)

The ATM having kept his card, Finch had no cash.

Shaunelle, *her confidence restored,* awaited the interview.

H. **Names or Other Words Used in Direct Address**

Tell us, *Marlene,* what solution you propose.

Mr. President, may we quote you on that?

I. ***Yes* and *No* at the Beginning of a Sentence**

Yes, these lines imply the poet's fear of death.

J. **Mild Interjections** (expressions of less than strong emotion):

Well, I think it could use more sauce.

Oh, just put it down anywhere.

Note: Strong interjections take exclamation points: *Hey!* Come back with my purse.

K. **Direct Quotations.** Generally, use a comma to set off a direct quotation (someone's exact words) from words that precede, follow, or interrupt it.

"You can't always get what you want," says the song.

"This," said Miss Marple, "is the final clue."

Punctuation of quotations is treated fully in sections 42–46, pages 136–138.

L. **Examples Introduced by *Such as, Especially, Particularly;* Expressions of Contrast**

She excelled in many sports, *particularly* track.

On weekends we offer several courses, *such as* Biology 101 and Music 210, for nontraditional students.

The class meets in Room 302, *not* 202.

Note: Some *such as* phrases are restrictive: Days *such as* this are rare.

29. Use a Comma Also

A. **In Place of Omitted or Understood Words** in structures such as

Hanoi was the northern capital; *Saigon, the southern.* [or, less formally, *Hanoi was the northern capital, Saigon the southern.*]

B. **Before a Confirmatory (Tag) Question**

The campus is safe after dark, *isn't it?*

C. **In Letters**

(1) *After the greeting of a friendly letter:* Dear Frank,

Note: Use a colon in a business letter: *Dear Mr. Coe:*

(2) *After the complimentary close in all letters:* Very truly yours,

D. **In Dates and Addresses.** In a month-day-year date, place the year within commas, as if it were parenthetical. Do the same with the state or country in an address:

In Skokie, *Illinois,* on July 4, *2001,* they were married.

Note: Do not use a comma in a month-year or a day-month-year date or between a state and a ZIP code: May 1967; 6 June 1944; Phoenix, AZ 85032.

E. For Clarity, to Prevent Misreading

By leaving Nora Helmer gained freedom. [Who left?]

By leaving, Nora Helmer gained freedom. [Nora left.]

By leaving Nora, Helmer gained freedom. [Mr. Helmer left.]

30. Do *Not* Use a Comma

A. To Separate Subject and Verb or Verb and Complement

WRONG: Many reference *books, are* now on CD-ROM.

RIGHT: Many reference *books are* now on CD-ROM.

WRONG: Municipal bonds *provide,* tax-free *income.*

RIGHT: Municipal bonds *provide* tax-free *income.*

B. To Join Two Independent Clauses in Place of a Coordinating Conjunction (*and, but, or, nor, for, yet, so*) or Semicolon. Avoiding this serious error, called a *comma splice,* is explained in section 26B, pages 91–92.

 **FLASH TEST**

PART 1

If **no comma** is needed in the bracketed space(s), leave the blank empty. If **one or more commas** are needed, write in the **reason** from the list below (only one reason per blank; use the abbreviations in parentheses).

independent clauses joined by conjunction **(ind)**	appositive **(app)**
introductory adverb clause **(intro)**	absolute phrase **(abs)**
series **(ser)**	direct address **(add)**
parenthetical expression **(par)**	mild interjection **(inter)**
nonrestrictive clause **(nr)**	direct quotation **(quot)**

EXAMPLES: The New England states include Vermont[ ] Maine[ ] and New Hampshire.   _____**ser**_____

The Secretary of State[ ] held a press conference.

1. *Cold Mountain*[ ] a novel by Charles Frazier[ ] recounts a Confederate deserter's homeward trek through the Appalachian Mountains. 1. _____

2. Professors[ ] who assign too many long papers[ ] may have small classes. 2. _____

3. Well[ ] I guess we'll have to leave without Ida. 3. _____

4. If there are no other questions[ ] let's begin our game. 4. _____

5. So you see[ ] Dr. Haywood[ ] I can't possibly pay your bill by next week. 5. _____

6. Phillip's father[ ] who is a religious man[ ] disapproves of many teenage antics. 6. _____

7. Dan and Marilyn[ ] however[ ] are hopeful for a 2008 victory. 7. _____

8. John Fitzgerald Kennedy[ ] the thirty-fifth President of the United States[ ] was assassinated on November 22, 1963. 8. _____

9. The Chinese are trained to write with their right hands[ ] for it is difficult to do Chinese calligraphy with the left hand. 9. _____

10. Before you meet clients for the first time[   ] learn all that you can about their company, their style, and their risk-taking ability.

    10. _____

11. He sat down at his desk last evening[   ] and made a preliminary draft of his speech.

    11. _____

12. Julie went into the library[   ] but she hurried out a few minutes later.

    12. _____

13. Lincoln spoke eloquently about government of the people[   ] by the people[   ] and for the people.

    13. _____

14. After she had listened to her favorite album[   ] she settled down to study.

    14. _____

15. The candidate gave a number of speeches in Illinois[   ] where she hoped to win support.

    15. _____

16. She had always wanted to visit the small village[   ] where her father lived, but she knew neither its name nor its location.

    16. _____

17. My instructor[   ] Dr. Ursula Tyler[   ] outlined the work for the current semester.

    17. _____

18. What you need[   ] David[   ] is a professional organizer to straighten out your office.

    18. _____

19. "Is this[   ]" she asked[   ] "the only excuse that you have to offer?"

    19. _____

20. Castles were cold and filthy[   ] according to historians[   ] because castles were built more for protection than convenience.

    20. _____

21. His hands swollen from five fire ant bites[   ] John swore that he would rid his yard of all ant hills.

    21. _____

22. Both potato and corn crops had a major impact on the life expectancy of Europeans[   ] living in the eighteenth century.

    22. _____

23. Ford's first Model T sold for $850 in 1908[   ] but the price dropped to $440 in 1915 because of mass production.

    23. _____

24. We were asked to read *The Grapes of Wrath*[   ] which John Steinbeck wrote in the 1930s.

    24. _____

25. Lorraine Hansberry[   ] the author of *A Raisin in the Sun*[   ] died at thirty-five.

    25. _____

FLASH TEST

PART 2

Write **C** if the punctuation in brackets is **correct.**

Write **X** if it is **incorrect.**

(Use only one letter for each answer.)

EXAMPLE: Since they had no further business there[,] they left.

    _____ C _____

1. The campaign hit a new low when the candidates began accusing each other of embezzlement[,] tax fraud[,] and even marital infidelity.

    1. _____

2. Her last day in the office[,] was spent sorting papers and filing manuscripts.

    2. _____

3. In preparation for the party[,] Carla began cleaning and cooking a week earlier.

    3. _____

4. Having turned on her word processor[,] Colleen began her great American novel.

    4. _____

5. Haven't you any idea[,] of the responsibility involved in running a household?

    5. _____

6. First-graders now engage in writing journals[,] in problem-solving activities[,] and in brief science experiments.

    6. _____

7. Shaking hands with his patient, the physician asked[,] "Now what kind of surgery are we doing today?"

    7. _____

8. Peter's goal was to make a short film in graduate school[,] and not worry about a future career.   8. _____

9. Erron and Nakita determined to find a less painful[,] but effective diet.   9. _____

10. The American cowboys' hats actually had many purposes besides shielding their faces from the sun and rain[,] for many cowboys used their hats as pillows and drinking cups.   10. _____

11. During conversations about controversial topics[,] our faces often communicate our thoughts, especially our emotional responses.   11. _____

12. Harry Rosen[,] a skilled, polished speaker[,] effectively used humor during his speeches.   12. _____

13. To understand how living arrangements affect student relationships[,] the psychology department completed several informal observational studies on campus.   13. _____

14. Many music lovers insist that the now-obsolete vinyl LP record produces better music[,] than the currently popular CD.   14. _____

15. The states with the largest numbers of dairy cows are Wisconsin[,] and California.   15. _____

16. Young Soo's mother was preparing *kimchi*[,] a pickled cabbage dish that is commonly eaten with Korean meals.   16. _____

17. Having friends must be an important aspect of our culture[,] for many popular television series focus on how a group of characters care for their friendships with one another.   17. _____

18. People beginning an intimate relationship use a significant number of affectionate expressions[,] but the frequency of these expressions drops as the relationship matures.   18. _____

19. Working hard to pay the mortgage, to educate their children, and to save money for retirement[,] many of America's middle class now call themselves the "new poor."   19. _____

20. The children could take martial arts classes near home[,] or they could decide to save their money for summer camp.   20. _____

21. Now only 68 percent of American children live with both biological parents[,] 20 percent of children live in single-parent families[,] and 9 percent live with one biological parent and a stepparent.   21. _____

22. Jeff was hungry for a gooey[,] chocolate brownie smothered in whipped cream and chocolate sauce.   22. _____

23. His thoughts dominated by grief[,] Jack decided to postpone his vacation for another month.   23. _____

24. "Oh[,] I forgot to bring my report home to finish it tonight," sighed Mary.   24. _____

25. People exercise because it makes them feel good[,] they may even become addicted to exercise.   25. _____

Answers to Exercises for: The Comma

Part 1

1. app	6. nr	11. —	16. —	21. abs
2. —	7. par	12. ind	17. app	22. —
3. inter	8. app	13. ser	18. add	23. ind
4. intro	9. ind	14. intro	19. quot	24. nr
5. add	10. intro	15. nr	20. par	25. app

Part 2

31–32 The Period [.]

31. Use a Period

A. After Every Sentence Except a Direct Question or an Exclamation

The *A* train goes to Harlem. [declarative sentence]

Take the *A* train. [imperative sentence]

I'll ask where the *A* train goes. [indirect question (a statement about a question); the direct question is "Where does the *A* train go?"]

B. After an Abbreviation or Initial

Mr., Mrs., U.S., Dr., Calif., M.D., Rev., lb.

Note: You may write *Ms.* either with or without a period, as long as you are consistent. *Miss* never takes a period.

Do **not** use a period with

✓ Many well-known sets of initials: IBM, FBI, NBC, NASA, UN, YWCA, CD-ROM

✓ Postal abbreviations of states: DE, AK, RI

✓ Radio and television stations: WSQK

✓ Money in even-dollar denominations: $40

✓ Contractions: ass'n, sec'y [for *association, secretary*. They may also be written *assn., secy.*]

✓ Ordinal numbers: 5th, 2nd, Henry VIII

✓ Nicknames: Rob, Pat, Sid, Pam

✓ Common shortened terms: memo, math, exam, lab, gym, TV [All these terms are colloquial; use the full words in formal writing.]

C. After a Number or Letter in a Formal Outline

    I. Influential Rock Groups

      A. The Rolling Stones

      B. U2

Note: Do *not* use a period

✓ If the number or letter is within parentheses: (1), (a)

✓ If the number is part of a title: Chapter 4

D. In a Spaced Group of Three (. . .) to Show

    (1) *Ellipsis* (the intentional omission of words) in a quoted passage. Retain necessary punctuation preceding the ellipsis:

✓ **Customary usage:**

George V. Higgins has written, "I think the only way to find out whether the story in your mind is any good is to sit down by yourself and try to put all of it on paper. . . . If the story interests you enough, . . . it will interest other people."

The first of the four periods after *paper* signals the end of the sentence. Follow this practice whether the omission is before or after such a period.

✓ **Latest Modern Language Association style:** Bracket the three periods of any ellipses in quotations to clarify that the ellipses were not in the original. See example, section 42F, page 136.

(2) Pause, hesitation, and the like in a dialogue and interrupted narrative (do not overuse this device):

This room. Yes, this room. . . . You . . . was it you?

. . . were going out to look for something. . . . The tree of knowledge, wasn't it?
                                                                                    —J. M. Barrie

E. After a Nonsentence. A **nonsentence** is a legitimate unit of expression lacking subject + predicate. It is found mostly in dialogue.

(1) A greeting: Good evening.
(2) A mild exclamation not within a sentence:
    Oh.   Darn.

(3) An answer to a question: Will you accept? *Perhaps.*

Note: A nonsentence is a correct expression. A fragment (a similar structure *un*intentionally lacking subject + predicate) is an error. Fragments are explained in section 26A, pages 90–91.

32. Do *Not* Use a Period after a title of a composition or report, even if that title is a sentence:

The Prospects for Campaign Finance Reform

Campaign Finance Can Be Reformed

Do, however, use a question mark or exclamation point where appropriate in a title: *Can Campaign Finance Reform Succeed?*

33–34 The Question Mark [?]

33. Use a Question Mark

A. After a Direct Question

Did you get a call? When? From Whom?

It was from Mr. Ward, wasn't it?

You testified earlier—do you recall?—that you didn't know him.

You met him at a party? [A question may be in declarative-sentence form; the question mark signals the tone in which it would be spoken.]

For use of the question mark in quotations, see section 45C, pages 137–138; in titles, see section 32, this page.

B. Within Parentheses to Indicate Doubt or Uncertainty

Joan of Arc was born in 1412 (?) and died in 1431.

34. Do *Not* Use a Question Mark

A.   After an Indirect Question (see section 31A, page 123, for definition)

Senator Henry asked what the program would cost.

B.   After a Polite Request in Question Form

Would you please sign the enclosed papers.

C.   Within Parentheses to Express Humor or Irony

WRONG: That purple suit shows his exquisite (?) taste.

35–36 The Exclamation Point [!]

35. Use an Exclamation Point after an emphatic word, sentence, or other expression:

Never!	He has a gun!
How gross!	What a night!

For use of the exclamation point in titles, see section 32, page 124. For its use in quotations, see section 45C, pages 137–138.

36. Do *Not* Use an Exclamation Point

A.   After a Mild Interjection or a Sentence That Suggests Only Mild Excitement or Emotion. The exclamation point is a strong signal, but one that quickly loses its effect if overused. Except in quoted dialogue, reserve the exclamation point mostly for expressions that begin with *what* or *how* (and are not questions). Elsewhere, use the less dramatic comma or period:

What a fool I was!   Why, I never knew that.

B.   More than Once, or with Other Pause or Stop Marks

WRONG: That's a lie!!! [One *!* is sufficient.]

WRONG: You failed again?! [Use either *?* or *!*.]

FLASH TEST

Write **C** if the punctuation in brackets is **correct.**

Write **X** if it is **incorrect.**

EXAMPLE: Is there any word from the Awards Committee yet[?]	C
1. You'd like that, wouldn't you[?]	1. _____
2. "Evacuate the dorm; there's a fire!" the resident assistant shouted[!]	2. _____
3. The police officer calmly inquired whether I had the slightest notion of just how fast I was backing up[?]	3. _____
4. Mr. Hall and Miss[.] James will chair the committee.	4. _____
5. The chem[.] test promises to be challenging.	5. _____
6. Where is the office? Down the hall on the left[.]	6. _____
7. Good afternoon, ma'am[.] May I present you with a free scrub brush?	7. _____

8. "How much did the owners spend on players' salaries?" the reporter asked[?]   8. _____

9. His next question—wouldn't you know[?]—was, "What do you need, ma'am?"   9. _____

10. "Wow! Does your computer have a video camera too[!]"   10. _____

11. "What a magnificent view you have of the mountains[!]" said he.   11. _____

12. Who said, "If at first you don't succeed, try, try again" [?]   12. _____

13. Would you please check my computer for viruses[?]   13. _____

14. HELP WANTED: Editor[.] for our new brochure.   14. _____

15. Pat, please type this memo[.] to the purchasing department.   15. _____

16. What? You lent that scoundrel Snively $10,000[?!]   16. _____

17. I asked her why, of all the men on campus, she had chosen him[?]   17. _____

18. Why did I do it? Because I respected her[.] Jackie worked hard to finish her degree.   18. _____

19. Footloose and Fancy Free[.] [title of an essay]   19. _____

20. Would you please send me your reply by e-mail[.]   20. _____

21. Your cat ate my goldfish[!!] Why didn't you tell me he was a murdering feline?   21. _____

22. Charlie was an inspiring [(?)] date. He burped all through dinner.   22. _____

23. My supervisor asked how much equipment I would need to update the computer center[.]   23. _____

24. The essay was "Computers: Can We Live Without Them[?]"   24. _____

25. I heard the news on station W[.]I[.]N[.]K.   25. _____

26. The postmark on the package read "Springfield, MA[.] 01102."   26. _____

27. The monarch who followed King George VI[.] was Queen Elizabeth II.   27. _____

28. According to Ramsey, "The election drew a light turnout[.] . . . Predictably, the Socialist Party won."   28. _____

29. You lost your wallet again[?] I don't believe it.   29. _____

30. The duke was born in 1576[(?)] and died in 1642.   30. _____

31. The bridge shook. Girders began to crack. The whole structure was collapsing[!!]   31. _____

32. Do you know when I may expect my refund[?]   32. _____

33. Could I have committed the crime? Never[.] I was on a business trip to St. Louis at the time.   33. _____

Answers to Exercises for: The Period, Question Mark, and Exclamation Point

1. C	8. X	15. X	22. X	29. C
2. X	9. C	16. X	23. C	30. C
3. X	10. X	17. X	24. C	31. X
4. X	11. C	18. C	25. X	32. C
5. X	12. C	19. X	26. X	33. C
6. C	13. X	20. C	27. X	
7. C	14. X	21. X	28. C	

37 The Semicolon [;]

FLASH SUMMARY

The semicolon signals a greater break in thought than the comma but a lesser break than the period. It is, however, closer to a period than to a comma in most of its uses and is often interchangeable with the period. The semicolon often gives your writing a formal tone, as the following examples suggest.

Use a Semicolon

A. Between Independent Clauses Not Joined by a Coordinating Conjunction

Commercial architects of the 1950s and 1960s designed huge, unadorned glass boxes; the Lever House in Manhattan is a landmark of this style.

The semicolon is particularly effective for showing balance or contrast between two clauses:

The woods abound with wildlife; the lakes teem with fish.

Freshmen think they know nothing; sophomores know they know everything.

B. Between Independent Clauses Joined by a Conjunctive Adverb (*therefore, however, nevertheless, thus, moreover, also, besides, consequently, meanwhile, otherwise, then, furthermore, likewise, in fact, still*):

Years ago many American college diplomas were written in Latin; *however,* today very few are.

For early feminists, voting rights were the key to equality; *consequently,* these women focused on suffrage.

Note: The comma after some conjunctive adverbs is optional.

Even when the conjunctive adverb moves into the second clause, the semicolon stays put between the clauses:

Years ago many American college diplomas were written in Latin; today, *however,* very few are.

C. Between Independent Clauses Joined by a Coordinating Conjunction When There Are Commas Within the Clauses

Today we take for granted automobile safety equipment such as air bags, collapsible steering columns, and antilock brakes; *yet* fifty years ago cars were not required even to have directional signals, seat belts, or outside rearview mirrors. [The semicolon marks the break between the independent clauses more clearly than another comma would.]

D. Between Items in a Series When There Are Commas Within the Items

The new officers are Verna Brooks, chair; Pedro Lopez, social director; Sam Lee, treasurer; and Sharon Grady, secretary.

FLASH TEST

PART 1

Write the **reason** for the semicolon in each sentence (use the abbreviations in parentheses). Use only one reason for each sentence.

between clauses lacking a coordinating conjunction **(no conj)**

between clauses joined by a conjunctive adverb **(conj adv)**

between clauses having commas within them **(cl w com)**

in a series having commas within the items **(ser w com)**

EXAMPLE: It was a glorious day for the North; it was a sad one for the South.   _____**no conj**_____

1. Congress has now voted to spend more to protect wildlife; however, it may be already too late for many species.   **1.** _____

2. The farmers are using an improved fertilizer; thus their crop yields have increased.   **2.** _____

3. Still to come were Perry, a trained squirrel; Arnold, an acrobat; and Mavis, a magician.   **3.** _____

4. "Negotiations," he said, "have collapsed; we will strike at noon."   **4.** _____

5. Study the manual carefully before the quiz; the lab instructor draws the questions from the manual.   **5.** _____

6. The average Internet user spends about six hours a week online; the majority of these users reach the Internet from work.   **6.** _____

7. Pam, who lives in the suburbs, drives her car to work each day; yet Ruben, her next-door neighbor, takes the bus.   **7.** _____

8. Changing your time-management habits requires determination; therefore, begin by writing down your goals.   **8.** _____

9. The play was performed in Altoona, Pennsylvania; Buckhannon, West Virginia; and The Woodlands, Texas.   **9.** _____

10. Flight 330 stops at Little Rock, Dallas, and Albuquerque; but Flight 440, the all-coach special, is an express to Phoenix.   **10.** _____

FLASH TEST

PART 2

Write **com** if you would insert a **comma** (or commas) in the brackets.

Write **semi** if you would insert a **semicolon** (or semicolons).

If you would insert nothing, leave the blank empty.

Write only one answer for each blank.

EXAMPLE: The milk had all gone sour[ ] we could not have our cappucino.   _____**semi**_____

1. The flood waters rose steadily throughout the night[ ] by dawn our kitchen was flooded to the countertops.   **1.** _____

2. Most Americans plan financially for retirement[ ] but many retire earlier than expected.   **2.** _____

3. Dr. Jones[ ] who teaches geology[ ] graduated from MIT.   **3.** _____

4. The Dr. Jones[ ] who teaches geology[ ] graduated from MIT.   **4.** _____

5. I met the woman[ ] who is to be president of the new junior college.   **5.** _____

6. She likes working in Washington, D.C.[ ] she hopes to remain there permanently.   **6.** _____

7. To the east we could see the White Mountains[ ] to the west, the Green.   **7.** _____

8. Read the article carefully[ ] then write an essay on the author's handling of the subject.

8. _____

9. The car company has produced a car paint[ ] that turns different colors depending on the light.

9. _____

10. The game being beyond our reach[ ] the coach told me to start warming up.

10. _____

11. We're going on a cruise around the bay on Sunday[ ] and we'd like you to come with us.

11. _____

12. If Amy decides to become a lawyer[ ] you can be sure she'll be a good one.

12. _____

13. Customer satisfaction is important[ ] therefore, the owners hired a consulting firm to conduct a customer survey.

13. _____

14. Li-Young registered for an advanced biology course[ ] otherwise, she might not have been admitted to medical school.

14. _____

15. The newest computers[ ] moreover[ ] are cheaper than last year's less powerful models.

15. _____

16. Portable phones are popular with most families[ ] but many of these phones do not work well in crowded urban areas.

16. _____

17. He began his speech again[ ] fire engines having drowned out his opening remarks.

17. _____

18. The best day of the vacation occurred[ ] when we took the children sled riding.

18. _____

19. Let me introduce the new officers: Phillip Whitaker, president[ ] Elaine Donatelli, secretary[ ] and Pierre Northrup, treasurer.

19. _____

20. We thought of every possible detail when planning the dinner party[ ] yet we didn't anticipate our cat's jumping into the cake.

20. _____

21. We have known the Floyd Archers[ ] ever since they moved here from New Jersey.

21. _____

22. The actor Hal Holbrook has successfully portrayed Mark Twain[ ] everywhere in the country for more than forty years.

22. _____

23. The drama coach was a serene person[ ] not one to be worried about nervous amateurs.

23. _____

24. To turn them into professional performers was[ ] needless to say[ ] an impossible task.

24. _____

25. "Yes, I will attend the review session," Jack said[ ] "if you can guarantee that the time spent will be worthwhile."

25. _____

Answers to Exercises for: The Semicolon

Part 1

1. conj adv	3. ser w com	5. no conj	7. cl w com	9. ser w com
2. conj adv	4. no conj	6. no conj	8. conj adv	10. cl w com

Part 2

1. semi	6. semi	11. com	16. com	21. —
2. com	7. semi	12. com	17. com	22. —
3. com	8. semi	13. semi	18. —	23. com
4. —	9. —	14. semi	19. semi	24. com
5. —	10. com	15. com	20. com	25. com

38. Use an Apostrophe with Possessive Nouns. Possessive nouns show "belonging to." If your cousin has (possesses) a car, the car belongs to your cousin. It is your cousin**'s** car, the car of your cousin. Possessive nouns always add an apostrophe ('). Singular possessive nouns normally also add an *s* ('s).

You can identify a possessive noun by trying it at the end of an *of* phrase; if it makes sense there, it is possessive: the beak *of a bird* → *a bird's* beak; the nose of Arthur → *Arthur's* nose; the team *of the girls* → the *girls'* team.

 **FLASH FOCUS**

A. Use Apostrophe + s ('s) with—	B. Use Apostrophe Alone (') with—
✓ Almost all singular nouns: a woman**'s** coat Ms. Bonilla**'s** cats Mr. Bates**'s** house an eagle**'s** nest a person**'s** legal right a fox**'s** bushy tail the class**'s** record	✓ Plural nouns ending in *s* the two girls**'**coats: the Bonillas**'** cats the Bateses**'** house all the eagles**'** nests the boys**'** gymnasium the foxes**'** bushy tails the classes**'** records
✓ Plural nouns that do not end in *s:* women**'s** rights the people**'s** voice the geese**'s** flight	✓ A few singular names that would sound awkward with another *s:* Ulysses**'** travels Sophocles**'** irony

Note: Some editors favor adding only an apostrophe to singular nouns ending in *s: Ms. Bates', class'.* Whichever system you follow, be consistent.

Caution: Do not confuse the ordinary plural of nouns with the possessive. Ordinary plural: I know the Bonillas. Possessive plural: The Bonillas' cat died. See section 40B, page 131.

C. **Use Possessives Before Gerunds (Verbal Nouns).** Just as you would say *Kirsch's action shocked everyone,* say **Kirsch's quitting** *shocked everyone* and *We were shocked by* **Kirsch's quitting** *without notice.* Other examples: *The UN protested the* **terrorists' bombing** *of the town. Horace disliked the* **store's closing** *early on weekends.*

D. **Note These Fine Points of Possession:**

(1) *Joint vs. individual possession:* If two or more nouns possess something jointly, only the last noun gets an apostrophe:

Jennifer and Rod's new baby is a girl.

If each noun possesses a separate thing, each noun gets its own apostrophe:

Jennifer's and Maria's babies are both girls.

(2) *Hyphenated words:* Add the apostrophe to the last word only:

Her *brother-in-law's* job was eliminated.

(3) *Possessive pronouns* can be confusing. Possessive indefinite and reciprocal pronouns take an apostrophe, just like nouns: *anybody's, someone's, each other's, one another's, someone else's, everybody else's,* . . . (see section 18D, page 62, for full list).

But possessive personal pronouns never take an apostrophe: *yours, his, hers, its, ours, theirs;* nor does *whose. Its* and *whose,* particularly, cause problems because they look much like the contractions for *it is* and *who is* (see section 39A and section 40A below; section 19F(3), page 65, and section 73, pages 183–192.)

(4) Words expressing time or amount usually form their possessives just as other nouns do: *a dollar's worth, a moment's rest, a week's pay, two weeks' pay.*

39. Use an Apostrophe Also

A. To Show Contractions and Other Omissions of Letters or Numerals

can't [cannot]	what's [what is]	it's [it is]
who's [who is]	we're [we are]	they're [they are]
you're [you are]	class of '05 [2005]	fishin' [fishing]

B. To Form the Plurals of Letters and Symbols

Her grades included three *A***'s** and two *B***'s.**

Use +**'s** and −**'s** on the test.

Use the apostrophe only where clarity demands it. You generally do not need it with figures (the 1990**s**, hitting in the .300**s**), words referred to as words (*if***s,** *and***s** or *but***s**), or initials (*YWCA***s**).

40. Do *Not* Use an Apostrophe

A. With Possessive Personal Pronouns (*his, hers, its, ours, yours, theirs*) or with *whose*

Whose sales team has surpassed *its* quota? Is it *hers, yours,* or *theirs?* It could be *ours.* [See section 19F(3), page 65, and section 73, pages 183–192, for *its/it's,* etc.]

B. With Ordinary Plurals or Verbs

The *Browns* went to the *stores.* Countless *stars* appeared. [ordinary plurals, not possessive]

The mayor *says* no, but she *means* perhaps. [verbs ending in *s*]

C. To Form the Possessives of Inanimate Objects (generally—unless an *of* phrase sounds awkward):

POOR: her *shoe's* sole

BETTER: the sole *of her shoe*

But

AWKWARD: the pay *of a week*

BETTER: *a week's* pay

 **FLASH TEST**

PART 1

In the first blank, write the number of the **correct** choice (**1** or **2**). In the second blank, write the **reason** for your choice (use the abbreviations in parentheses; if your choice for the first blank has no apostrophe, leave the second blank empty).

singular possessive (**sing pos**)	contraction (**cont**)
plural possessive (**pl pos**)	plural of letter or symbol used as a word (**let/sym**)

EXAMPLES: The fault was (1) **Jacob's** (2) **Jacobs'**.

1	sing pos
2	sing pos

The fault was (1) **your's** (2) **yours**.

1. There (1) **wasn't** (2) **was'nt** even a trace of blood on the knife. **1.** _____ _____

2. The (1) **Smith's** (2) **Smiths** have planned a murder-mystery party. **2.** _____ _____

3. The (1) **James'** (2) **Jameses** are moving to Seattle. **3.** _____ _____

4. My (1) **brother-in-law's** (2) **brother's-in-law** medical practice is flourishing. **4.** _____ _____

5. The (1) **Russo's** (2) **Russos'** new home is spacious. **5.** _____ _____

6. (1) **Its** (2) **It's** important to exercise several times a week. **6.** _____ _____

7. (1) **Who's** (2) **Whose** responsible for the increased production of family-oriented movies? **7.** _____ _____

8. The two (1) **girl's** (2) **girls'** talent was quite evident to everyone. **8.** _____ _____

9. Parents across the nation hope that college tuition costs will stop increasing in the decade of the (1) **2000s** (2) **2000's**. **9.** _____ _____

10. It will be a two-(1) **day's** (2) **days'** drive to Galveston. **10.** _____ _____

11. The dispute over the last clause caused a (1) **weeks** (2) **week's** delay in the contract signing. **11.** _____ _____

12. Mary accidentally spilled tea on her (1) **bosses** (2) **boss's** report. **12.** _____ _____

13. After the long absence, they fell into (1) **each others'** (2) **each other's** arms. **13.** _____ _____

14. Each woman claimed that the diamond ring was (1) **her's** (2) **hers**. **14.** _____ _____

15. Geraldine uses too many (1) **ands** (2) **and's** in most of her presentations. **15.** _____ _____

16. His (1) **O's** (2) **Os** have a solid black center; his typewriter needs to be cleaned. **16.** _____ _____

17. (1) **Wer'ent** (2) **Weren't** you surprised by the success of her book? **17.** _____ _____

18. Which is safer, your van or (1) **ours** (2) **our's**? **18.** _____ _____

19. Georgiana insisted, "I (1) **have'nt** (2) **haven't** seen Sandy for weeks." **19.** _____ _____

20. He bought fifty (1) **cents** (2) **cents'** worth of bubblegum. **20.** _____ _____

FLASH TEST

PART 2

For each bracketed apostrophe, write **C** if it is **correct**; write **X** if it is **incorrect**. Use the first column for the first apostrophe, the second column for the second apostrophe.

EXAMPLE: **Who[']s** on first? Where is **todays[']** lineup?

C	X

1. Everyone **else[']s** opinion carries less weight with me than **your[']s**. **1.** _____ _____

2. **Mrs. Jackson[']s** invitation to the **William[']s** must have gone astray. **2.** _____ _____

3. He **would[']nt** know that information after only two **day[']s** employment. **3.** _____ _____

4. **Were[']nt** they fortunate that the stolen car wasn't **their[']s**? **4.** _____ _____

5. **It[']s** a pity that the one bad cabin would be **our[']s**. **5.** _____ _____

6. **We[']re** expecting the **Wagner[']s** to meet us in Colorado for a ski trip. **6.** _____ _____

7. Mark McGwire's home run **total[']s** were higher than those of Sammy Sosa, but McGwire had fewer **RBI[']s**. **7.** _____ _____

8. **Does[']nt** the student realize that he **won[']t** be able to take the final early? **8.** _____ _____

9. The two sisters had agreed that **they[']d** stop wearing each **others[']** shoes. **9.** _____ _____

10. She[']s not going to accept **anybody[']s** advice, no matter how sound it may be.

10. _____ _____

11. The three **students[']** complaints about the **professor[']s** attitude in class were finally addressed by the administration.

11. _____ _____

12. He[']s hoping for ten **hours[']** work a week in the library.

12. _____ _____

13. The idea of a cultural greeting card business was not **our[']s;** it was **Lois[']s.**

13. _____ _____

14. There are three *i*[']s in the word *optimistic;* there are two *r*[']s in the word *embarrass.*

14. _____ _____

15. The computer printout consisted of a series of **1[']s** and **0[']s.**

15. _____ _____

16. Their advisor sent two dozen yellow **rose[']s** to the Women Student **Association[']s** meeting.

16. _____ _____

17. I really **did[']nt** expect to see all of the **drivers[']** finish the race.

17. _____ _____

18. **Hav[']ent** you heard about the theft at the **Jone[']s** house?

18. _____ _____

19. The popular **mens[']** store established in 1923 **was[']nt** able to compete with the large discount stores in the nearby mall.

19. _____ _____

20. I'm sure that, if **he[']s** physically able, **he[']ll** be at the volunteer program.

20. _____ _____

Answers to Exercises for: The Apostrophe

Part 1

1.	1	cont	5.	2	pl pos	9.	1	—	13.	2	sing pos	17.	2	cont
2.	2	—	6.	2	cont	10.	2	pl pos	14.	2	—	18.	1	—
3.	2	—	7.	1	cont	11.	2	sing pos	15.	1	—	19.	2	cont
4.	1	sing pos	8.	2	pl pos	12.	2	sing pos	16.	1	let/sym	20.	2	pl pos

Part 2

1.	C	X	5.	C	X	9.	C	X	13.	X	C	17.	X	X
2.	C	X	6.	C	X	10.	C	C	14.	C	C	18.	X	X
3.	X	X	7.	X	X	11.	C	C	15.	X	X	19.	X	X
4.	X	X	8.	X	C	12.	C	C	16.	X	C	20.	C	C

41 Italics (Underlining)

FLASH SUMMARY

Italic type, or *italics,* is slanted type, like the first words of this sentence. Generally, in your word processing, typing, or handwriting, indicate italics by underlining: <u>Cold Mountain</u>, <u>Cold Mountain</u>.

Note: Some publications, especially some magazines and newspapers, follow styles that omit all or most italics. Although not wrong, such alternative styles are not recommended.

Use Italics to Designate

A. Titles of Separate Publications

(1) **Books:** Our readings include Ellison's *Invisible Man.*

(2) Magazines, newspapers, and journals: Her subscriptions range from the *Village Voice* to *Popular Mechanics.*

Note: The word *the* is not capitalized or italicized in a newspaper or magazine title.

(3) Bulletins, pamphlets, and newsletters: County Conservation Tips.

(4) Plays, films, TV and radio programs, and musical productions:

Ragtime [play or musical production]

The Talented Mr. Ripley [film]

America's Castles [TV or radio program. For a single segment or episode in a series, use quotation marks: "The Hearst Estate."]

(5) Poems long enough to be published alone as books: Homer's *Iliad*

(6) Electronic publications (tapes, compact disks, computer programs, CD-ROMs, online databases . . .): New York Times Online

Note: Do not underline (or put within quotation marks) the title at the beginning of a composition or research paper unless the title contains words that would be underlined anyway, such as the title of a novel:

Symbolism in Steinbeck's Early Stories

Symbolism in Steinbeck's *East of Eden*

B. Names of Ships, Aircraft, and Spacecraft

The *Alaska Princess* sails from Vancouver.

The space shuttle *Endeavour* landed on schedule.

C. Titles of Paintings and Sculptures

Morning Sun Michelangelo's *David* *The Blue Boy*

D. Foreign Words Not Yet Anglicized

The lovers bade each other *sayonara.*

Note: Generally, if a word is listed in a reputable English dictionary, it is considered Anglicized and needs no italics. Do not underline the common abbreviations a.m., p.m., A.D., viz., vs., etc., i.e., e.g.

E. Words, Letters, Figures, or Symbols Referred to as Such

Remember the *d* when spelling *supposed to.*

His license number contained two *J*'s and a *9.*

Avoid using *&* for *and* in formal writing.

F. Emphasis, where you cannot convey it by the order or choice of your words:

Ms. Coe said that she *might* reconsider the grade. [The emphasis on *might* stresses the uncertainty.]

Note: Avoid overuse of italics for emphasis.

FLASH TEST

In each sentence, **underline** the word(s) that should be in italics.

EXAMPLE: The cover of <u>Newsweek</u> depicted African refugees.

1. One of the most popular CDs of the century's end was The Duke Ellington Centennial Edition.

2. Deciding to come home by ship, we made reservations on the Queen Elizabeth II.

3. Geraldine went downtown to buy copies of Esquire and Field and Stream.

4. "It's time for a change!" shouted the candidate during the debate.

5. Show Boat, a revival of a 1920s musical, did very well on Broadway.

6. The New York Times must have weighed ten pounds last Sunday.

7. The Mystery Theater series on public television promises amateur sleuths a weekly escape into murder and intrigue.

8. For my birthday a friend gave me the book Ladder of Years by Ann Tyler.

9. Among the magazines scattered in the room was a copy of Popular Mechanics.

10. Maya Angelou's first published work, I Know Why the Caged Bird Sings, is an autobiography describing her first sixteen years.

11. When I try to pronounce the word statistics, I always stumble over it.

12. I still have difficulty remembering the difference between continual and continuous.

13. "I'll never stop fighting for my rights," Megan Morton thundered. "And I mean never."

14. Picasso's Guernica depicts the horrors of war.

15. The Thinker is a statue that many people admire.

16. Spike Lee's film Malcolm X inspired me.

17. You'll enjoy reading "The Man of the House" in the book Fifty Great Short Stories.

18. The British spelling of the word humor is h-u-m-o-u-r.

19. "How to Heckle Your Prof" was an essay in John James's How to Get Thrown Out of College.

20. Michelangelo's Last Judgment shows "the omnipotence of his artistic ability."

21. The source of the above quotation is the Encyclopaedia Britannica.

22. The fourth opera in this winter's series is Verdi's Don Carlo.

23. Her argument was ad hominem.

24. Perry won the spelling bee's award for creative expression with his rendition of antidisestablishmentarianism.

25. The instructor said that Sam's 7s and his 4s look very much alike.

Answers to Exercises for: Italics

1. *The Duke Ellington Centennial Edition*

2. *Queen Elizabeth II*

3. *Esquire, Field and Stream*

4. *change*

5. *Show Boat*

6. *New York Times*

7. *Mystery Theater*

8. *Ladder of Years*

9. *Popular Mechanics*

10. *I Know Why the Caged Bird Sings*

11. *statistics*

12. *continual, continuous*

13. the second *never*

14. *Guernica*

15. *The Thinker*

16. *Malcolm X*

17. *Fifty Great Short Stories*

18. *humor, h-u-m-o-u-r*

19. *How to Get Thrown Out of College*

20. *Last Judgment*

21. *Encyclopaedia Britannica*

22. *Don Carlo*

23. *ad hominem*

24. *antidisestablishmentarianism*

25. *7, 4*

42–46 Quotation Marks [" "]

FLASH SUMMARY

Quotation marks enclose the exact words of a speaker, certain titles, or words used in a special sense. Quotation marks are always (with one small exception) used in pairs.

42. Use Regular (Double) Quotation Marks [" "] to Enclose a Direct Quotation.

A. Use Quotation Marks Around a Speaker's Exact Words. Note that commas set off each quotation:

She said, "I'll see you in court."

"I'll see you in court," she said.

She said, "I'll see you in court," and left.

Note: Do not use quotation marks with an *indirect* quotation (a paraphrase or summary of a speaker's words): She told him that she would see him in court.

B. With an Interrupted Quotation, use quotation marks around only the quoted words:

"I'll see you," she said, "in court."

C. With an *Un*interrupted Quotation of More Than One Sentence, use quotation marks only before the first sentence and after the last:

WRONG: She said, "You can't deny me my rights." "I'll see you in court."

RIGHT: She said, "You can't deny me my rights. I'll see you in court."

D. With an *Un*interrupted Quotation of Several Paragraphs, use either of the following forms:

✓ Put quotation marks at the beginning of *each* paragraph but at the end of only the *last* paragraph.

✓ Use no quotation marks at all; instead, type the entire quotation as an indented block. See section 55C, page 155.

E. With a Short Quotation That Is Only Part of a Sentence, use no commas:

They had promised to "show some muscle."

F. Use Three Spaced Periods to Show Omission of unimportant or irrelevant words from a quotation (ellipsis—see section 31D(1), pages 123–124).

✓ **Customary usage:**

Emerson wrote, "Is it so bad, then, to be misunderstood? . . . To be great is to be misunderstood."

✓ **Latest Modern Language Association style,** using brackets to show that the ellipsis was not in the original (keep all the original punctuation in its proper place outside the brackets):

Emerson wrote, "Is it so bad, then, to be misunderstood? [. . .] To be great is to be misunderstood."

G. To Insert Your Explanatory Words Into a Quotation, use brackets (not parentheses). See section 52A, page 143.

H. When Quoting Dialogue, start a new paragraph with each change of speaker:

"The lead guitarist is superb," she remarked.

"He sounds tinny to me," I replied.

I. **When Quoting Poetry,** use quotation marks only for very short passages (three or fewer lines) that are run into your text. Use a slash mark (with a space before and after) to show the end of each line of the poem:

Emily Dickinson compares exultation to "the going/Of an inland soul to sea."

For quotations of more than three lines, do not use quotation marks; type the lines as an indented block as explained in section 55C (page 155).

43. Use Double Quotation Marks Also to Enclose

A. **Titles of Short Written Works: Poems, Articles, Essays, Short Stories, Chapters, Songs**

"My Lost City" is an essay in *The Crack-Up.*

Chapter 10 of *Stuart Little* is titled "Springtime."

"Daddy's Little Girl" is a favorite wedding song.

B. **Definition of Words**

The word *nice* once meant "foolish or wanton."

C. **Words Used in a Special Sense or for a Special Purpose**

[A]ntidrug agents detained two brothers accused of being [. . .] producers of methamphetamines, or "speed."

—New York Times

If you are using the word several times within a short paper or chapter, you need quotation marks only the first time.

Note: Occasionally you will see a slang expression or nickname enclosed in quotation marks, indicating that the writer recognizes the expression to be inappropriately informal. Avoid this apologetic use of quotation marks.

44. Use Single Quotation Marks [' '] to enclose a quotation within a quotation. Think of this construction as a box within a box. Ordinary double quotation marks [" "] provide the wrapping around the outer box; single quotation marks [' '] provide the wrapping around the inner box. Be sure to place end punctuation within the correct box:

"Who said, 'Alas! poor Yorick'?" the dean asked.

45. Use Other Marks with Quotation Marks as Follows:

A. **Periods and Commas.** Always put these marks *inside* closing quotation marks:

"Stocks are up," he said. "Bonds may fall."

B. **Colons and Semicolons.** Always put these marks *outside* closing quotation marks:

He announced, "Stocks are up"; then they fell.

There have been three popular recordings of "All Along the Watchtower": Bob Dylan's, Jimi Hendrix's, and U2's.

C. **Question Marks, Exclamation Points, and Dashes.** Place these marks *inside* the quotation marks when they belong to the quotation, *outside* otherwise:

Luz asked, **"**Which key do I press**?"** [The quotation is the question.]

Did Luz say, **"**I clicked the mouse**"**? [The part outside the quotation is the question.]

Did Luz ask, **"**Which key do I press**"**? [Both the quotation and the outside part are questions. Use only one question mark—the outside one.]

"It's perfect**!"** Luz exclaimed.

How wonderful it was when Luz said, **"**Now I understand**"**!

"I don't see how—**"** Luz began, but she kept trying.

"Now**"**—Luz grabbed the printout—**"**let's see it.**"**

46. Do *Not* Use Quotation Marks

A. **To Enclose the Title Introducing a Composition or Research Paper** (unless the title is a quotation):

WRONG: "The Presidential Election of 2000"

RIGHT: The Presidential Election of 2000

B. **To Show Intended Irony, Humor, or Emphasis.** Your irony or humor will be more effective if not so blatantly pointed out:

WRONG: His "golden" voice emptied the opera house.

RIGHT: His golden voice emptied the opera house.

For emphasis, use italics (see section 41F, page 134).

 **FLASH TEST**

PART 1

Insert quotation marks at the proper places in each sentence.

EXAMPLE: She wrote "Best Surfing Beaches" for *Outdoor* magazine.

1. The November issue of the *Atlantic Monthly* contained a stimulating article, Pre-Empting the Holocaust.

2. Murder in the Rain Forest, which appeared in *Time* magazine, told of the death of a courageous Brazilian environmentalist.

3. W. C. Fields's dying words were I'd rather be in Philadelphia.

4. The poem The Swing was written by Robert Louis Stevenson.

5. Be prepared, warned the weather forecaster, for a particularly harsh winter this year.

6. Childhood Memories is a chapter in the reader *Growing Up in the South*.

7. In Kingdom of the Skies, in the magazine *Arizona Highways,* Joyce Muench described the unusual cloud formations that enhance Arizona's scenery.

8. The word *cavalier* was originally defined as a man on a horse.

9. One of the most famous American essays is Emerson's Self-Reliance.

10. One of my favorite short stories is Eudora Welty's A Worn Path.

11. The song The Wind Beneath My Wings was sung to inspire mentors to stay with the literacy program.

12. The World Is Too Much with Us is a poem by William Wordsworth.

13. The New Order is an article that appeared in *Time* magazine.

14. An article that appeared in the *Washington Post* is Can We Abolish Poverty?

15. Cousins' essay The Right to Die poses the question of whether suicide is ever an acceptable response to life circumstances.

16. The Love Song of J. Alfred Prufrock is a poem by T. S. Eliot.

17. The dictionary of slang defines *loopy* as slightly crazy.

18. The concluding song of the evening was Auld Lang Syne.

19. We read a poem by Alice Walker titled Women.

20. Police Chief Busted is the title of an editorial in the *Wall Street Journal.*

 FLASH TEST

PART 2

Write **C** if the punctuation in brackets is **correct.**

Write **X** if it is **not.**

EXAMPLE: "What time is it["?] wondered Katelyn.   _____X_____

1. The stadium announcer intoned[, "]Ladies and gentlemen, please rise for our national anthem."   1. _____

2. When the job was finished, the worker asked, "How do you like it[?"]   2. _____

3. In the first semester we read Gabriel García Márquez's short story "Big Mama's Funeral[".]   3. _____

4. "Where are you presently employed?[",] the interviewer asked.   4. _____

5. "When you finish your rough draft," said Professor Grill[, "]send it to my e-mail address."   5. _____

6. Who was it who mused, "Where are the snows of yesteryear["?]   6. _____

7. Dr. Nelson, our anthropology teacher, asked, "How many of you have read *The Autobiography of Malcolm X*[?"]   7. _____

8. "We need more study rooms in the library[,"] declared one presidential candidate in the student government debate.   8. _____

9. "Write when you can[,"] Mother said as I left for the airport.   9. _____

10. To *dissuade* means "to persuade someone not to do something[."]   10. _____

11. "Ask not what your country can do for you[;"] ask what you can do for your country."   11. _____

12. "Our language creates problems when we talk about race in America.[" "]We don't have enough terms to explain the complexities of cultural diversity."   12. _____

13. "Do you remember Father's saying, 'Never give up[?'] she asked.   13. _____

14. She began reciting the opening line of one of Elizabeth Barrett Browning's sonnets: "How do I love thee? Let me count the ways[."]   14. _____

15. Gwendolyn Brooks's poem ["]The Bean Eaters["] is one of her best.   15. _____

16. ["]*The Fantasticks*["] is the longest-running musical play in American theater.   16. _____

17. "Want to play ball, Scarecrow[?"] the Wicked Witch asked, a ball of fire in her hand.   17. _____

18. "Shall I read aloud Whitman's poem 'Out of the Cradle Endlessly Rocking[?"] she asked.   18. _____

19. Have you read Adrienne Rich's poem "Necessities of Life[?"]   19. _____

20. When Susan saw the show about America's homeless, she exclaimed, "I have to find a way to help[!"]   20. _____

Answers to Exercises for: Quotation Marks

Part 1

1. "Preempting the Holocaust."
2. "Murder . . . Forest,"
3. "I'd . . . Philadelphia."
4. "The Swing"
5. "Be prepared," . . . "for . . . year."
6. "Childhood Memories"
7. "Kingdom of the Skies,"
8. "a man on a horse."
9. "Self-Reliance."
10. "A Worn Path."
11. "The Wind . . . Wings"
12. "The World . . . Us"
13. "The New Order"
14. "Can . . . Poverty?"
15. "The Right to Die"
16. "The . . . Prufrock"
17. "slightly crazy."
18. "Auld Lang Syne."
19. "Women."
20. "Police Chief Busted"

Part 2

1. C
2. C
3. X
4. X
5. C
6. C
7. C
8. C
9. C
10. C
11. X
12. X
13. C
14. C
15. C
16. X
17. C
18. C
19. X
20. C

47–48 The Colon [:]

47. Use a Colon to Introduce

A. **A List That Follows a Grammatically Complete Statement.** The list is usually in apposition to some word in the statement:

Their journey took them to four countries: Turkey, Iran, Pakistan, and India. [The four names are in apposition to *countries*.]

Only one traveler was a native Asian: Ibrahim. [*Ibrahim* is a one-item "list" in apposition to *traveler*.]

Often *the following* or *as follows* precedes the colon:

Their papers included *the following*: passports, visas, health records, and driver's licenses.

Do *not* use a colon after an *in*complete statement (one that lacks, for example, a needed complement or object of preposition), or after *such as* or *for example*:

WRONG: Their papers included: passports, visas, health records, and driver's licenses.

RIGHT: Their papers included passports, visas. . . .

WRONG: Their journey took them to countries *such as*: Turkey, Iran, Pakistan, and India.

RIGHT: Their journey took them to countries *such as* Turkey, Iran. . . .

B. **A Long Quotation** (one or more paragraphs):

In *The Sketch Book* Washington Irving wrote: "English travelers are the best and the worst in the world. Where no motives of pride or interest intervene, none can equal them." [Quotation continues for one or more paragraphs.]

C. A Formal Quotation or Question

Cutting the tape, the governor declared: "The Greenport-Springview Bridge is officially open."

The basic question is: where [or *Where*] is our country headed?

D. A Second Independent Clause That Explains or Illustrates the First Clause

There is a way to win the election: we [or *We*] can play up the incumbent's shady past.

E. The Body of a Business Letter (after the greeting):

Dear Madam: Dear Dr. Schwartz:

Note: Use a comma after the greeting of a personal (friendly) letter.

F. The Details Following an Announcement

For rent: room with kitchen, near campus.

G. A Formal Resolution, After the Word *Resolved*

Resolved: That the club spend $50 for decorations.

H. The Words of a Speaker in a Play (after the speaker's name):

ROSALIND: Nay, but who is it?

48. Use a Colon to Separate

A. Parts of a Title, Reference, or Numeral

TITLE: The Cold War: A Reinterpretation

REFERENCE: Isaiah 10:3–15 [or, in MLA style, 10.3–15]

NUMERAL: 11:25 p.m.

B. Certain Parts of a Bibliography Entry

Sowell, Thomas. <u>Conquests and Cultures: An International History.</u> New York: Basic, 1988.

Colón, Rafael Hernández. "Doing Right by Puerto Rico." *Foreign Affairs* 77.4 (1998): 112–114.

49 The Dash [—]

FLASH SUMMARY

The dash is a dramatic mark, signaling an abrupt break in the flow of a sentence. Do not use it for an ordinary pause or stop, in place of a comma, period, or semicolon. When typing, make a dash by using two strokes of the hyphen key, with no spaces before, between, or after--like this.

Use a Dash

A. To Show a Sudden Break in Thought

I'm sure it was last Novem—no, it was October.

If you don't apologize at once, I'll—

"My dear constituents, I greet you—" the senator began, but he was stopped by a chorus of boos.

B. **To Set Off a Parenthetical Element** that is long, that sharply interrupts the sentence, or that otherwise would be hard to distinguish:

World War I—my grandfather called it "the big war"—was shorter than World War II.

The pieces on view at Tiffany—in an exhibition called "The Jewelry of Louis Comfort Tiffany: Explorations of Color, Nature and the Exotic," which closes on August 29—celebrate not only his jewelry designs but also the 150th anniversary of his birth.

—*New York Times*

C. **To Emphasize an Appositive**

He had only one goal—stardom. [or . . . *goal: stardom.*]

Sarah, Vera, Maria, Tammy—all have found better jobs.

Three majors—literature, writing, and linguistics—are offered in this department.

Note: The colon can also emphasize an appositive, but it imparts a more formal tone than the dash.

D. **To Precede the Author's Name After a Direct Quotation**

"So we beat on, boats against the current, borne back ceaselessly into the past."

—F. Scott Fitzgerald

50–51 Parentheses [( )]

50. Use Parentheses (Always in Pairs)

A. **To Set Off Incidental Information or Comments**

Representative Rizzo (R., Florida) spoke against the bill.

The old washing machine (it predates Woodstock and probably the Beatles) still does three loads a day.

Note: Do not overuse parentheses. Use commas to set off ordinary parenthetical (interrupting) expressions. Do not use an opening capital letter or closing period with a sentence in parentheses within a larger sentence.

B. **To Enclose**

(1) Letters or figures in enumeration:

The secretary must (1) take minutes at meetings, (2) do all typing, and (3) keep records.

(But see section 31C, page 123.)

(2) References and directions:

The amoeba (see figure 6) reproduces asexually.

(3) A question mark indicating uncertainty:

She was born in China in 1778(?) and died in 1853.

C. **For Accuracy, in Legal Documents and Business Letters**

Please remit the sum of fifty dollars ($50).

D. **With Other Punctuation Marks as Follows:**

(1) The comma, semicolon, and period follow the closing parenthesis in a sentence:

Her longest novel **(687 pages),** it is also her best.

She knows Greek **(**her family's tongue**);** he knows Russian.

The heat grew unbearable **(**it broke the record**).**

(2) ***The question mark and the exclamation point*** go inside the parentheses if the mark belongs to the parenthetical element; otherwise, they go outside:

The book mentions Mechthild of Magdeburg **(**died 1282**?).**

Have you read much of Samuel Butler **(**died 1680**)?**

Sid asked me to lend him fifty dollars **(**what nerve**!).**

51. Do Not Use Parentheses

A. **To Indicate Deletions.** Instead draw a line through the deleted words:

WRONG: George Bush was elected in 1988 **(and 1992)**.

RIGHT: George Bush was elected in 1988 and 1992.

B. **To Enclose Your Editorial Comment.** Use brackets for this purpose, as explained in the next section.

52 Brackets [[ ]]

Use Brackets

A. **To Enclose Your Editorial or Explanatory Remarks Within a Direct Quotation**

According to Antonia Fraser, "As Queen, however, she **[**Katherine Howard**]** had new ways of enjoying herself: the exercise of patronage, for example."

See section 42F, page 136, for use of brackets with ellipses in quotations.

B. **With *sic* to Mark the Original Writer's Error in Material You Are Quoting**

His letter said, "I'm not use **[**sic**]** to rejection."

Sic is Latin for "Thus it is." Its use clarifies that the error was made not by you but by the person you are quoting.

C. **To Enclose Stage Directions**

JUAN **[***striding to the door***]:** Someone must help them.

FLASH TEST

PART 1

Write **C** if the colon is used **correctly**.

Write **X** if it is used **incorrectly**.

EXAMPLE: This bus runs via: Swan Street, Central Avenue, and North Main.   <u>   **X**   </u>

1. Casey's first question was: Can anybody here play this game?   **1.** _____

2. The coach signaled the strategy: we would try a double steal on the next pitch.   **2.** _____

3. Dear Sir:
    My five years' experience as a high school English teacher qualifies me to be the editor of your newsletter.   **3.** _____

4. Dearest Rodney:

　　My heart yearns for you so greatly that I can hardly bear the days until we're in each other's arms again.

5. Laurie's shopping list included these items: truffles, caviar, champagne, and a dozen hot dogs.

6. The carpenter brought his: saw, hammer, square, measuring tape, and nails.

7. College students generally complain about: their professors, the cafeteria food, and their roommates.

8. She began her letter to Tom with these words: "I'll love you forever!"

9. Her train reservations were for Tuesday at 3:30 p.m.

10. The dean demanded that: the coaches, the players, and the training staff meet with him immediately.

11. Tonight's winning numbers are: 169, 534, and 086.

12. She was warned that the project would require two qualities: creativity and perseverance.

13. The project has been delayed: the chairperson has been hospitalized for emergency surgery.

14. If Smith's book is titled *The World Below the Window: Poems 1937–1997*, must I include both the title and subtitle in my Works Cited list?

15. I packed my backpack with: bubble bath, a pair of novels, and some comfortable clothes.

4. _____
5. _____
6. _____
7. _____
8. _____
9. _____
10. _____
11. _____
12. _____
13. _____
14. _____
15. _____

FLASH TEST

PART 2

Set off the boldfaced words by inserting the correct punctuation: **dash(es)** , **parentheses,** or **brackets**.

EXAMPLE:　Senator Aikin **(Dem., Maine)** voted for the proposal.

1. In my research paper I quoted Wilson as observing, "His **Fitzgerald's** last years became a remarkable mix of creative growth and physical decline." [Punctuate to show that the boldfaced expression is inserted editorially by the writer of the research paper.]

2. Holmes had deduced **who knew how?** that the man had been born on a moving train during the rainy season. [Punctuate to indicate a sharp interruption.]

3. He will be considered for **this is between you and me, of course** one of the three vice-presidencies in the firm. [Punctuate to indicate merely incidental comment.]

4. I simply told her **and I'm glad I did!** that I would never set foot in her house again. [Punctuate to indicate merely incidental comment.]

5. Campbell's work on *Juvenal* **see reference** is an excellent place to start.

6. At Yosemite National Park we watched the feeding of the bears **from a safe distance, you can be sure.** [Punctuate to achieve a dramatic effect.]

7. Her essay was entitled "The American Medical System and It's **sic** Problems."

8. The rules for using parentheses **see page 7** are not easy to understand.

9. We traveled on foot, in horse-drawn wagons, and occasionally **if we had some spare cash to offer, if the farmers felt sorry for us, or if we could render some service in exchange** atop a motorized tractor. [Punctuate to indicate that this is *not* merely incidental comment.]

10. The statement read: "Enclosed you will find one hundred dollars **$100** to cover damages."

11. David liked one kind of dessert **apple pie.**

12. **Eat, drink, and be merry** gosh, I can hardly wait for senior week.

13. The essay begins: "For more than a hundred years **from 1337 until 1453** the British and French fought a pointless war." [Punctuate to show that the boldface expression is inserted editorially.]

14. The concert begins at **by the way, when does the concert begin?**

15. Getting to work at eight o'clock every morning **I don't have to remind you how much I dislike getting up early** seemed almost more than I cared to undertake. [Punctuate to indicate merely incidental comment.]

16. She said, "Two of my friends **one has really serious emotional problems** need psychiatric help." [Punctuate to achieve a dramatic effect.]

17. Within the last year, I have received three **or was it four?** letters from her. [Punctuate to indicate merely incidental comment.]

18. Julius was born in 1900 **?** and came west as a young boy.

Answers to Exercises for: The Colon, The Dash, Parentheses, and Brackets

Part 1

1. C	4. X	7. X	10. X	13. C
2. C	5. C	8. C	11. X	14. C
3. C	6. X	9. C	12. C	15. X

Part 2

1. [ ]	5. ( )	9. – –	13. [ ]	17. ( )
2. – –	6. –	10. ( )	14. –	18. ( )
3. ( )	7. [ ]	11. –	15. ( )	
4. ( )	8. ( )	12. –	16. – –	

53 The Hyphen [-]

Use a Hyphen

A. To Join Certain Compound Words

sister-in-law will-o'-the-wisp Scotch-Irish

A good dictionary will show which compounds are hyphenated. Generally, if the compound is not in the dictionary, write it as two words, with no hyphen: *tree trunk*.

B. To Join Words Used as a Single Adjective Before a Noun

a well-known author late-model cars fifty-dollar bill

a now-you-see-me-now-you-don't office presence

cat-and-mouse game

Note: Do not hyphenate such a modifier when it *follows* a noun as a subjective complement: Hanley is *well known*. Do not use a hyphen between an *-ly* adverb and an adjective: *freshly baked* bread.

With a series of hyphenated modifiers, omit the part after the hyphen until the last item: *ten-, twenty-, and fifty-dollar bills*.

C. **When Writing Out Two-Word Numbers from Twenty-One to Ninety-Nine and Two-Word Fractions**

thirty-three   sixty-seven
ninety-eighth   four-fifths

But other words in the number take no hyphen:

four hundred fifteen   four hundred twenty-five
five twenty-fourths   one thousand four hundred twenty-five

Also hyphenate a compound adjective containing a number:

ten-year-old boy   forty-hour week
hundred-yard dash   ten-dollar bill

two- and three-room apartments

D. **To Avoid Ambiguity**

AMBIGUOUS: Mitchell was the *senior housing director.* [*senior director of housing* or *director of housing for seniors?*]

CLEAR: Mitchell was the *senior-housing director.* [director of housing for seniors. For the other meaning, use *senior director of housing.*]

E. **With the Prefixes** *ex-* **(When It Means "Former"),** *self-*, **and** *all-*, **and the Suffix** *-elect*

ex-manager   self-pity
all-county   Mayor-elect Bobbs

Note: Today nearly all prefixes and suffixes are joined to root words without hyphens, except where ambiguity *(recover, re-cover)* or awkwardness might result or where the root is capitalized *(anti-American, Europe-wide).* Examples of current usage are *antiterrorist, noninterventionist, semiliterate* (but *semi-independent,* to avoid an awkward double *i*), *bimonthly, citywide.*

F. **To Indicate Words That Are Spelled Out and Hesitation or Stammering**

"It's her time for b-e-d," the child's mother said.

"It's c-c-cold in h-here," he stammered.

G. **To Divide a Word That Will Not Fit at the End of a Line.** For an example, see line 6 of section 55B, page 155.

Note: Always put the hyphen at the end of the first line, not at the beginning of the second line. Do not guess where a word should divide; consult your dictionary. See section 59, page 162, for more details on syllabication.

54 The Slash (Virgule) [/]

Use a Slash

A. **Between Two Lines of Poetry Quoted in Running Text**

Dickinson described death as "the supple Suitor / That wins at last." [Leave a space before and after the slash.]

See section 42I, page 137.

B. Between Alternatives

This subway line stops at Sixth Avenue/Avenue of the Americas [alternative names for the same street].

The new Dodge/Plymouth is on special sale [different brand names for the same car].

For *and/or*, see section 71, page 180. Do not use the slash for a hyphen: *Boston-Miami* (not *Boston/Miami*) flights.

C. To Mean *per*: *$1.65/lb.*

D. In Fractions: 5/8, x/2.

FLASH TEST

Write **C** if the use or omission of a hyphen or slash is **correct.**

Write **X** if it is **incorrect.**

EXAMPLE: Seventy six trombones led the big parade.   **X**

1. Alexander Pope wrote, "The learn'd is happy nature to **explore / The** fool is happy that he knows no more."   1. _____

2. "I **c-c-can't** breathe because of my asthma," panted the patient.   2. _____

3. The **eleven-year-old** girl planned to be an astronaut.   3. _____

4. One refers to the monarch of Britain as "**his/her** majesty."   4. _____

5. The speaker was **well known** to everyone connected with administration.   5. _____

6. The **well-known** author was autographing his latest novel in the bookstore today.   6. _____

7. The team averaged over **fifty-thousand** spectators a game.   7. _____

8. The contractor expects to build many **five-** and **six-room** houses this year.   8. _____

9. The senator composed a **carefully-worded** statement for a press conference.   9. _____

10. I sent in my subscription to a new **bi-monthly** magazine.   10. _____

11. Sam's **brother-in-law** delighted in teasing his sister by belching at family dinners.   11. _____

12. We'll have a chance to see two top teams in action at tonight's **Bulls/Pistons** game.   12. _____

13. He made every effort to **recover** the missing gems.   13. _____

14. After the children spilled blueberry syrup on her white sofa, Letitia had to **recover** it.   14. _____

15. At **eighty-four,** Hartley still rides his motorcycle in the mountains on sunny days.   15. _____

16. Charles will run in the **hundred yard** dash next Saturday.   16. _____

17. "The children are not to have any more **c-a-n-d-y,**" said Mother.   17. _____

18. After he graduated from college, he became a manager of the **student-owned** bookstore.   18. _____

19. The idea of a **thirty hour** week appealed to the workers.   19. _____

20. Baird played **semi-professional** baseball before going into the major leagues.   20. _____

21. Customers began avoiding the **hot-tempered** clerk in the shoe department.   21. _____

22. Al's main problem is that he lacks **self-confidence.**   22. _____

23. The **brand-new** vacuum cleaner made a loud squealing noise every time we turned it on.   23. _____

24. The word processing software was **brand new.**   24. _____

25. Mr. Pollard's major research interest was **seventeenth-century** French history.   25. _____

Answers to Exercises for: The Hyphen and The Slash

1. C	6. C	11. C	16. X	21. C
2. C	7. X	12. X	17. C	22. C
3. C	8. C	13. C	18. C	23. C
4. C	9. X	14. X	19. X	24. C
5. C	10. X	15. C	20. X	25. C

FLASH TEST

PUNCTUATION REVIEW: UNIT II

PART 1

Write **T** for each statement that is **true.**

Write **F** for each that is **false.**

EXAMPLE: A period is used at the end of a declarative sentence.   _____T_____

1. **Three spaced periods** are used to indicate an omission (ellipsis) in quoted material.   1. _____

2. **Possessive personal pronouns** contain an apostrophe.   2. _____

3. The **question mark** is always placed inside closing quotation marks.   3. _____

4. The sentence "Dellene searched for her friend, Mitch," means that Dellene has only one friend.   4. _____

5. A **dash** is used before the author's name on the line below a direct quotation.   5. _____

6. **Parentheses** are used to enclose editorial remarks in a direct quotation.   6. _____

7. A **restrictive clause** is not set off within commas.   7. _____

8. A **semicolon** is used to set off an absolute phrase from the rest of the sentence.   8. _____

9. The use of **brackets** around the word *sic* indicates an error occurring in quoted material.   9. _____

10. Mild interjections should be followed by an **exclamation point**; strong ones, by a **comma.**   10. _____

11. An indirect question is followed by a **period.**   11. _____

12. A **semicolon** is used after the expression *Dear Sir.*   12. _____

13. The title of a magazine article should be underlined to designate the use of **italics.**   13. _____

14. *Ms.* may take a **period** but *Miss* does not.   14. _____

15. **Single quotation marks** are used around a quotation that is within another quotation.   15. _____

16. Both *Mr. Jones'* and *Mr. Jones's* are acceptable **possessive forms** of *Mr. Jones.*   16. _____

17. The title at the head of a composition should be enclosed in **double quotation marks.**   17. _____

18. **No apostrophe** is needed in the following greeting: "Merry Christmas from the Palmers." 18. _____

19. The **possessive** of *somebody else* is *somebody's else.* 19. _____

20. The **possessive** of *mother-in-law* is *mother's-in-law.* 20. _____

21. A **semicolon** is normally used between two independent clauses joined by *and* if one or both clauses contain internal commas. 21. _____

22. A quotation consisting of several sentences takes **double quotation marks** at the beginning of the first sentence and at the end of the last sentence. 22. _____

23. A quotation consisting of several paragraphs takes **double quotation marks** at the beginning and end of each paragraph. 23. _____

24. Generally, a **foreign word** is not italicized if it can be found in a reputable American dictionary. 24. _____

25. The word *the* is **italicized** in the name of a newspaper or a magazine. 25. _____

26. A polite request in the form of a question is followed by a **period.** 26. _____

27. **Single quotation marks** may be substituted for double quotation marks around any quoted passage. 27. _____

28. The **comma** is always placed outside quotation marks. 28. _____

29. The **colon** and **semicolon** are always placed outside quotation marks. 29. _____

30. A **comma** is always used to separate the two parts of a compound predicate. 30. _____

31. The expression *such as* is normally followed by a **comma.** 31. _____

32. The **nonsentence** is a legitimate unit of expression and may be followed by a **period.** 32. _____

33. An **exclamation point** and a **question mark** are never used together. 33. _____

34. **Parentheses** are used around words that are to be deleted from a manuscript. 34. _____

35. A **comma** is used between two independent clauses not joined by a coordinating conjunction. 35. _____

36. A **semicolon** is used after the salutation of a friendly letter. 36. _____

37. The subject of a sentence should be separated from the predicate by a **comma.** 37. _____

38. An overuse of **underlining** (italics) for emphasis should be avoided. 38. _____

39. The **contraction** of the words *have not* is written thus: *hav'ent.* 39. _____

40. Nonrestrictive clauses are always set off with **commas.** 40. _____

41. **Double quotation marks** are used around the name of a ship. 41. _____

42. A **comma** is used before the word *then* when it introduces a second clause. 42. _____

43. The prefix *semi* always requires a **hyphen.** 43. _____

44. **No comma** is required in the following sentence: "Where do you wish to go?" he asked. 44. _____

45. A **dash** is a legitimate substitute for all other marks of punctuation. 45. _____

46. A **slash** is used to separate two lines of poetry quoted in a running text. 46. _____

47. A **dash** is placed between words used as alternatives. 47. _____

48. Every introductory prepositional phrase is set off by a **comma.** 48. _____

49. An introductory adverbial clause is usually set off with a **comma.** 49. _____

50. A **colon** may be used instead of a **semicolon** between two independent clauses when the second clause is an explanation of the first. 50. _____

FLASH TEST

PART 2

Write **C** if the punctuation in brackets is **correct.**

Write **X** if it is **incorrect.**

EXAMPLE: The last question on the test [,] counted 30 points.   <u>   X   </u>

1. Abner Fenwick found, to his chagrin, that Physics 101 was quite difficult[;] but, because he put in maximum effort, he earned a *B.*   1. _____

2. The Messicks were late[,] their car battery having gone dead.   2. _____

3. I wondered why we couldn't get rid of the computer virus[?]   3. _____

4. Dear Dr. Stanley[;] Thank you for your letter of May 10.   4. _____

5. Rafael enjoyed inviting his friends[,] and preparing elaborate meals for them; however, most of his attempts were disasters.   5. _____

6. When the benefits officer described the new medical insurance package, everyone asked, "How much will this new policy cost us["?]   6. _____

7. I remembered the job counselor's remark: "If you send out three hundred inquiry letters in your hometown without even one response, relocate[."]   7. _____

8. "Despite the recession," explained the placement counselor[,] "health-care, construction, and business services still promise an increase in employment opportunities."   8. _____

9. A novella by Conrad, a short story by Lawrence, and some poems of Yeats[,] were all assigned for the last week of the semester.   9. _____

10. In Corning, New York[,] there is a large museum of glass objects from many lands and times.   10. _____

11. Why is it that other children seem to behave better than our[']s?   11. _____

12. The relief workers specifically requested food, blankets, and children['s] clothing.   12. _____

13. Approximately seven million Americans visit their doctor each year[;] seeking an answer for why they feel so tired.   13. _____

14. Whenever he speaks, he's inclined to use too many *and-uh*[']s between sentences.   14. _____

15. The auditor requested to review[:] the medical receipts, our childcare expenses, and any deductions for home improvement.   15. _____

16. The last employee to leave the office is responsible for the following[,] turning off the machines, extinguishing all lights, and locking all executives' office doors.   16. _____

17. Everywhere there were crowds shouting anti[-]American slogans.   17. _____

18. Private colleges and universities are concerned about dwindling enrollment[;] because their tuition costs continue to climb while requests for substantial financial aid are also increasing.   18. _____

19. During the whole wretched ordeal of his doctoral exams[;] Charles remained outwardly calm.   19. _____

20. More than twenty minutes were cut from the original version of the film[,] the producers told neither the director nor the writer.   20. _____

21. The mock-epic poem "Casey at the Bat" was first published June 3, 1888[,] in the *Examiner.*   21. _____

22. We were married on January 1, 2000[,] in Tahiti.   22. _____

23. The temperature sinking fast as dusk approached[;] we decided to seek shelter for the night.

23. _____

24. By the year 2000, only about half of Americans entering the workforce were native born and of European stock[;] thus this country is truly becoming a multiracial society.

24. _____

25. My only cousin[,] who is in the U.S. Air Force[,] is stationed in the Arctic.

25. _____

26. Any U.S. Air Force officer[,] who is stationed in the Arctic[,] receives extra pay.

26. _____

27. Hey! Did you find a biology book in this classroom[?!]

27. _____

28. Charles Goodyear, the man who gave the world vulcanized rubber, personified the qualities of the classic American inventor[:] he spent nine years experimenting to find a waterproof rubber that would be resistant to extreme temperatures.

28. _____

29. Murphy was commended by his boss for his frankness and spunk[;] then Murphy was fired.

29. _____

30. The first well-known grocery store group was[,] the Atlantic and Pacific Tea Company, founded in 1859.

30. _____

31. Fernando jumped and squealed with delight[,] because he found a new pair of roller blades under his bed as a present from his family's Three Kings celebration.

31. _____

32. The movies[,] that I prefer to see[,] always have happy endings.

32. _____

33. At the Powwow Anna and her friends entered the Fancy Shawl Dance competition[;] for they wanted to dance in their new dresses and moccasins.

33. _____

Answers to Punctuation Review for: Unit 2

1. T	11. T	21. T	31. F	41. F
2. F	12. F	22. T	32. T	42. F
3. F	13. F	23. F	33. T	43. F
4. T	14. T	24. T	34. F	44. T
5. T	15. T	25. F	35. F	45. F
6. F	16. T	26. T	36. F	46. T
7. T	17. F	27. F	37. F	47. F
8. F	18. T	28. F	38. T	48. F
9. T	19. F	29. T	39. F	49. T
10. F	20. F	30. F	40. T	50. T

Part 2

1. C	8. C	15. X	22. C	29. C
2. C	9. X	16. X	23. X	30. X
3. X	10. C	17. C	24. C	31. X
4. X	11. X	18. X	25. C	32. X
5. X	12. C	19. X	26. X	33. X
6. X	13. X	20. X	27. X	
7. C	14. X	21. C	28. C	

FLASH FOCUS

When you complete Unit III, you should be able to:

✓ Understand the basics of capitalization, abbreviation, and other mechanics

✓ Use various techniques to improve your spelling

✓ Understand how to apply the principles of mechanics and good spelling to your writing

"Grammar is a piano I play by ear. All I know about grammar is its power."

—Joan Didion

"Arguments over grammar and style are often as fierce as those over IBM versus MAC, and as fruitless as Coke versus Pepsi and boxers versus briefs."

—Jack Lynch

FLASH TEST

Before you begin studying the sections in Unit III, take the diagnostic tests on mechanics and spelling to test your knowledge. If you answer eight or more questions incorrectly, be sure to note where you need extra help or explanation and pay close attention to those particular sections in Unit III.

PART 1: DIAGNOSTIC TEST: CAPITALIZATION

In each blank, write **C** if the boldfaced word(s) **follow** the rules of capitalization.

Write **X** if the word(s) **do not follow** the rules.

EXAMPLE: The Mormons settled in what is now Salt Lake **City.**   C

1. I read a book about the *Titanic.*   1. _____
2. My **college** days were stressful.   2. _____
3. He attends Taft **high school.**   3. _____
4. The **President** vetoed the bill.   4. _____
5. They drove **east** from Tucson.   5. _____
6. We presented **Mother** with a bouquet of roses.   6. _____
7. I finally passed **spanish.**   7. _____
8. She is in France; **He** is at home.   8. _____
9. "Are you working?" **she** asked.   9. _____
10. I love **Korean** food.   10. _____
11. We saluted the **american** flag.   11. _____
12. Last **Summer** I drove to California.   12. _____
13. My birthday was **Friday.**   13. _____
14. I am enrolled in courses in **philosophy** and Japanese.   14. _____
15. She went **North** for Christmas.   15. _____

16. Please, **Father,** lend me your car.   16. _____

17. "But he's my **Brother,**" she wailed.   17. _____

18. "Stop!" **shouted** the officer.   18. _____

19. Jane refused to be **Chairperson** of the committee.   19. _____

20. "If possible," he said, "**Write** the report today."   20. _____

PART 2: DIAGNOSTIC TEST: ABBREVIATIONS AND NUMBERS

Write **C** if the boldfaced abbreviation or number is used **correctly.**

Write **X** if it is used **incorrectly.**

EXAMPLE: They drove through **Tenn.**   ____X____

1. **Three million** people have visited the park.   1. _____

2. I participated in a **five-hour** workshop on interpersonal communications. 2. _____

3. The play begins at **7 p.m.**   3. _____

4. Aaron was born on November **11th,** 1988.   4. _____

5. The rent is **$325** a month.   5. _____

6. The interest comes to **8** percent.   6. _____

7. **Sen.** Levy voted against the bill.   7. _____

8. There are **nineteen** women in the club.   8. _____

9. **1999** was another bad year for flooding.   9. _____

10. I wrote a note to **Dr.** Rhee.   10. _____

11. [Opening sentence of a news article] The **ACDYM** has filed for bankruptcy. 11. _____

12. She lives on Buchanan **Ave.**   12. _____

13. We consulted Ricardo Guitierrez, **Ph.D.**   13. _____

14. Our appointment is at **4** o'clock.   14. _____

15. I slept only **3** hours last night.   15. _____

PART 3: SPELLING

In each sentence, one boldfaced word is **misspelled.** Write its number in the blank.

EXAMPLE: (1) **Its** (2) **too** late (3) **to** go.   ____1____

1. Jane's (1) **independent** attitude sometimes was a (2) **hindrence** to the (3) **committee.**   1. _____

2. (1) **Approximatly** half of the class noticed the (2) **omission** of the last item on the (3) **questionnaire.**   2. _____

3. The (1) **mischievous** child was (2) **usualy** (3) **courteous** to adults.   3. _____

4. At the office Jack was described as an (1) **unusually** (2) **conscientous** and (3) **indispensable** staff member.   4. _____

5. Even though Dave was (1) **competent** in his (2) **mathematics** class, he didn't have the (3) **disipline** required to work through the daily homework.   5. _____

6. The sociologist's (1) **analysis** of the (2) **apparent** (3) **prejudise** that existed among the villagers was insightful.   6. _____

7. She was (1) **particularly** (2) **sensable** about maintaining a study (3) **schedule.**　7. _____

8. It was (1) **necesary** to curb Tad's (2) **tendency** to interrupt the staff discussion with (3) **irrelevant** comments.　8. _____

9. (1) **Personaly,** it was no (2) **surprise** that (3) **curiosity** prompted the toddler to smear lipstick on the bathroom mirror.　9. _____

10. Tim developed a (1) **procedure** for updating our (2) **bussiness** (3) **calendar.**　10. _____

11. As a (1) **sophomore** Sue had the (2) **perseverence** and (3) **sacrifice** needed to work three part-time jobs and to raise her three sons.　11. _____

12. Her (1) **opinion,** while (2) **fascinating,** revealed an indisputable (3) **hypocricy.**　12. _____

13. Every day our (1) **secretery** meets a colleague from the (2) **Psychology** Department at their favorite campus (3) **restaurant.**　13. _____

14. During (1) **adolescence** we often (2) **condemm** anyone who offers (3) **guidance.**　14. _____

15. Based on Bill's (1) **description,** his dream vacation sounded (2) **irresistable** and guaranteed to (3) **fulfill** anyone's need to escape.　15. _____

Answers to Diagnostic Test on Capitalization (Part 1)

1. C	5. C	9. C	13. C	17. X
2. C	6. C	10. C	14. C	18. C
3. X	7. X	11. X	15. X	19. X
4. C	8. X	12. X	16. C	20. X

Answers to Diagnostic Test on Abbreviations and Numbers (Part 2)

1. C	4. X	7. X	10. C	13. C
2. C	5. C	8. C	11. X	14. X
3. C	6. C	9. X	12. X	15. X

Answers to Diagnostic Test on Spelling (Part 3)

1. 2	4. 2	7. 2	10. 2	13. 1
2. 1	5. 3	8. 1	11. 2	14. 2
3. 2	6. 3	9. 1	12. 3	15. 2

 FLASH SUMMARY

The technical conventions that apply only to the written form of our language, such as capitalization and number form, are called mechanics. (Punctuation too is part of mechanics but warrants a division of its own in this book.) Attention to spelling and other mechanical details signals that you are a careful writer, concerned about your paper's appearance, readability, and clarity.

55 Manuscript Form

A. Handwritten Papers. Use white, lined paper that is $8\frac{1}{2}$ by 11 inches. Write on one side of the paper only, using black or blue ink. Do not use paper torn from notebooks. Write legibly; a word difficult to decipher may be marked as an error. Clearly distinguish between capital and lowercase letters.

B. **Papers Typed or Done on Computers.** If working on a typewriter, use a fresh black ink ribbon and unlined, white, nonerasable, 16- or 20-pound bond paper; type on one side only. If working on a computer, use a fresh ink cartridge and high-quality paper (20-pound or business weight if possible). Set your printer to a dark setting (not "draft" or "speed"). Choose a plain font such as Courier and a type size of 10 or 12 points. If necessary, adjust the paper in the printer to give adequate top and bottom margins. Turn on pagination if available.

C. **Spacing.** Whether handwriting, typing, or word processing, use double spacing and leave one-inch margins all around. To begin a paragraph, indent five spaces ($\frac{1}{2}$ inch in handwriting). Do not indent the first line of a page unless it begins a paragraph. Do not crowd lines at the bottom of a page; use a new sheet.

Separate from the text any prose quotations longer than four lines or verse quotations longer than three lines; use no quotation marks, indent ten spaces from the left margin (one inch in handwriting), and maintain double spacing. Keep shorter quotations in the body of your text, and enclose them in quotation marks. See section 42I, page 137.

D. **Titles and Page Numbers.** Placement of titles: MLA Style—Unless instructed otherwise, put your heading (your name, instructor's name, class, and date) at the top left of page 1. Center the title below that; do not repeat the title on subsequent pages. APA Style—Unless instructed otherwise, start with a separate title page with the title of the paper, your name (with middle initial) and your school. This information (title of paper, name, and school) should be on separate lines and centered on the page. Count this page as page 1. In the upper right corner of this page and every page, put the first few key words of your title and the page number. At the beginning of the first page of text, repeat the title. For punctuation and capitalization of titles, see section 32, page 124; section 46A, page 138; and section 56F, page 156.

Number all pages with Arabic numerals (1, 2 . . .) in the upper right corner, with no periods or parentheses. If using MLA style, precede each page number with your last name; if using APA, instead of your last name use a short form of your title.

E. **Justifying and Word Dividing.** *Right justifying* means making every line of text end precisely at the right margin. (Most word-processing systems can do this.) However, unless your instructor permits, do *not* right justify your papers. Also, unless your instructor permits, do not divide a word at the end of a line when the whole word will not fit. Put it on the next line. (Most computers do this automatically or have a command that will cancel hyphenation.)

F. **Proofreading.** Before handing in a paper, examine it several times for errors in typing, spelling, punctuation, wording, and sentence construction. Computer spell-checkers are generally not advanced enough to catch homonyms (*there* for *their*) or wrong words correctly spelled (*drams* for *dreams*), and grammar checkers can be wildly imprecise. If you have many errors, redo the page or even the whole paper, especially if you are word processing. If you have only a few minor errors, make changes neatly, as follows:

(1) Deletions. Draw a horizontal line through words to be deleted. Do not use parentheses. See section 51A, page 143.

(2) Insertions. Above the line write the words to be inserted, and just below the line use a caret (^) to show the point of insertion.

(3) Paragraphing. Use the ¶ sign to show the point at which you wish to begin a paragraph. Write *NO* ¶ if you wish to remove a paragraph indention.

56. Capitalize Words

A. **The First Word of Every Sentence,** including quoted sentences:

The network declared, "**T**he war has definitely ended."

But do **not** capitalize the first word of

✓ An indirect quotation (paraphrase): The network declared *that the war had ended.*

✓ A fragmentary quotation: The network declared that the war had "**d**efinitely ended."

✓ A sentence in parentheses within another sentence: The network declared (**e**veryone assumed it true) that the war had ended. This rule applies also with dashes; see section 49B, page 142.

B. **The First Word of a Line of Poetry** (unless the poet has used lowercase):

Unhappy we the setting sun deplore,

So glorious once, but ah! it shines no more.

—Phyllis Wheatley

C. **Words and Phrases Used as Sentences**

When? **N**ever. **N**o, not you. **O**f course.

D. **The First Word of a Formal Question or Statement After a Colon**

The border guard questioned us: **W**hat is your destination? **H**ow long will you stay?

Hemingway said it best: **C**ourage is grace under pressure.

E. **The First Word of Each Item in a Formal Outline**

I. **E**xercises to develop shoulder muscles

    A. **L**ateral raise

    B. **P**ullover

F. **Important Words in a Title**

Death Comes for the Archbishop [book]

"**S**ex, **B**etrayal, and **M**urder" [article]

Always capitalize the first and the last word. Capitalize all other words *except*

(1) *Articles (***a, an,** *and* **the***):*
*Death of **a** Salesman*

(2) *Prepositions (***on, in, to** *. . .)* *and* **to** *in an infinitive:*
*Light **in** August A Night **to** Remember*

(3) *Coordinating conjunctions (***and, but** *. . .)*
*The Sound **and** the Fury*

Note: Some authorities favor capitalizing prepositions of five or more letters, such as *about: Much Ado About Nothing.* Most authorities favor not capitalizing *the* beginning a newspaper or magazine title: The story was in *the San Francisco Chronicle.* Always capitalize the first word following a dash or colon in a title: *Tokyo at Night: A Guide to Restaurants and Clubs.*

G. **The First and Last Words in the Salutation (Greeting) of a Letter and the First Word in the Complimentary Close**

My dearest **S**on, **V**ery truly yours,

The Pronoun *I* and the Interjection *O* (but not *oh*) :

To thee, **O** Lord, **I** pray.   Why, oh why?

57. Capitalize Proper Nouns

A proper noun, as distinguished from a common noun, is the name of a specific person, place, or thing: *Milton, America, Eiffel Tower.* (A proper adjective, derived from a proper noun, is also capitalized: *Miltonic, American.*)

Proper Noun	*Common Noun*
Tamara	woman
Rapid City	city
October	month
Saddleback College	college
Rockville Fire Brigade	organization

A. **Specific Persons, Ethnic Groups, Tribes, Nationalities, Religions, and Languages**

Joyce Carol Oates	Caucasian	Hispanic
Navajo	Vietnamese	Islam

Note: Most style manuals, although not all, favor lowercasing *black, white, aborigine,* and other racial descriptions. Whichever style you choose, be consistent with all races.

B. **Specific Places** (countries, states, cities, geographic sections; oceans, lakes, and other bodies of water; streets, buildings, rooms, parks, monuments, and so forth):

Tanzania	Arctic Ocean	South Main Street
South Carolina	the Pacific Rim	the Barr Building
Greenville	Room 67	Lake Huron
Hyde Park	the Vietnam Memorial	

Lakes Erie and Huron (but *the Hudson and Mohawk Rivers*)

C. **Specific Organizations, Companies, and Brand Names**

The White Sox	United Nations	Board of Health
Baptist Church	the Red Cross	Yoho Ski Club
Republican Party	Supreme Court	Ace Tire Corp.

Juicy Fruit gum [lowercase the product]

D. **Days of the Week, Months, Holidays, and Holy Days**

Tuesday	March	Fourth of July	Mother's Day
Labor Day	Easter	Yom Kippur	Ramadan

E. **Religious Names Considered Sacred**

God (but the *gods*)   the Almighty   the Virgin   Allah

Note: The modern tendency is not to capitalize pronouns referring to the Deity except to avoid ambiguity: Trust in **H**im. But *May God shed **h**is grace on you.*

F. **Historical Events, Periods, and Documents**

the Civil War	the Battle of Waterloo
the Great Depression	the Renaissance

Magna Carta   Civil Rights Act

But *twentieth century, feminist movement, mysticism*

G. Educational Institutions, Departments, Specific Courses, Classes of Students, and Specific Academic Degrees

Tulane University Biology 101 [but see section 58D, page 159]

Junior Class Ph.D. Department of Music

H. Flags, Awards, and School Colors

the Stars and Stripes   the Emmy Award

the Pulitzer Prize   the Blue and Gold

I. Stars and Planets

the North Star   Saturn   the Big Dipper

Note: Do not capitalize *sun* and *moon* unless they are personified (considered as persons). Do not capitalize *earth* unless it is personified or considered as one of the planets.

J. Ships, Trains, Aircraft, and Spacecraft

U.S.S. *Missouri Silver Meteor Endeavour*

K. Initials and Other Letter Combinations indicating time, divisions of government, letter equivalents of telephone numbers, call letters of radio and TV stations, and certain other well-known letter combinations:

B.C. (or B.C.E.)	TV	1-800-**SKI HERE**
FBI	O.K. (or OK)	AIDS
KDKA	A.D. (or C.E.)	NBC

L. Personifications

Mother Nature Old Man Winter the hand of Death

M. Titles Preceding Names

Professor Che-Tsao Chang   Chief Justice Rehnquist

General Powell   the Reverend Peale

Do not capitalize a title *following* a name unless the title shows very high national or international distinction:

Che-Tsao Chang, professor of art

Elizabeth II, Queen of Great Britain

You may capitalize a title of very high distinction when used instead of the person's name. Be consistent in this usage:

The President greeted the Pope.

Capitalize an abbreviated title before or after a name:

Prof. Maura Ryan, Ph.D.   Sen. Homer Page, Jr.

58. Do *Not* Capitalize

A. Points of the Compass

The trail led north by northwest.

But do capitalize such words when referring to sections of the nation or world (usually preceded by *the*):

States in the **W**est and **S**outheast are gaining population.

The **M**iddle **E**ast's perspective differs from the **W**est's.

B. **Seasons** (unless personified):

The South is warm in **w**inter, hot in **s**ummer.

. . . crown old **W**inter's head with flowers.

—Richard Crashaw

C. **Words Denoting a Family Relationship,** when they follow a possessive noun or pronoun:

She is Jorge's **a**unt. My father has just left.

But do capitalize when the family relationship is used as a title preceding a name or by itself as a name:

Jorge greeted **A**unt Julia. Come back, **F**ather.

D. **Names of Academic Disciplines** (unless they are part of specific course titles or proper nouns):

The college offers courses in **f**inance and **m**arketing.

The college offers **F**inance 101 and **M**arketing 203. [specific course titles]

Course in **C**hinese and **J**apanese are also available. [proper nouns]

E. **Common Nouns** (unless they are part of proper nouns):

The **f**ire **d**epartment from an **u**pstate **c**ounty won the **f**irefighting **c**ontest at the local **h**igh **s**chool.

The **S**ilton **F**ire **B**rigade from **A**dams **C**ounty won the **A**ll-Idaho **F**irefighters' **C**ontest at **S**locum **H**igh **S**chool.

F. **Common Words Derived from Proper Nouns**

french fries   **c**hina [dishes]   **r**oman numerals

G. **The First Word After a Semicolon**

She wanted to travel; **h**e wanted to stay put.

H. **The First Word in the Latter Part of an Interrupted Quotation** (unless that word begins a new sentence):

"English 405," Ralph insisted, "**w**ill do wonders for your writing." [All quoted words are one sentence.]

"Take English 405," Ralph insisted. "**I**t will do wonders for your writing." [*It* begins a new quoted sentence.]

I. **The First Word of a Quotation That Is Only Part of a Sentence**

Her courage was called "**a**bove and beyond duty."

J. **The Second Part of Most Compound Words** (unless the second part is a proper noun):

Thirty-**f**ifth Avenue	Mayor-**e**lect Hirsch
Secretary-**d**esignate Rae Rand	anti-**A**merican

K. **A Word That You Want to Emphasize** (use italics instead):

WRONG: You were told NOT to go there.

RIGHT: You were told *not* to go there.

FLASH TEST

PART 1

Write **C** if the boldfaced word(s) are **correct** in use or omission of capital letters.

Write **X** if the word(s) are **incorrect.**

EXAMPLE: Cajuns speak a dialect of **french.** _____X_____

1. They met at the North Side **Jewish** Center. 1. _____
2. DiNapoli wanted to attend a California **college.** 2. _____
3. The **turkish** bath is closed. 3. _____
4. Hyeon Woo's uncle is a Buddhist **Monk.** 4. _____
5. When will **Congress** convene? 5. _____
6. She is a **Junior** at the University of Houston. 6. _____
7. Gregory looked forward eagerly to visiting his **Mother-in-Law.** 7. _____
8. He always disliked **Calculus.** 8. _____
9. Joe constantly reads about the **Civil War.** 9. _____
10. I made an appointment with **Professor** Allen. 10. _____
11. She met three **Professors** today. 11. _____
12. "Did you save your paper on the disk?" **she** asked. 12. _____
13. Each **Spring** I try a new sport. 13. _____
14. The deaths were reported in the *Times.* 14. _____
15. I worked in the **Southwest.** 15. _____
16. Her **Aunt Miriam** has returned. 16. _____
17. He's late for his **anthropology** class. 17. _____
18. John was **Secretary** of his class. 18. _____
19. Woods was promoted to **Major.** 19. _____
20. The bookstore has a special sale on Hewlett-Packard **Computers.** 20. _____

FLASH TEST

PART 2

In the first blank write the number of the **first** correct choice (**1** or **2**) .

In the second blank write the number of the **second** correct choice (**3** or **4**) .

EXAMPLE: Wandering (1) **West** (2) **west,** Max met (3) **Milly** (4) **milly.** __2__ __3__

1. The Holbrook (1) **Company** (2) **company** is having a great sale on Italian (3) **Shoes** (4) **shoes.** 1. _____ _____
2. Her (1) **Father** (2) **father** went (3) **South** (4) **south** on business. 2. _____ _____
3. The new (1) **College** (2) **college** is seeking a (3) **Dean** (4) **dean.** 3. _____ _____
4. Children are taught to begin letters with "My (1) **Dear** (2) **dear** (3) **Sir** (4) **sir.**" 4. _____ _____

5. Business letters often end with "Very (1) **Truly** (2) **truly** (3) **Yours** (4) **yours.**"   5. _____ _____

6. After (1) **Church** (2) **church**, we walked across the Brooklyn (3) **Bridge** (4) **bridge.**   6. _____ _____

7. The (1) **Politician** (2) **politician** declared that the protester was (3) **Un-American** (4) **un-American.**   7. _____ _____

8. The young (1) **Lieutenant** (2) **lieutenant** prayed to the (3) **Lord** (4) **lord** for courage in the battle.   8. _____ _____

9. My (1) **Cousin** (2) **cousin** now lives in the (3) **East** (4) **east.**   9. _____ _____

10. The (1) **President** (2) **president** addresses (3) **Congress** (4) **congress** tomorrow.   10. _____ _____

11. Joan Bailey, (1) **M.D.,** (2) **m.d.,** once taught (3) **Biology** (4) **biology.**   11. _____ _____

12. Dr. Mikasa, (1) **Professor** (2) **professor** of (3) **English** (4) **english,** is writing a murder mystery.   12. _____ _____

13. The (1) **Comet** (2) **comet** can be seen just below (1) **The Big Dipper** (4) **the Big Dipper.**   13. _____ _____

14. "I'm also a graduate of North Harris (1) **College** (2) **college**," (3) **She** (4) **she** added.   14. _____ _____

15. The (1) **Rabbi** (2) **rabbi** of (3) **Temple** (4) **temple** Beth Emeth is a leader in interfaith cooperation.   15. _____ _____

16. Vera disagreed with the review of "(1) **The** (2) **the** War Chronicles" in (3) *The* (4) *the New York Times.*   16. _____ _____

17. The club (1) **Treasurer** (2) **treasurer** said that the financial report was "(3) **Almost** (4) **almost** complete."   17. _____ _____

18. The (1) **Girl Scout** (2) **girl scout** leader pointed out the (3) **Milky Way** (4) **milky way** to her troop.   18. _____ _____

19. Students use the textbook *Writing* (1) *For* (2) *for* Audience (3) *And* (4) *and Purpose.*   19. _____ _____

20. Educational Support Services is in (1) **Room** (2) **room** 110 of Yost (3) **Hall** (4) **hall.**   20. _____ _____

Answers to Exercises for: Capitalization

Part 1

1. C	5. C	9. C	13. X	17. C
2. C	6. X	10. C	14. C	18. X
3. C	7. X	11. X	15. C	19. X
4. X	8. X	12. C	16. C	20. X

Part 2

1. 1 4	5. 2 4	9. 2 3	13. 2 4	17. 2 4
2. 2 4	6. 2 3	10. 1 3	14. 1 4	18. 1 3
3. 2 4	7. 2 4	11. 1 4	15. 2 3	19. 2 4
4. 2 3	8. 2 3	12. 2 3	16. 1 4	20. 1 3

59 Syllabication

FLASH SUMMARY

The need to divide a word that will not fit at the end of a line has been eliminated in most word processing, which can automatically move the whole word to the next line (see section 55E, page 155). Nevertheless, knowledge of word-division principles is important for other writing occasions.

Avoid dividing any words if at all possible; especially avoid breaking two successive lines. When breaking a word is unavoidable, mark the division with a hyphen (made with one keyboard stroke [-]). A good dictionary is your most reliable guide to the hyphenation of words. Remembering the following rules, however, will reduce your need to consult the dictionary.

59. Syllabication

A. **Divide According to Pronunciation; Always Divide Between Syllables.** Leave enough of a word at the end of the first line to suggest the sound and meaning of the whole word: *con-vince, irreg-ular, change-able*.

B. **Divide Compound Words Between the Parts:** *hand-book, book-keeper, rattle-snake*. If a compound word is already hyphenated, break it at an existing hyphen: *sister-in-law, self-portrait*.

C. **Do Not Divide a One-Syllable Word of any Length:** *thoughts, straight, clashed, twelfths*

D. **Do Not Set Off a Single Letter as a Syllable.**

> **WRONG:** a-part, dough-y **RIGHT:** apart, doughy

60–62 Numbers

60. Generally, Write Out a Number in Words When

A. **It Uses Only One or Two Words**

forty hours, *sixty-three* athletes, *six hundred* members, *twenty-seventh* floor

B. **It Is Part of a Compound Adjective**

a *five-day* week, a *three-month-old* baby, a *two-bedroom* apartment

C. **It Is a Fraction Without a Whole Number**

one-tenth of the voters; *three-fourths* full

But use figures when a whole number precedes: The stock market fell $5\frac{3}{8}$ points.

D. **It Begins a Sentence**

Four hundred fifty-two people attended the concert.

Never begin a sentence with a figure. If the number is a long one, rewrite the sentence to place the number elsewhere: Attendance at the concert was *1,287*.

61. Use Figures

A. **Any Number Needing Three or More Words if Written Out**

The concert drew *452* people.

Use commas to separate every set of three digits (except in serial and telephone numbers, addresses, years in dates, and page numbers). Count from the right or the decimal point:

1,287 copies $2,383,949.96

A.D. 1066   2258 Ocean Road

Write very large round numbers as follows:

two million   23 million   4.2 trillion

B. **Numbers in These Special Uses:** Addresses; room numbers; telephone numbers; TV and radio stations; chapter, page, and line numbers; serial numbers; decimals and percentages; route numbers; times; statistics; precise measurements:

May 10, 2001	276 Fox Road	Room 217
459-7245	chapter 7	Route 66
67.6	Channel 6 98.6°F	5:02 a.m.
8 percent	82 for; 47 against	Giants 8, Bucs 7
6 by 3.2 inches [but six feet long]		

Note: Observe these cautions:

✓ Do not use -st, -th, etc. after figures in dates:

WRONG: March 15th, 2004

RIGHT: March 15, 2004 [but the fifteenth of March]

✓ In formal writing, do not use the form 3/15/04 for a date.

✓ In writing a time, use figures with a.m. and p.m. and when emphasizing an exact time. Generally, use words otherwise:

3 p.m.	at 9:45 tomorrow
from 2:30 to 3:00 p.m.	the 8:02 train
four o'clock	around half-past five

The times 12 a.m. and 12 p.m. are ambiguous; which is noon and which is midnight? Say noon or midnight instead (and give both days that midnight separates): noon Sunday, midnight Sunday/Monday, midnight June 3/4.

C. **Groups of Numbers in the Same Passage** (do not mix words and figures):

The control group's scores were 196, 57, 122, 10, and 43.

62. Write Amounts of Money as Follows:

I earn ninety-five dollars a day. I earn $95.50 a day.

I earn $310 a week. I won $40, $30, and $5 at the races.

She won a million dollars. She won $6 million.

She won $6,889,346.

63–64 Abbreviations

FLASH SUMMARY

Abbreviations are intended mainly for limited spaces, such as signs, lists, and documentation. In ordinary writing, avoid abbreviations except for those listed in section 63.

63. In Ordinary Writing, Abbreviate

A. Certain Titles Before Proper Names: *Mr., Mrs., Ms., Dr., St. (saint), Messrs., Mmes. . . . :*

Mr. Joel Sachs *Mr.* Sachs *Ms.* Wong

Mmes. Wong and Howe

St. Teresa *Rev.* Hector Gomez *Hon.* Ida Ives

But write *Reverend* and *Honorable* in full if they follow *the:*

the *Reverend* Hector Gomez the *Honorable* Ida Ives

Abbreviate military and civil titles unless you use only the person's last name:

Lt. Col. Fabian Farley *Sen.* Clara Chisolm

Lieutenant Colonel Farley *Senator* Chisolm

B. Degrees and Certain Other Titles After Proper Names: *Sr. (senior), Jr., Esq., M.A., Ph.D. . . . :*

Ralph Grabowski, *Sr.,* visited Ramez Audi, *D.D.S.*

C. Certain Expressions Used with Numerals: *a.m., p.m., B.C., A.D., No. (number), $:*

9:30 *a.m.* *A.D.* 1054 325 *B.C.* *No.* 97 *$*37.50

Do not use such abbreviations without a numeral:

WRONG: She arrived this *a.m.*

RIGHT: She arrived this *morning.*

Note: You may choose to write *B.C.E. (before the common era)* and *C.E. (common era)* instead of *B.C.* and *A.D. (A.D.* precedes the year; the others follow.) You may also choose to write any of these sets of initials without periods; whatever your choices, be consistent in style.

D. Certain Latin Phrases: *i.e., (that is), viz. (namely), e.g. (for example), cf. (compare), etc. (and so forth), vs. (versus) .*

Note: Publishers tend to discourage the use of these abbreviations in the text of formal writing; you will do better to write out the English equivalents unless space is restricted (as in notes). Never write *and etc.;* it is redundant.

E. Certain Government Agencies and Other Well-Known Organizations (usually without periods): *CIA, NASA, NAACP, ABC, IBM.* To be sure that your reader knows the meaning of such initials, give the full title at first mention, preferably followed by the initials in parentheses:

The *American Automobile Association (AAA)* is campaigning for more highway funds. . . . Officials of the *AAA* are optimistic.

64. In Ordinary Writing, Do *Not* Abbreviate

A. Names of States, Countries, Months, Days, or Holidays:

WRONG: *Calif.* had a flood last *Tues., Xmas* Eve.

RIGHT: *California* had a flood last *Tuesday, Christmas* Eve.

B. Personal Names:

George (not *Geo.*) Washington slept here.

C. **The Words** *Street, Avenue, Road, Park,* **and** *Company,* especially as part of proper names:

WRONG: The Brooks *Co.* moved to Central *Av.*

RIGHT: The Brooks *Company* moved to Central *Avenue.*

D. **The Word** *and,* except in names of firms and in American Psychological Association reference list citations:

Ways *and* Means Committee; the Brooks & Logan Corporation.

E. **References to a School Subject**

WRONG: The new *psych.* class is filled.

RIGHT: The new *psychology* class is filled.

E. **The Words** *Volume, Chapter,* **and** *Page,* except in documentation, tabulations, and technical writing.

FLASH TEST

Write the number of the **correct** choice.

EXAMPLE: The book was (1) **3** (2) **three** days overdue.   _____2_____

1. (1) **365** (2) **Three hundred sixty-five** was the final attendance count.   1. _____

2. The odometer showed that it was (1) **5½** (2) **five and one-half** miles from the campus to the beach.   2. _____

3. (1) **Prof.** (2) **Professor** Hilton teaches Asian philosophy.   3. _____

4. Lincoln was born in (1) **Ky.** (2) **Kentucky.**   4. _____

5. Builders are still reluctant to have a (1) **thirteenth** (2) **13th** floor in any new buildings.   5. _____

6. The exam will be held at noon on (1) **Fri.** (2) **Friday.**   6. _____

7. The (1) **P.O.** (2) **post office** on campus always has a long line of international students mailing letters and packages to their friends and families.   7. _____

8. Judd has an interview with the Sherwin Williams (1) **Co.** (2) **Company.**   8. _____

9. Nicole will study in Germany, (1) **Eng.** (2) **England,** and Sweden next year.   9. _____

10. Evan Booster, (1) **M.D.,** (2) **medical doctor,** is my physician.   10. _____

11. Frank jumped 22 feet, (1) **3** (2) **three** inches at the Saturday meet.   11. _____

12. For the laboratory, the department purchased permanent markers, legal pads, pencils, (1) **etc.** (2) **and other office supplies.**   12. _____

13. For (1) **Xmas** (2) **Christmas,** the Fords planned a quiet family gathering rather than their usual ski holiday.   13. _____

14. Travis needed to leave for work at exactly 8:00 (1) **a.m.** (2) **o'clock.**   14. _____

15. John's stipend was (1) **$2,145** (2) **two thousand one hundred forty-five dollars.**   15. _____

16. She will graduate from medical school June (1) **2,** (2) **second,** 1998.   16. _____

17. He and his family moved to Vermont last (1) **Feb.** (2) **February,** didn't they?   17. _____

18. Over (1) **900** (2) **nine hundred** students attend Roosevelt Junior High School.   18. _____

19. Brad loved all of his (1) **phys. ed.** (2) **physical education** electives.   19. _____

20. Next year, the convention will be held on April (1) **19,** (2) **19th,** (3) **nineteenth,** in Burlington.   20. _____

21. The service included an inspiring homily by the (1) **Rev.** (2) **Reverend** Spooner. 21. _____

22. The lottery prize has reached an astonishing (1) **twenty-four million dollars** (2) **$24 million.** 22. _____

23. The family next door adopted a (1) **two-month-old** (2) **2-month-old** baby girl from China. 23. _____

24. We had an opportunity to meet (1) **Sen.** (2) **Senator** Lester at the convention. 24. _____

25. The diagram was on (1) **pg.** (2) **page** 44. 25. _____

26. One of my friends will do her student teaching in (1) **TX.** (2) **Texas** this spring. 26. _____

27. When we offered tickets to a baseball game for our raffle, we had (1) **one-third** (2) **1/3rd** of the employees purchase tickets. 27. _____

28. Jack's dissertation was (1) **two hundred fifty** (2) **250** pages. 28. _____

29. The plane expected from (1) **LA early this a.m.** (2) **Los Angeles early this morning** is late. 29. _____

30. The bus arrives at 10:55 a.m. and leaves at (1) **11:00 a.m.** (2) **eleven a.m.** 30. _____

31. Ben earned (1) **three hundred dollars,** (2) **$300,** saved $80, and spent the rest on books and movies. 31. _____

32. Rachel's name was (1) **twenty-sixth** (2) **26th** on the list of high school graduates. 32. _____

33. Private Bailey wanted a (1) **3-day** (2) **three-day** pass to see Lorena. 33. _____

Answers to Exercises for: Numbers and Abbreviations

1. 2	8. 2	15. 1	22. 2	29. 2
2. 1	9. 2	16. 1	23. 1	30. 1
3. 2	10. 1	17. 2	24. 2	31. 2
4. 2	11. 1	18. 2	25. 2	32. 1
5. 1	12. 2	19. 2	26. 2	33. 2
6. 2	13. 2	20. 1	27. 1	
7. 2	14. 1	21. 2	28. 2	

65–69 Spelling

FLASH SUMMARY

To a reader, misspellings are the most obvious of writing errors, yet to the writer, they are among the easiest to overlook. Do not trust a computer's spell-checker to do the job; most cannot distinguish *clam* from *calm* or *passed* from *past*. Rely on (1) using a reputable dictionary for words of which you are not sure and (2) very careful proofreadings—more than two or three. Proofread at least once backward, word for word from the end, so that the paper's flow of thought does not divert your mind from your proofreading task.

65. Spelling Improvement Techniques

A. Visualize the Correct Spelling of a Word. Look attentively at a word; then look away from it and try to see the printed word in your mind.

B. Practice Pronouncing Troublesome Words. Say each word aloud, syllable by syllable, a number of times.

ath-let-ic	quan-ti-ty	gov-ern-ment
ac-ci-den-tal-ly	di-sas-trous	e-quip-ment
val-u-a-ble	tem-per-a-ture	min-i-a-ture

C. **Practice Writing Troublesome Words.** Practice each word several times. Begin slowly and increase your speed until the correct form comes easily. You will need this drill to substitute correct spelling habits for faulty ones. Keep a corrected list of your misspelled words.

D. **Distinguish Between Words Similar in Sound or Spelling.** See section 73, pages 183–192, for explanations of the following and many other such distinctions: *to/too/two, their/there/they're, its/it's, your/you're, loose/lose, whose/who's.*

E. **Think of Related Words.** Often you can determine whether to end a word with -*er* or -*ar*, -*ence* or -*ance*, -*able* or -*ible*, and so forth, by thinking of a related form of the word. For example, if you think of *definition*, you can be fairly sure that *definite* ends in -*ite.* Examine these pairs:

famili**a**rity	famili**a**r	aud**i**tion	aud**i**ble
gramm**a**tical	gramm**a**r	stimul**a**tion	stimul**a**nt
peculi**a**rity	peculi**a**r	symb**o**lic	symb**o**l
regul**a**rity	regul**a**r	confid**e**ntial	confid**e**nt
imagin**a**tion	imagin**a**ry	exist**e**ntial	exist**e**nce
desper**a**tion	desper**a**te		

Exception: sensation—sensible, sensitive

F. **Create and Use Memory Devices.** Associate one word with another, find a word within a word, or make up jingles or nonsense sentences; such **mnemonics** can help you over the trouble spots in your problem words. Here are some examples:

Emma is in a *dil**emma**.*

She put a **dent** in the *superinten**dent**.*

*Station**e**ry* is pap**er**.

A *princi**ple*** is a ru**le**.

Poor *gram**mar*** will **mar** your writing.

It is **vile** to have no *pri**vile**ges.*

The *vi**lla**in* owns a **villa in** Spain.

There is **a rat** in *sep**arat**e* and in *comp**arat**ive*.

I have **lice** on my *lice**nse***!

There is **iron** in the *env**iron**ment.*

There is a **meter** in the *ce**meter**y.*

Tim has great *op**tim**ism.*

With any *pro**f**essor,* one **F** is enough.

Group words with similar characteristics, such as two sets of double letters (*accommodate, embarrass, possess*) or three *i*'s (*optimistic, primitive*) or names of occupations (*author, censor, conductor, emperor, investor, sponsor, professor*) or the three -*ceed* words (*proceed, exceed, succeed.* All other words ending in the same sound are spelled with -*cede*, except *supersede).*

66. The Five Basic Rules

A. **The *ie* Rule.** You probably know the old jingle:

Put *i* before *e* except after *c*,

Or when sounded like *a* as in *neighbor* and *weigh*.

That is, normally use *ie:*

achieve	field	niece
believe	grief	relieve
chief	hygiene	yield
friend	mischief	mischievous

But after a *c*, use *ei:*

ceiling	deceive	receive
conceive	perceive	receipt

Use *ei* also when the two letters sound like *AY:*

freight	neighbor	vein
weigh	sleigh	heir

Actually, *ei* is usual when the two letters have any sound other than *EE: counterfeit, forfeit, foreign, height, neither* (the British say *NYE-ther*), *leisure* (British *LEZZ-ure*).

Troublesome exceptions: finan**cie**r, so**cie**ty, spe**cie**s; prot**ei**n, s**ei**ze, w**ei**rd.

B. **The Final *-e* Rule:** Drop a final silent *e* before a suffix beginning with a vowel (*a, e, i, o, u*, and here *y*) :

write + ing = writing	fame + ous = famous
love + able = lovable	scare + y = scary
hope + ed = hoped	come + ing = coming

Exception: mileage

But keep the *e* before a vowel suffix in these cases:

(1) ***After c and g*** (to keep a "soft" sound) before a suffix beginning with *a* or *o*: noti**ce**/able, chan**ge**/able, coura**ge**/ous, outra**ge**/ous, ven**ge**/ance.

(2) ***To avoid confusion with other words:*** singe + ing = singe/ing (to avoid confusion with *singing*); dye + ing = dye/ing.

And keep the *e* when the suffix does not begin with a vowel: hope/*ful*, love/*less*, lone/*ly*, safe/*ty*, state/*ment*, same/*ness*.

Exceptions: judgment, argument, acknowledgment, truly, duly

C. **The Final *-y* Rule:** Change a final *y* to *i* before any suffix except *-ing:*

happy + ness = happiness	cry + ed = cried
busy + ly = busily	lady + es = ladies

cry/ing bury/ing try/ing

But ignore this rule if a vowel precedes the *y:*

chimn**ey**/s   ann**oy**/ed   monk**ey**/s

Exceptions: lay, la**i**d; pay, pa**i**d; say, sa**i**d.

D. **The Doubling Rule:** Double a final consonant before a suffix beginning with a vowel (including *y*) if the original word does both of the following:

(1) ends in consonant-vowel-consonant (cvc):

   CVC   CVC   CVC

drop, drop/**p**ing bat, bat/**t**er hum, hum/**m**able

(2) and (if more than one syllable) is accented on the last syllable:

  CVC   CVC   CVC

occUR occUR/**r**ed occUR/**r**ence

  CVC   CVC   CVC

reFER reFER/**r**ed reFER/**r**al

  CVC   CVC   CVC

beGIN beGIN/**n**ing beGIN/**n**er

Otherwise, do not double:

         VVC   VVC   VCC

Not *cvc:* droop/ing, preVAIL/ing, dent/ed

Not accented on last syllable:

OFFer/ing, BENefit/ed, RECKon/ing

Note: If the accent jumps back to an earlier syllable when the suffix is added, do not double: *conFER, CONfer/ence; reFER, REFer/ence.*

E. **The Let-It-Alone Rule.** When adding prefixes or suffixes or combining roots, do not add or drop letters unless you know that one of the spelling rules applies or that the word is irregular (see section 69, pages 170–171):

Prefix + Root	*Root + Suffix*	*Root + Root*
dis/appear	careful/ly	book/keeper
dis/satisfied	immediate/ly	grand/daughter
mis/spell	comical/ly	
re/commend	state/ment	
un/necessary	achieve/ment	

67. Forming Plurals

To form most plurals, add *-s* to the singular (*toy, toys; dollar, dollars;* Donna *Remington,* the *Remingtons*). The following generalizations cover most other plurals. Consult your dictionary in other cases or when in doubt.

A. **Add *-es* if You Hear an Added Syllable** when you say a plural: *bush, bush/**es**; fox, fox/**es**; buzz, buzz/**es**; church, church/**es.***

B. **Add *-es* When the Final *-y* Rule Applies** (see section 66C): *sky, skies; liberty, liberties.*

C. **Change Final *f* or *fe* to *v* and Add *-es*** in the following and a few other similar nouns: *calf, cal**ves**; knife, kni**ves**; wife, wi**ves**; loaf, loa**ves**; wharf, whar**ves**; half, hal**ves**; life, li**ves**.*

D. **Add *-es* to Certain Singular Nouns Ending in *o*:**
tomato, tomato**es**; potato, potato**es**; hero, hero**es**

With musical terms, with words having a vowel before the *o*, and with most other singular nouns ending in *o*, add just *-s:*

solo, solo**s**;	piano, piano**s**;	alto, alto**s**;
radio, radio**s**;	studio, studio**s**;	rodeo, rodeo**s**

With some words, you may use either -s or -es:

domino, dominos, dominoes; zero, zeros, zeroes

Consult a dictionary for other final -o word plurals.

E. Change Final -is to -es in Many Words:

basis, bases; synopsis, synopses; oasis, oases;
hypothesis, hypotheses; thesis, theses; axis, axes;
parenthesis, parentheses; analysis, analyses; crisis, crises

F. Make Compound Words Plural as Follows:

(1) With solid (unhyphenated) compounds, add the -s to the very end: cupfuls, mouth-fuls

(2) With hyphenated compounds, add the -s to the noun: fathers-in-law, passers-by

G. Use the Foreign Plural for Some Nouns of Foreign Origin: *alumnus, alumni (male); alumna, alumnae (female); stimulus, stimuli; stratum, strata; curriculum, curricula*

With many other such nouns, you may use either the foreign or English plural:

radius, radii or radiuses; stadium, stadia or stadiums; octopus, octopi or octopuses; index, indices or indexes; appendix, appendices or appendixes; antenna, antennae (of insects) or antennas (of electronic devices); phenomenon, phenomena or phenomenons; criterion, criteria or criterions; vertebra, vertebrae or vertebras.

Many of these use the foreign plural in scholarly or technical writing and the English plural in general writing. Your dictionary may specify when each should be used.

Note: Remember that *criteria, phenomena,* and *media* are plurals and require plural verbs. Most authorities also consider *data* plural in formal English. For the singular, use *body of data,* or, if appropriate, *database.*

H. For Clarity, Use -'s for Plurals of Letters and Symbols

Optimistic has three *i*'s. [not *three is*]

See section 39B, page 131.

68. Nonstandard and Alternative Spellings

A. Avoid Nonstandard Spellings, such as *nite, lite, rite* (for *right*), and *thru,* which occur mostly in product names. Do not use them elsewhere.

B. Use Preferred Spellings. Some words have alternative correct spellings: *programmer, programer; kidnapper, kidnaper; dialogue, dialog; catalogue, catalog.* When the dictionary lists two or more spellings, you are safer using the first, which is considered preferred.

69. 100 Problem Words

Many bothersome spelling words have been explained in the suggestions and rules above. Others, pairs of look-alikes or sound-alikes such as *advice* and *advise,* are clarified in section 73, pages 183–192. Below are one hundred more "demons."

absence	across	apologize
acknowledge	adolescence	apparent
acquaintance	amateur	approximately
acquire	analysis	argument

article	hypocrisy	psychology
auxiliary	independent	pursue
business	indispensable	questionnaire
calendar	irrelevant	reminisce
category	irresistible	repetition
committee	knowledge	restaurant
competent	maintenance	rhythm
condemn	management	ridiculous
conscientious	maneuver	sacrifice
courteous	mathematics	schedule
criticism	meant	secretary
criticize	mischievous	sensible
curiosity	necessary	sincerely
definite	ninety	sophomore
description	ninth	souvenir
desperate	nucleus	supposed to
develop	omission	suppression
discipline	opinion	surprise
doesn't	opportunity	synonym
eighth	parallel	tendency
erroneous	particularly	tragedy
exaggerate	perform	truly
excellent	permanent	twelfth
existence	permissible	unusually
fascinating	perseverance	used to
forty	persistent	vacuum
fulfill	personally	
guarantee	playwright	
guidance	prejudice	
height	prevalent	
hindrance	procedure	

FLASH TEST

PART 1

Write the number of the **correctly spelled** word.

EXAMPLE: A knowledge of (1) **grammar** (2) **grammer** is helpful. _____1_____

1. We received an insufficient (1) **quantity** (2) **quanity** of antibiotics. 1. _____

2. Glenn hopes to add (1) **playright** (2) **playwright** to his list of professional credentials. 2. _____

3. No one thought that a romance would (1) **develope** (2) **develop** between those two. 3. _____

4. Mrs. Smith will not (1) **acknowlege** (2) **acknowledge** whether she received the check. 4. _____

5. I love to (1) **surprise** (2) **suprise** the children with small presents. 5. _____

6. After three well-played quarters, the Bruins had a (1) **disasterous** (2) **disastrous** fourth quarter. 6. _____

7. One of the volunteers will be (1) **ninety** (2) **ninty** years old next week. 7. _____

8. The salary will depend on how (1) **competant** (2) **competent** the employee is. 8. _____

9. I loved listening to Grandpa's tales about his childhood because he always (1) **exagerated** (2) **exaggerated** the details.

9. _____

10. It's important to accept valid (1) **criticism** (2) **critcism** without taking the comments personally.

10. _____

11. It was (1) **ridiculous** (2) **rediculous** to expect Fudgley to arrive on time.

11. _____

12. (1) **Approximately** (2) **Approximatly** fifty families attended the adoption support group meeting.

12. _____

13. The murder was a (1) **tradegy** (2) **tragedy** felt by the entire community.

13. _____

14. The Statue of Liberty is a (1) **symbel** (2) **symbol** of the United States.

14. _____

15. Everyone could hear the (1) **argument** (2) **arguement** between the two young lovers.

15. _____

16. Tim asked several questions because he wasn't sure what the professor (1) **ment** (2) **meant** by a "term paper of reasonable length."

16. _____

17. The professor was offended by the (1) **ommission** (2) **omission** of his research data.

17. _____

18. Carrying a portable telephone seems a (1) **necessary** (2) **neccessary** precaution.

18. _____

19. Every time I visit Aunt Nan, she likes to (1) **reminisce** (2) **reminice** about her youth.

19. _____

20. Meeting with a tutor for an hour before the examination was a (1) **desperate** (2) **desparate** attempt by Tom to pass his math class.

20. _____

21. Susan was excited about her (1) **nineth-** (2) **ninth-**grade graduation ceremony.

21. _____

22. Sally needed a lot of (1) **repetition** (2) **repitition** in order to memorize the formulas for her next chemistry test.

22. _____

23. How (1) **definite** (2) **defenite** is their decision to return to Texas?

23. _____

24. The weight loss program offered a (1) **guarantee** (2) **garantee** that I would lose at least ten pounds.

24. _____

25. Jake hoped his temporary job would become a (1) **permenent** (2) **permanent** position.

25. _____

FLASH TEST

PART 2

If the word is spelled **incorrectly**, write the **correct spelling** in the blank.

If the word is spelled **correctly**, leave the blank empty.

EXAMPLES: hindrance
vaccum

	vacuum

1. unusualy

1. _____

2. oppinion

2. _____

3. criticize

3. _____

4. familar

4. _____

5. proceedure

5. _____

6. thru

6. _____

7. pursue

7. _____

8. accross

8. _____

9. confident

9. _____

10. maneuver   10. _____
11. relieve   11. _____
12. absense   12. _____
13. sacrefice   13. _____
14. mischievious   14. _____
15. prevalent   15. _____
16. parallel   16. _____
17. noticeable   17. _____
18. disasterous   18. _____
19. indepindent   19. _____
20. bussiness   20. _____
21. acquire   21. _____
22. truly   22. _____
23. government   23. _____
24. appologize   24. _____
25. controlling   25. _____

Answers to Exercises for: Spelling

Part 1

1. 1	6. 2	11. 1	16. 2	21. 2
2. 2	7. 1	12. 1	17. 2	22. 1
3. 2	8. 2	13. 2	18. 1	23. 1
4. 2	9. 2	14. 2	19. 1	24. 1
5. 1	10. 1	15. 1	20. 1	25. 2

Part 2

1. unusually	6. through	11. –	16. –	21. –
2. opinion	7. –	12. absence	17. –	22. –
3. –	8. across	13. sacrifice	18. disastrous	23. –
4. familiar	9. –	14. mischievous	19. independent	24. apologize
5. procedure	10. –	15. –	20. business	25. –

FLASH TEST

MECHANICS AND SPELLING REVIEW: UNIT III

In each of the following paragraphs, correct all errors in **capitalization, number form, abbreviations, syllabication,** and **spelling.** Cross out the incorrect form and write the correct form above it, as section 60, Manuscript Form, directs.

1. Martha's Vineyard is an Island off cape Cod, Mass., that covers aproximately two hundred sixty sq. kilometers. The first europeans to settle there were the English, in 1642. In the 18th Century Fishing and Whaling came into existance as its cheif sources of employment. By the 18 ninteys its developement as a Summer resort was under way. Wealthy people from N.Y. and Boston vacationed on its beaches and sailed around its harbors. John D. Rockefeller, jr., and other socialites visited there, usually in Aug., the most populer vacation month. It was a favorite spot of the Kennedy Family. Today the year-round population is about 6 thousand. Its communitys include Oak Bluffs, Tisbury, and W. Tisbury. Martha's Vineyard also contains a State Forest.

2. A hurricane is a cyclone that arises in the Tropics, with winds exceeding seventy-five mph, or 121 kilometers per hour. The term *Hurricane* is usually applied to cyclones in the N. Atlantic ocean, whereas those in the western Pacific are called typhoons. Some hurricanes, however, arise in the eastern Pacific, off the West coast of Mexico, and move Northeast. In an average yr. three point five hurricanes will form off the east coast of North America, maturing in the Caribbean sea or the gulf of Mexico. Such hurricanes are most prevelent in Sept. One of the most destructive of these storms slammed into the United States in 1938, causing 100s of deaths in the Northeast. In the nineteen-nineties Hurricane Andrew devastated southern Fla., including Everglades national park. Homes, Churches, schools, and wharfs were ripped apart. Hurricanes can last from 1 to thirty days, weakening as they pass over land. Over the warm Ocean, however, their fury intensifies, and they often generate enormous waves that engulf Coastal areas. To learn more about hurricanes, read *Hurricanes, Their Nature And History*.

3. Turkey is a unique Country. Though partly in Europe, it is ninety seven % in Asia; thus it combines elements of European, middle eastern, and Asiatic cultures. Though the country's Capital is Ankara, its most-famous city is Istanbul, which was for 100s of yrs. called Constantinople and before that Byzantium. To the west of Turkey lies the Aegean sea; to the s.e. lie Iran, Iraq, &Syria. The vast majority of Turks are Muslim, but there are also small numbers of christians and Spanish Speaking Jews. Modern Turkey came into being after the downfall of the Ottoman empire in world war I; its present boundaries were established by the treaty of Lausanne in nineteen twenty-three. 17 years later the nation switched from the arabic to the roman Alphabet. In Government Turkey has a two house Legislature and a head of State.

Answers to Mechanics and Spelling Review for Unit 3

1. (Count 25 items) . . . island . . . Cape . . . Massachusetts . . . approximately 260 square . . . Europeans . . . eighteenth century fishing and whaling [*count* fishing *and* whaling *together as one item*] . . . existence . . . chief . . . 1890s . . . development . . . summer . . . New York . . . Jr. . . . August . . . popular . . . family . . . six . . . communities . . . West . . . state forest

2. (Count 25 items) . . . tropics . . . 75 miles per hour . . . *hurricane* . . . North . . . Ocean . . . west . . . northeast . . . year 3.5 . . . Sea . . . Gulf . . . prevalent . . . September . . . hundreds . . . 1990s . . . Florida . . . National Park . . . churches . . . wharves . . . one . . . ocean . . . coastal . . . *and*

3. (Count 25 items) . . . country . . . 97 percent . . . Middle Eastern . . . capital . . . most famous . . . hundreds . . . years . . . Sea . . . southeast . . . and . . . Christians . . . Spanish-speaking . . . Empire . . . World War . . . Treaty . . . 1923. Seventeen . . . alphabet . . . government . . . two-house legislature . . . state

FLASH FOCUS

When you complete Unit IV, you should be able to:

✓ Understand how choosing the right words can make your writing clearer and more expressive

✓ Understand how to use appropriate language in your writing

✓ Understand how to distinguish between similar sounding words

"The beautiful part of writing is that you don't have to get it right the first time, unlike say, a brain surgeon. You can always do it better, find the exact word, the apt phrase, the leaping simile."

—Robert Cormier

"Slang is a language that rolls up its sleeves, spits on its hands, and goes to work."

—Carl Sandburg

"I would hurl words into the darkness and wait for an echo. If an echo sounded, no matter how faintly, I would send other words to tell, to march, to fight."

—Richard Wright

FLASH TEST

Before you begin studying the sections in Unit IV, take the diagnostic test on word choice to test your knowledge. If you answer eight or more questions incorrectly, be sure to note where you need extra help or explanation, and pay close attention to those particular sections in Unit IV.

DIAGNOSTIC TEST: WORD CHOICE

To be correct, the boldfaced expression must be standard, formal English and must not be sexist or otherwise discriminatory.

Write **C** if the boldfaced word is used **correctly.**

Write **X** if it is used **incorrectly.**

EXAMPLES:	The counsel's **advice** was misinterpreted.	C
	They **could of** made the plane except for the traffic.	X

1. Her car is different **than** mine. 1. _____

2. I'm not sick; I'm **alright.** 2. _____

3. The plane began its **descent** for Denver. 3. _____

4. Economic problems always **impact** our enrollment. 4. _____

5. My glasses **lay** where I had put them. 5. _____

6. We didn't play **good** in the last quarter. 6. _____

7. I selected a **nice** birthday card. 7. _____

8. The float **preceded** the band in the parade. 8. _____

9. No one predicted the **affects** of the bomb. 9. _____

10. My aunt always uses unusual **stationery.**

11. I dislike **those kind** of cookies.

12. We are going to **canvas** the school district for the scholarship fund.

13. The computer **sits** on a small table.

14. College men and **girls** are warned not to drink and drive.

15. The **principal** spoke to the students.

16. I **had ought** to learn to use that software.

17. He made **less** mistakes than I did.

18. The family **better** repair the furnace.

19. The package had **burst** open.

20. Mrs. Grundy **censured** so much of the play that it was unintelligible.

21. We are taught to consider the feelings of our **fellow man.**

22. **Irregardless** of the warning, I drove in the dense fog.

23. The next **thing** in my argument concerns my opponent's honesty.

24. The new carpet **complements** the living room furniture.

25. A different **individual** will have to chair the service project.

26. I **ought to of** made the flight arrangements.

27. **Numerical statistical figures** show that an asteroid may collide with Earth.

28. **Due to the fact that** it rained, the game was canceled.

29. **That sort of** person is out of place in this salon.

30. The water was dull **gray in color.**

10. _____
11. _____
12. _____
13. _____
14. _____
15. _____
16. _____
17. _____
18. _____
19. _____
20. _____
21. _____
22. _____
23. _____
24. _____
25. _____
26. _____
27. _____
28. _____
29. _____
30. _____

Answers to Diagnostic Test for: Word Choice

1. X	7. X	13. C	19. C	25. X
2. X	8. C	14. X	20. X	26. X
3. C	9. X	15. C	21. X	27. X
4. X	10. C	16. X	22. X	28. X
5. C	11. X	17. X	23. X	29. C
6. X	12. X	18. X	24. C	30. X

 FLASH SUMMARY

The clarity, style, and tone of your writing, and its acceptance by your audience, depend largely on your choice of words.

70. Be Concise, Clear, and Original

A large vocabulary is an asset, but using too many "big words" can weaken your writing. Use words not to impress but to convey meaning accurately, clearly, and concisely, and with originality.

A. Cut Needless Words.

(1) Redundancy (needless repetition) in general:

WORDY: *In* the first chapter *of the book, for all intents and purposes, it* sets the scene *for the future* events to come *in the book. In my opinion, I think that* the *large* purple mansion, garish *in color,* is an *absolutely* perfect setting for mysterious *happenings and occurrences.*

CONCISE: The first chapter sets the scene. The garish purple mansion is a perfect setting for mysterious events to come.

CAUTION: Not all repetition is redundancy. Sometimes you must repeat for clarity or emphasis.

UNCLEAR: The three computer programs contained several innovations. The first attracted the most attention. [first program or first innovation?]

CLEAR: The three computer programs contained several innovations. The first program attracted the most attention.

ESL *(2) Double negatives, double subjects, and double **that**:*

They *had* (not *hadn't*) hardly enough for survival. [*Hardly, barely,* and *scarcely* mean *almost not* and thus act as negatives.]

After the trial the lawyer congratulated us.

The editorial claimed *that*, despite the nationwide decrease in crime, our city was unsafe.

B. **Purge Overblown Diction.** Use plain, direct wording. It is generally clearer and carries more force than elaborate language. Avoid filling your writing with words ending in *-ion, -ity, -ment,* or *-ize,* such as *situation* or *utilize.* Examples:

Overblown	*Concise*
crisis situation	crisis
make a decision	decide
underwent a conversion	converted
determine the veracity of	verify
attain the lunar surface	reach the moon
utilize the emergency audible warning system	press the alarm button

OVERBLOWN AND OBSCURE: Implementation of federally mandated reorganization procedures within designated departments, with the objective of downsizing, is anticipated in the near future. It is the company's intention to attempt the consequent organizational framework adjustments with minimal negative impact upon company personnel.

CONCISE AND CLEAR: Our company must soon begin federally ordered cutbacks in some departments, but we intend to do so with the fewest layoffs possible. [This version gains force also by using active voice *(we intend)* instead of passive *(is anticipated)*. See section 15B, pages 45–46.]

Gear your vocabulary to your intended audience. Do not talk down to them, but do not talk over their heads either. Avoid *jargon* (technical or other terms unknown to most general readers, such as *multi-modality approach to ESL*) unless your audience are specialists in the subject. If you must use such a term, define it in parentheses following its first use.

Here are some common expressions that can be pared down:

Redundant, Wordy, or Overblown	*Concise*
absolutely perfect, **very** unique	perfect, unique [see section 17B, page 59]
maintenance **activity**	maintenance
actual fact, true fact	fact
and etc.	etc. [see section 71, page 181]
Where is the car **at**?	Where is the car?

at this (that) point in time	now (then)
on the **basis of** this report	from this report
but yet, but however	but *or* yet *or* however
each and every	*use only one:* each *or* every
in the **event that**	if
residential **facility**	residential building, home
the **fact that** she had no cash; **due to the fact that** he knew; **except for the fact that it** was void	her lack of cash; because he knew; except that it was void
take the rainfall **factor** into consideration	consider rainfall
general consensus of opinion	consensus
generally (*or* **usually**) always	always *or* generally *or* usually
that **kind** (*or* **sort**) **of a** man	that kind (*or* sort) of man
jumped **off of** the wall	jumped off the wall
continue **on**	(*usually*) continue
Meet me **outside of** the house.	Meet me outside the house.
Their romance is **over with.**	Their romance is over.
the registration **procedure,** the education **process**	registration, education
for the **purpose of** studying	to study; for studying
The **reason** they died **was because** no help came.	They died because no help came.
They know the **reason why** he lied.	They know why he lied.
refer back to	refer to
in (with) regard(s) to this matter	about (*or* concerning) this matter
round **in shape;** blue **in color;** 6′11″ tall **in height**	round; blue; 6′11″ tall
The crime **situation** is improving.	Crime is down.
My financial **situation** is very poor.	I have little money.
connect **up;** road ends **up;** climb **up;** meet **up with**	connect; ends; climb; meet
She got good **usage** from her car. She **utilized** her cell phone to call home.	good use; used her cell phone. Usage *means "customary use," as in* English usage. Utilize *is for special uses:* Ground-up glass is utilized for paving.

C. **Be Specific.** A **general** term covers a wide grouping: *disease, music, science.* A **specific** term singles out one of that grouping: *malaria, "Old Man River," archaeology.* (Of course, there may be intermediate terms: music ➔ song ➔ show tune ➔ "Old Man River.")

Sometimes you must generalize, as in topic and summary sentences:

The nation has seen urban crime decrease markedly.

But to avoid vagueness, you need, in accompanying sentences, specifics that will support your generalization:

Murder is down by half and rape by twenty percent.

(See section 75B, pages 201–204, for examples in paragraphs.) Be as specific as your context allows: a *reddish purple* (not *colorful*) sunset; *two dozen* (not *many*) onlookers; his *dazzling whirls and leaps* (not his *fine dancing*).

General or Vague	*More Specific*
many, a number of, some, a lot of	more than 100, about forty thousand, fewer than twenty, nearly half . . .
thing	item, detail, article, idea, deed, quality, event, incident, point (*for* thing she said), foods (*for* things to eat), sights (*for* things to see) . . .
fine, nice, wonderful, great	sunny, friendly, considerate, record-setting, inspiring

D. **Use Fresh, Original Wording.**

(1) *Avoid trite, overused expressions (clichés),* such as *last but not least,* which bore readers and signal your lack of originality. Be suspicious of expressions that pop too readily into your mind—they may well be clichés. Watch also for words you tend to use too often, such as *very* (try *quite, rather,* or *extremely;* or better, specify a degree: not *very cold* but *so cold that our eyelids froze*).

Some Common Clichés to Avoid

add insult to injury	my mind was a blank
better late than never	quick as a wink
between a rock and a hard place	raining cats and dogs
down but not out	soft as silk
easier said than done	time flew by
hungry as a horse	tried and true
in this day and age	water under the bridge

(2) *Use imaginative language.* For originality, create some imaginative comparisons—**similes** and **metaphors:**

SIMILE (uses *like* or *as*): Earning a Ph.D. is *like climbing Everest barefoot.*

METAPHOR: The subway train, *a red-eyed dragon,* roared into the station.

E. **Consider Connotation.** *Thrifty, frugal, stingy,* and *parsimonious* all refer to holding on to one's money, but each has a different **connotation,** or implied meaning: you would convey a negative rather than a positive connotation if you used *parsimonious* instead of *thrifty.*

71. Maintain the Appropriate Language Level

Some words and expressions are considered unsuitable for formal writing (such as a research paper) and speaking (such as a graduation address).
Among these are

✓ **Colloquialisms** (used only in informal, casual conversation or writing intending a casual tone). Included among colloquialisms are shortened forms of words, such as *exam, prof, chem, ID* (for *identification*):

COLLOQUIAL (**INFORMAL**): The chem prof ID's everyone before the exam.

FORMAL: The chemistry professor checks everyone's identification before the examination.

✓ **Regionalisms** and **dialect words** (known only within certain geographic areas or population groups): *pop* (for *soda*), *leastways*, thanks *a heap*.

✓ **Slang** (used only among certain social groups, such as teenagers). Most slang fades fast, and thus may be unknown to many readers. Who today refers to a *gat* or a *schmo*?

SLANG: He must have paid *mad benjamins* for a *crib* like that.

STANDARD: He must have paid *plenty of money* for a *house* like that.

✓ **Nonstandard** (ungrammatical) expressions (always to be avoided): *ain't got no money*

Note: The lines separating colloquial, slang, and nonstandard expressions are sometimes blurry: authorities may differ, or words may over time slide up or down the acceptability scale. Moreover, there is no sharp line dividing formal and informal: the *New York Times's* sports pages are less formal than a scholarly journal article. Consider the following list as guidelines rather than ironclad rules.

Common Expressions Not Suitable in Formal Writing

[Most are colloquial. Regionalisms are labeled (R), nonstandard terms (N).]

alright. Say *all right.*

red **and/or** green. (Acceptable in legal and business writing but not in general formal writing; also sometimes unclear.) Say *green, red,* or *both.*

anyways, anywheres, everywheres, nowheres, somewheres (N). Say *anyway* or *any way, anywhere, everywhere. . . .*

aren't I. Say *am I not.*

awful. Say *quite bad, ugly, shocking. . . .*

awful(ly) good. Say *quite, very, extremely.* See section 16A, page 56.

want it **badly.** Say *greatly, very much.*

being as (how), being that. Say *because, since.*

you **better** do it. Say *you had better, you'd better.*

between you and I, for him and I. . . . After a preposition say *you and me, him and me.* See section 19C, page 63–64.

a **bunch** of people. Say *group, crowd.*

I **bust, busted, bursted** balloons (N). Say *I burst balloons* (present and past), *I have burst balloons.*

He had no doubt **but that (but what)** she knew it. Say *He had no doubt that.*

can't hardly (scarcely, barely). Say *can hardly, scarcely, barely.* See section 70A(2), page 177.

can't help but love you. Say *can't help loving you.*

Contact me tomorrow. Say *Call, See, E-mail.* . . . (Some authorities do accept the verb *contact* in formal usage, to mean "get in touch with." *Contact* as a noun is acceptable formally.)

cop(s). Say *police officer, police.*

could of, may of, might of, must of, should of, would of, ought to of (N). Say *could have, may have, might have* . . . or, informally, *could've, may've, might've.* . . .

a couple of friends, days, problems. . . . Say *two friends, three days, several problems.* . . . Save *couple* for a joined pair, such as *an engaged couple.*

Due to the time, we left. Say *Because of the time.* . . . (*Due to* is acceptable after *be* or *seem: The delay was due to* rain. See section 70B, page 178.)

He **enthused (was enthused)** about it. Say *He was enthusiastic about it.*

reading Baldwin, Walker, **etc.** In paragraph writing, say *and others* or *and so forth,* or say *reading writers such as Baldwin and Walker.*

every bit as old as. Say *just as old as.*

every so often, every once in a while. Say *occasionally, from time to time.*

every which way. Say *every way.*

She has a **funny** accent. Say *peculiar, odd.*

If I **had of** known (N). Say *had known.*

He **had ought** to go (N). Say *He ought to.*

a half a page. Say *a half page, half a page.*

They **have got** the answer. Say *have the answer.*

hisself, ourselfs, yourselfs, themself(s), theirself(s), theirselves (N). Say *himself, ourselves, yourselves, themselves.*

Hopefully, the bus will come. Say *We hope the bus will come.* (Strictly, *hopefully* means "full of hope." The bus is not full of hope.)

if and when I go. Generally, say either *if I go* or *when I go.*

Sinatra's music **impacted (on)** three generations. Say *greatly affected, influenced, brought happiness to.* . . . *Impact* as a noun (a great *impact*) is acceptable.

irregardless (N). Say *regardless.*

is when, is where. See section 27E, page 95.

It being late, we left. Say *Since it was* or *Because it was.* See section 26A, page XX.

kid(s). Say *child(ren).*

kind of (sort of) soft. Say *rather soft, somewhat soft,* or just *soft.*

a lot (often misspelled *alot*) **of, lots of.** Say *much, many;* better, say *fifty* or *dozens of.* See section 70C, page 179.

mad at you. Say *angry with you. Mad* means "insane."

most all the books. Say *almost all.*

nowhere near ready. Say *not nearly* ready.

O.K., OK, okay. Say *all right, correct* (adj.); *approval* (noun); *approve* (verb).

everyone **outside of** John. Say *except John.*

plan on going. Say *plan to go.*

plenty good. Say *quite good.* (*Plenty* is acceptable as a noun: *plenty* of fish.)

I'm going, **plus** Nan. He felt sick; **plus,** he had no money. Say *Nan and I are going. He felt sick; besides (also, moreover), he had no money.*

a **pretty** sum; a **pretty** long ride. Say *a very large sum, a fairly long ride.*

real good, **real** smooth. Say *very, quite.*

They were **right** tired (R). They went **right** home. Say *quite* tired, *directly* home.

seeing as how, seeing that. Say *since, because.*

It **seldom ever** changed. Say *seldom or never, seldom if ever, hardly ever.*

in bad **shape.** Say *in poor condition.*

They were **so** happy. Say *They were so happy that they wept.* See section 27C, page 94.

She ran **so** she could stay fit. Say *so that she could.*

The bill was vague, **so** the President vetoed it. (Frequently joining independent clauses with *so* gives your writing an informal tone. Try recasting the sentence: The President vetoed the bill *because* it was vague.)

Woods is **some** golfer! He worried **some.** Say *Woods is quite a golfer! He worried somewhat* or *a little.*

It was **such** a loud noise. There is **no such a** place. Say *such a loud noise that her ears hurt* [see section 27C, page 94]. *There is no such place.*

This would **sure** help. Say *surely help.* See section 16A, page 56.

terribly sad, a **terrific** win. Say *extremely sad, a last-minute win, an exciting win.*

them weapons (N). Say *those weapons.*

these kind (sort, type), those kind. Say *this kind, that kind, this sort, that type.* (*Kind, type,* and *sort* are singular; they must take singular modifiers. For plurals, say *these kinds, those types,* etc.)

this (these) here, that (those) there (N). Say *this, that, these, those.*

Try and win. Be **sure and** vote. Say *Try to win. Be sure to vote.*

It was **very** appreciated. Say *very much, greatly.*

She **waited on** a bus (R). Say *waited for.* But *She waited on* (served) *the mayor's table.*

Jones read in the newspaper **where** Smith had died (N). Say *that Smith had died.*

If *Seinfeld* **would have** continued, it **would have** stayed popular (N). See section 14B(7), page 44.

Keep your language level consistent within a paper. Determine the right tone for each of your writings from its nature (research paper, informal essay, chatty letter), its purpose (to amuse, to arouse to action, to stimulate thought), and its intended audience. Be especially alert for colloquial expressions creeping into your formal papers.

72. Use Nondiscriminatory Terms

 A. **Nonsexist Terms.** A word or expression is considered sexist if it wrongly excludes, diminishes, or denigrates the role of one sex (usually women) in its context: *A buyer should shop around for the car he wants. The mailman is here.* [Women too buy cars and deliver mail.] *They sent a lady plumber.* [*Lady* seems to imply that women are not expected to be plumbers or that they are not good ones.] You can avoid sexist usage as follows:

(1) *Pronouns.* The traditional use of *he, his,* and *him* in contexts applicable to both sexes (*Every student needs his calculator*) is now widely regarded as sexist. Substituting for these pronouns may present a problem, however, because English lacks common-gender equivalents. Try either of the following solutions, taking care to preserve clarity and consistency with context:

✓ *Shift to the plural where possible:* Buyers should shop around for the cars *they* want. All *students* need *their* calculators.

✓ *Remove gender where possible:* Shopping around for a car will ensure a good buy. Student calculators are required. A worker's attitude affects job performance.

Other solutions are less satisfactory. Using *he or she, his or her, her or him* (Every student needs *his or her* calculator) sounds clumsy after a number of repetitions. Substituting *you* or *your* (in that class *you* need a calculator) is colloquial. Using *they, their, them* with a singular noun (Every *student* needs *their* calculator), although common colloquially, is generally not accepted in formal English.

> **(2) Nouns.** Where both sexes are or may be included, replace single-sex nouns with gender-neutral ones:

Single-sex	Inclusive
mankind	humankind
seaman	sailor
policeman	(police) officer
mailman	mail carrier
fireman	firefighter
repairman	repairer
housewife	homemaker
waitress	server
the average man	the average person

Use *ladies* only as a parallel to *gentlemen.* Omit *lady* or (generally) *woman* before *pilot, engineer,* and the like. Refer to females sixteen and older as *(young) women,* not *girls.* Avoid expressions that put women in a lower category, such as *farmers and their wives* [the wives work the farm too; say just *farmers* or *farm families*], *man and wife* [say *husband and wife*].

B. Other Nondiscriminatory Terms

> **(1) Ethnic, racial, religious.** Avoid ethnic stereotypes and negative terms such as *wetback, half-breed, redneck, culturally deprived.* Avoid terms that place Europe at the center of the world (say *East Asian,* not *Far Eastern* [that is, far east of Europe] or *Oriental*) or that cast one race as dominant: *nonwhite* may imply that white is the racial standard; *flesh-colored*—meaning white flesh—ignores most of the world; words that equate black with bad *(a black mark, blacklist)* imply African American racial inferiority. Call racial, national, ethnic, and religious groups by the names they prefer: *African Americans, American Indians* (or *Native Americans*), *Inuit* (for *Eskimos*). Omit hyphens in terms such as *Italian American* and *Chinese American.* Do not label a religion a cult; say *house of worship,* not *church* (unless referring specifically to Christians).

> **(2) Disabilities.** Avoid calling persons with disabilities *crippled, deformed,* or the like; focus on the person, not the impairment: *a wheelchair user,* not *an amputee; a person with a mental disorder,* not *a mental case.*

73. Distinguish Between Similar Words

Below are sets of two (or more) words that may cause confusion because of their similar appearance, sound, spelling, or meaning.

a, an. See section 16E(1), page 57.

accept, except. *Accept* (verb) means "to receive": The Grateful Dead *accepted* the Grammy Award.
> *Except* (usually preposition) means "excluding": Peace prevailed in all Europe *except* the Balkans.

Note: *Except* is occasionally a verb, meaning "to exclude": The judge told the lawyers to *except* the disputed testimony from their summation.

adapt, adopt. *Adapt* means "to adjust or make suitable": She *adapted* her office to accommodate computers.

Adopt means "to take as one's own": She *adopted* the jargon of computer hackers. They *adopted* a girl.

advice, advise. *Advice* (noun) means "counsel": I was skeptical of the salesperson's *advice*.

Advise (verb) means "to give advice": The salesperson *advised* me to buy the larger size.

affect, effect. Most commonly, *affect* (verb) means "to have an effect on": Mostly, the disease *affected* poor people.

Most commonly, *effect* (noun) means "a result, consequence, outcome": The disease had a devastating *effect* on the poor.

Note: Less commonly, *affect* (as a verb) means "to pretend or imitate": He *affected* a British accent. *Effect* (as a verb) means "to accomplish, to bring about": The medicine *effected* a cure.

afterward, afterwards. Use either; be consistent.

aisle, isle. An *aisle* is a passage between rows of seats: the side *aisle*.

An *isle* is an island: the Emerald *Isle*.

all ready, already. *All ready* means "fully ready": the runner was *all* [fully] *ready* for the marathon.

Already means "previously" or "by this time": Karl had *already* crossed the finish line.

all together, altogether. *All together* means "in a group": We were *all together* at the reunion.

Altogether means "wholly, completely": Custer was *altogether* surprised at Little Big Horn.

allusion, illusion, delusion. *Allusion* means "an indirect reference": The play has many Biblical *allusions*.

Illusion means "a temporary false perception or a magic trick": It was an optical *illusion*.

Delusion refers to a lasting false perception or belief about oneself or other persons or things: He had the *delusion* of expecting success without effort.

among. See *between*.

amoral, immoral. *Amoral* means "not concerned with morality": An infant's acts are *amoral*.

Immoral means "against morality": Murder is *immoral*.

amount, number. *Amount* refers to things in bulk or mass: a large *amount* of grain; no *amount* of persuasion.

Number refers to countable objects: a *number* of books.

ante-, anti-. Both are prefixes. *Ante-* means "before": *anteroom, antedate, antecedent*. *Anti-* means "against": *antibody, antisocial, antidote*.

anxious, eager. *Anxious* conveys worry or unease: Forecasters grew *anxious* about the oncoming storm.

Eager conveys strong desire: They were *eager* to marry.

any more, anymore. *Any more* means "additional": Is there *any more* fuel? There isn't *any more*.

Anymore means "at present" or "any longer": He doesn't write home *anymore*.

any one, anyone. *Any one* refers to any single item of a number of items: You may take *any one* of these courses.

> *Anyone* means "any person": Has *anyone* here seen Kelly?

apt, likely, liable. *Apt* refers to probability based on normal, habitual, or customary tendency: He was *apt* to throw things when frustrated.

> *Likely* indicates mere probability: It is *likely* to rain.
>
> *Liable,* strictly, refers to legal responsibility: Jaywalkers are *liable* to arrest. Informally, it is used also with any undesirable or undesired risk: He's *liable* to get into trouble.

as, because, since. For expressing cause, *because* is most precise; *since* and *as* may ambiguously convey either time or cause: *Since* he's been put in charge, three people have quit.

Note: Although many schoolchildren have been told never to begin a sentence with *because,* it is quite all right to do so—as long as you avoid a fragment.

as, like. See *like.*

awhile, a while. Do not use the adverb *awhile* after *for* or *in.* One may stay *awhile* (adverb), stay *a while* (noun), stay for a *while* (noun), but not for *awhile* (adverb).

bad, badly. See section 16C, page 57.

because. See *as, because, since.*

beside, besides. *Beside* (preposition) means "at the side of": My lawyer stood *beside* me [at my side] in court.

> *Besides* (preposition, conjunctive adverb) means "other than" or "in addition (to)": *Besides me,* only my lawyer knew. My lawyer is clever; *besides,* she is experienced.

between, among. *Between* implies *two* persons or things in a relationship; *among* implies *three* or more: Emissaries shuttled *between* London and Moscow. A dispute arose *among* the four nations.

born, borne. Use *born* (with *be*) only to mean "have one's birth": They *were born* [had their birth] in Brazil.

> Use *borne* before *by* and elsewhere: The baby was *borne by* a surrogate mother. She has *borne* two sons. Zullo has *borne* the burdens of office well.

brake, break. *Brake* refers to stopping: Apply the *brake. Brake* the car carefully.

> *Break* refers to destroying, damaging, exceeding, or interrupting: Don't *break* the glass. I'll *break* the record. Take a ten-minute *break.*

bring, take. In precise usage, *bring* means "to come (here) with," and *take* means "to go (there) with": *Take* this check to the bank, and *bring* back the cash.

can, may. In formal usage, *can* means "to be able to" (They *can* solve any equation), and *may* means "to have permission to" (You *may* leave now). *May* also expresses possibility: It *may* snow tonight.

canvas, canvass. A *canvas* is a cloth: Buy a *canvas* tent. *Canvass* means "to solicit": *Canvass* the area for votes.

capitol, capital. Use *capitol* for the building where a legislature meets: The governor's office is in the *capitol.*

> Elsewhere, use *capital:* Topeka is the state *capital* [seat of government]. The firm has little *capital* [money]. It was a *capital* [first-rate] idea.

Murder can be a *capital* offense [one punishable by death].

carat, caret, carrot. Gold and gems are weighed in *carats.*

A *caret* (^) signals an omission: I ^ going home.

A *carrot* is a vegetable: Eat your *carrots.*

casual, causal. *Casual* means "occurring by chance, informal, unplanned"; *causal* means "involving cause."

censor, censure. To *censor* is to examine written, visual, recorded, or broadcast material to delete objectionable content: Many parents want to *censor* violent television shows.

To *censure* is to criticize or blame: The senator was *censured* for unethical conduct.

cite, site, sight. *Cite* means "to quote an authority or give an example": Did you *cite* all your sources in the paper?

Site means "location": Here is the new building *site*.

Sight refers to seeing: The ship's lookout *sighted* land. Use your *sight* and hearing.

classic, classical. *Classic* means "of the highest class or quality": *Hamlet* is a *classic* play.

Classical means "pertaining to the art and life of ancient Greece and Rome": *Classical* Greek art idealized the human figure. *Classical* music refers to symphonies and the like.

coarse, course. *Coarse* means "rough, not fine": *coarse* wool.

A *course* is a path or a series of lessons: race *course*, art *course*.

compare to, compare with. *Compare to* means "to liken, to point out one or more similarities": Earning a Ph.D. has been *compared to* climbing Everest barefoot.

Compare with means "to examine to determine similarities and differences": The report *compares* United States medical care *with* that of Canada.

compliment, complement. *Compliment* means "to express praise": The dean *complimented* Harris on her speech.

Complement means "to complete, enhance, or bring to perfection": The illustrations should *complement* the text.

The nouns *compliment* and *complement* are distinguished similarly. Free tickets are *complimentary*.

comprise, compose, include. Strictly, *comprise* means "to be made up of (in entirety)": Our university *comprises* eight colleges.

Compose means "to make up, to constitute": Eight colleges *compose* our university. Our university is *composed* of eight colleges.

Include means "to contain (but not necessarily in entirety)": Our university *includes* colleges of business and pharmacy.

continual, continuous. *Continual* means "frequently repeated": She worked in spite of *continual* interruptions.

Continuous means "without interruption": The explorers could hear the *continuous* roar of the falls.

convince, persuade. *Convince* emphasizes changing a person's belief: *Convince* me of your sincerity.

Persuade emphasizes moving a person to action: The activist *persuaded* bystanders to join the protest.

correspond to, correspond with. *Correspond to* means "to be similar or analogous to": The German gymnasium *corresponds to* the American prep school.

Correspond with means "to be in agreement or conformity with": His behavior did not *correspond with* our rules. It also means "to communicate with by exchange of letters."

council, counsel, consul. *Council* means "a deliberative assembly": The Parish *Council* debated the issue.

Counsel (noun) means "advice" or "attorney": He sought the *counsel* of a psychologist. She is the *counsel* for the defense.

Counsel (verb) means "to advise": They *counseled* us to wait before marrying. *Consul* means "an officer in the foreign service": The distinguished guest was the *consul* from Spain.

credible, credulous, creditable. *Credible* means "believable": A witness's testimony must be *credible*.

Credulous means "too ready to believe; gullible": A *credulous* person is easily duped.

Creditable means "praiseworthy": The young pianist gave a *creditable* performance of a difficult work.

decent, descent. *Decent* means "proper, right": This is not a *decent* film for children. *Descent* means "a going down" or "ancestry": The plane's *descent* was bumpy. He's of Guyanese *descent*.

delusion. See *allusion*.

device, devise. A *device* (noun) is an invention or a piece of equipment: This *device* turns the lights on at dusk.

To *devise* (verb) is to invent: *Devise* a new mousetrap.

different from, different than. Formal usage requires *different from*: His paper is hardly *different from* yours.
Note: *Different than* is gaining acceptance when introducing a clause: The scores were *different than* we expected (smoother than *different from what*).

differ from, differ with. *Differ from* expresses unlikeness: His paper *differs* greatly *from* mine.

Differ with expresses divergence of opinion: The President *differed with* Congress regarding welfare.

disinterested, uninterested. *Disinterested* means "not influenced by personal interest; impartial, unbiased": A *disinterested* judge gives fair rulings.

Uninterested means simply "not interested": The *uninterested* judge dozed on the bench.

dived, dove. *Dived* is the preferred past tense and past participle of *dive*: The pelicans dived (not *dove*) into the sea.

each other, one another. *Each other* refers to *two* persons or things; *one another*, to *three or more*.

eager. See *anxious*.

effect. See *affect*.

emigrate, immigrate. *Emigrate* means "to leave a country"; *immigrate* means "to enter a new country": Millions *emigrated* from Europe. They *immigrated* to America.

eminent, imminent. *Eminent* means "distinguished": She's an *eminent* surgeon. *Imminent* means "about to happen": Rain is *imminent*.

ensure, insure. *Ensure* is preferred for "make sure, guarantee": to *ensure* your safety, wear seat belts.

Insure refers to insurance (protection against loss): *Insure* your valuables.

envelop, envelope. To *envelop* is to surround: Fog *envelops* us.
An *envelope* holds a letter: Seal the *envelope*.

every one, everyone. Use *everyone* wherever you can substitute *everybody*: *Everyone* (*everybody*) left early.

Elsewhere, use *every one* (usually followed by *of*): *Every one* of the flights was delayed.

except. See *accept*.

famous, notable, notorious. *Famous* means "widely known": it usually has favorable connotations.

> *Notable* means "worthy of note" or "prominent"; a person can be *notable* without being *famous*.
>
> *Notorious* means "widely known in an unfavorable way": Jesse James was a *notorious* bandit.

farther, further. *Farther* refers to physical distance: Roadblocks kept the troops from going *farther.*

> *Further* means "to a greater extent or degree": The UN decided to discuss the issue *further.*

fewer, less. *Fewer* refers to number; use it with countable things: *Fewer* lakes are polluted these days.

> Use *less* with things that are not countable but are considered in bulk or mass: *Less* wheat grew this year.

formally, formerly. *Formally* means "according to proper form": Introduce us *formally.*

> *Formerly* means "previously": They *formerly* lived here.

former, latter; first, last. *Former* and *latter* refer to the first and second named of only two items: Concerning jazz and rock, she prefers the *former* [jazz], but he prefers the *latter* [rock]. In a series of three or more, use *first* and *last.*

forth, fourth. *Forth* means "forward": Go *forth* and conquer. *Fourth* is 4th: They paraded on the *Fourth* of July.

good, well. See section 16C, page 57.

hanged, hung. Strict usage requires *hanged* when you mean "executed": She was *hanged* as a spy.

> Elsewhere, use *hung.* They *hung* the flag high.

healthy, healthful. *Healthy* means "possessing health": The children are *healthy.*
Healthful means "conducive to health": Bran is *healthful.*

historic, historical. Strictly, *historic* means "famous or important in history": July 4, 1776, is an *historic* date.

> *Historical* means "pertaining to history": Good *historical* novels immerse us in their times.

if, whether. When presenting alternatives, use *whether* for precision: Tell us *whether* (not *if*) you pass or fail. Also, drop an unneeded *or not* after *whether:* He was unsure *whether* or not to go.

illusion. See *allusion.*

immigrate. See *emigrate.*

imminent. See *eminent.*

immoral. See *amoral.*

imply, infer. Writers or speakers *imply* (state indirectly or suggest): The union's statement *implied* that the management was lying.

> Readers or listeners *infer* (draw a conclusion or derive by reasoning): From these data we *infer* that a recession is near.

in, into. Use *into* with movement from outside to inside: The nurse ran *into* Wilcox's room.

> Elsewhere, use *in:* Wilcox lay quietly *in* his bed.

include. See *comprise.*

incredible, incredulous. A fact or happening is *incredible* (unbelievable): Astronomical distances are *incredible.*

A person is *incredulous* (unbelieving): He was *incredulous* when told how far the Milky Way extends.

individual, person, party. Do not use *party* or *individual* when you mean simply *person*: They heard from a certain *person* (not *individual* or *party*) that she was engaged. Except in legal and telephone-company usage, and when you mean "one taking part," do not use *party* to refer to one person.

Use *individual* only when emphasizing a person's singleness: Will you act with the group or as an *individual?*

ingenious, ingenuous. *Ingenious* means "clever"; *ingenuous* means "naive, having childlike frankness": *Ingenious* swindlers forged a deed to the Brooklyn Bridge and sold it to an *ingenuous* out-of-towner.

instance, instants, instant's. *Instance* means "a case or example": She noted each *instance* of violence. [plural: *instances*]

Instants is the plural of *instant*, meaning "a brief time, a particular moment": She did it in a few *instants*.

Instant's is the possessive of *instant*: They came at an *instant's* notice.

insure. See *ensure*.

isle. See *aisle*.

its, it's. *Its* is the possessive of *it*: The dog wagged *its* tail.

It's is the contraction of *it is*. Use *it's* only if you can correctly substitute *it is* in your sentence: *It's* (*it is*) ready.

last, latter. See *former*.

later, latter. *Later*, the comparative form of *late*, means "more late."

For *latter*, see *former*.

lay. See *lie*.

lead, led. *Lead* (rhymes with *need*) is the present tense of the verb meaning "to conduct, to go at the head of, to show the way": Browne can *lead* us to prosperity.

Led is the past tense and past participle of the same verb: Browne (has) *led* us to prosperity.

Lead (rhymes with *dead*) is a metal: I need a *lead* pipe.

learn, teach. *Learn* means "to acquire knowledge": Toddlers must *learn* not to touch electrical outlets.

Teach means "to impart knowledge": Parents must *teach* toddlers not to touch electrical outlets.

leave, let. *Leave* means "to depart": I must *leave* now.

Let means "to permit": *Let* me go.

less. See *fewer*.

lessen, lesson. To *lessen* is to diminish: His pain *lessened*.

A *lesson* is a unit of learning: Study your *lesson*.

liable, likely. See *apt*.

lie, lay. *Lie* means "to rest" and is an intransitive verb (it never takes an object): Don't *lie* on the new couch. The islands *lie* under the tropical sun. Here *lies* Jeremiah Todd.

Lay means "to put, to place" and is a transitive verb (it must take an object): *Lay* your *head* on this pillow. Let me *lay* your *fears* to rest.

To complicate matters, the past tense of *lie* is spelled and pronounced the same as the present tense of *lay*:

Yesterday Sandra *lay* [*rested*] too long in the sun. She should not have *lain* [*rested*] there so long. Yesterday the workers *laid* [*placed*] the foundation. They have *laid* [*placed*] it well.

Present	Past	Past Participle
lie [rest]	lay [rested]	(has) lain [rested]
lay [place]	laid [placed]	(has) laid [placed]

like, as. In formal English, do not use *like* (preposition) where *as* (conjunction) sounds right: The old house had remained just *as* (not *like*) I remembered it. It happened just *as* (not *like*) [it did] in the novel. Act *as if* (not *like*) you belong here.

loose, lose. *Loose* (usually adjective—rhymes with *goose*) is the opposite of *tight* or *confined*: The *loose* knot came undone. The lions are *loose!*
    Loose is also sometimes a verb: *Loose* my bonds.
    Lose (verb—rhymes with *news*) is the opposite of *find* or *win*: Did you *lose* your keys? We may *lose* the battle.

may. See *can*.

maybe, may be. *Maybe* is an adverb meaning "perhaps": *Maybe* Professor Singh will be absent. Do not confuse it with the verb *may be*: He *may be* at a conference.

moral, morale. *Moral* (as an adjective) means "righteous, ethical": To pay his debts was a *moral* obligation.
    Moral (as a noun) means "a lesson or truth taught in a story": The *moral* of the story is that greed is wrong.
    Morale (noun) means "spirit": Our *morale* sagged.

notable, notorious. See *famous*.

number. See *amount*.

one another. See *each other*.

oral. See *verbal*.

party, person. See *individual*.

passed, past. *Passed* (verb) is from *pass*: I *passed* the test.
    Past (noun) means "a former time": Forget the *past*.
    Past (preposition) means "by, beyond": Walk *past* it.

percent, percentage. Use *percent* with a specific figure: 45 *percent*. Otherwise, use *percentage*: a small *percentage* of it.
Note: The *percentage* is singular: The *percentage* of deaths *is* small. A *percentage* is either singular or plural, depending on what follows: A *percentage* of the fruit *is* spoiled. A *percentage* of the men *are* here.

personal, personnel. *Personal* means "private": This is a *personal* matter, not a public one.
    Personnel are employees: Notify all *personnel*.

persuade. See *convince*.

practical, practicable. *Practical* means "useful, sensible, not theoretical"; *practicable* means "feasible, capable of being put into practice": *Practical* people with *practical* experience can produce a *practicable* plan.

precede, proceed. To *precede* is to come before: X *precedes* Y.
    Proceed means "to go forward": The parade *proceeded*.

presence, presents. *Presence* means "being present; attendance": Their *presence* at the ball was noted.
    Presents are gifts, such as birthday *presents*.

principle, principal. A *principle* is a rule or a truth (remember: *principLE* = *ruLE*):

The Ten Commandments are moral *principles*. Some mathematical *principles* are difficult.

Elsewhere, use *principal,* meaning "chief, chief part, chief person": All *principal* roads are closed. At 8 percent, your *principal* will earn $160 interest. The *principal* praised the students.

quiet, quite. *Quiet* means "not noisy": This motor is *quiet*.

Quite means "very, completely": I'm not *quite* ready.

raise, rise. *Raise, raised, raised* ("to lift; make come up") is a transitive verb (takes an object): They *raise tomatoes*. The teacher *raised* the *window*. *Raise* our *salaries!*

Rise, rose, risen ("to ascend") is an intransitive verb (never has an object): The sun is *rising*. Salaries *rose*.

respectfully, respectively. *Respectfully* means "in a manner showing respect": Act *respectfully* in church. *Respectfully* yours.

Respectively means "each in the order given": Use it only as a last resort in clarifying order:

WEAK: Brooks, McIntyre, and Black won the award in 1999, 2000, and 2001, *respectively*.

BETTER: Brooks won the award in 1999, McIntyre in 2000, and Black in 2001.

right, rite, write. *Right* means "correct": the *right* answer.

A *rite* is a ceremony, such as an initiation *rite*.

To *write* is to put words on paper: *Write* us from Hawaii.

sight, site. See *cite*.

since. See *as, because, since*.

sit, set. *Sit, sat, sat* is an intransitive verb (takes no object) meaning "to be seated": They *sat* on the floor.

Set, set, set is generally a transitive verb (needs an object) meaning "to put or place": She *set* her book on the desk. (*Set* is equivalent to *sit* only in regard to a hen's *setting* on her eggs.)

stationary, stationery. *Stationary* means "not moving; not movable": *Stationary* targets are easily hit.

Stationery is writing paper.

take. See *bring*.

teach. See *learn*.

than, then. *Than* (conjunction) is used in comparing: She was more fit *than* he [was]. See section 19C(4), page 64.

Then is an adverb meaning "at (or after) that time" or "in that case; therefore": They *then* replicated the study. The vote may be tied; *then* the chair must decide.

that. See *who*.

their, there, they're. *Their* is a possessive pronoun: The litigants arrived with *their* lawyers. *Their* faces were tense.

There is an adverb of place: Sit *there*. It is also an expletive (an introductory word): *There* is no hope.

They're is a contraction of *they are*: *They're* suing her.

threw, through. *Threw* is the past of *throw*. I *threw* the ball. For *through*, see next entry.

through, thorough, thought. *Through* means "from end to end or side to side of": *through* the tunnel.

Thorough means "complete, exact": a *thorough* search.

Thought refers to thinking: a clever *thought*.

to, too, two. *To* is a preposition: They drove *to* Miami. *To* also introduces an infinitive: They wanted *to* find work.

    Too is an adverb meaning "also" or "excessively": They took her *too*. He was *too* old to care. Do not use *too* for *very*: She didn't seem *very* (not *too*) happy.

    Two is a number: Take *two* of these pills.

toward, towards. Use either, but be consistent.

uninterested. See *disinterested*.

verbal, oral. Strictly, *verbal* means "expressed in words, either written or spoken": Many computer programs use pictorial instead of *verbal* commands. (For the grammatical term *verbal*, see section 14D, page 44.)

    Oral means "spoken": Give *oral*, not written, responses.

weak, week. *Weak* means "not strong": *weak* from the flu.

    A *week* is seven days.

weather, whether. *Weather* refers to rain, sunshine, and so forth.

    Whether introduces alternatives: *whether* they win or lose. See also *if, whether*.

well. See section 16C, pages 56–57.

whether. See *if, whether; weather*.

which. See *who*.

while, though, whereas. The basic meaning of *while* is "during the time that." Avoid using it to mean *and, but, though,* or *whereas*, especially if two times are involved: This test proved negative, *whereas* (or *though* or *but*, but not *while*) last month's was positive.

who, which, that. Use *who* to refer to persons; use *which* only for things; use *that* for persons or things: The player *who* (or *that*, but not *which*) scores lowest wins.

who, whom. See section 19D, E, pages 64–65.

whose, who's. *Who's* is a contraction of *who is*: *Who's* that?

    Whose is the possessive of *who*: *Whose* hat is this?

woman, women. *Woman*, like *man*, is singular: that *woman*.

    Women, like *men*, is plural: those *women*.

write. See *right, rite, write*.

your, you're. *Your* is the possessive of *you*: Wear *your* hat.

    You're is a contraction of *you are*: *You're* late.

FLASH TEST

PART 1

Rewrite each sentence in the space below it, **replacing** or **eliminating** all redundant, overblown, vague, or clichéd expressions. You may use a dictionary, and you may invent specifics if necessary.

EXAMPLES: We find our general consensus of opinion to be that the governor should resign.
        <u>Our consensus is that the governor should resign.</u>

        She looked really nice.
        <u>She wore jet-black jeans and a trim white blouse, and her broad smile would melt an iceberg.</u>

1. The director she believes that within a few months that she can increase profits by 25 percent.

2. As a small child of three years of age, I was allowed outside to play only during the hours from eight to eleven a.m. in the morning and from three to five p.m. in the afternoon.

3. Lady Macbeth returned back to the deadly murder scene to leave the daggers beside the grooms.

4. In the Bible it says that we should not make a judgment about others.

5. Except for the fact that my grandmother is on Medicaid, she would not be able to afford living in her very unique senior citizens' residential facility.

6. The deplorable condition of business is due to the nature of the current conditions relevant to the economic situation.

7. The thing in question at this point in time is whether the initial phase of the operation is proceeding with a sufficient degree of efficiency.

8. She jumped off of the wall and continued on down the lane so that she could meet up with me outside of my domicile.

9. The house was blue in color and octagonal in shape.

10. She couldn't hardly lose her way, due to the fact that the road was intensely illuminated.

FLASH TEST

PART 2

Write the number of the **correct** choice (use standard, formal English).

EXAMPLE: Lincoln had no doubt (1) **but that** (2) **that** the South would secede.   _____2_____

1. (1) **Irregardless** (2) **Regardless** of the weather, I plan to drive to Florida for the   1. _____
   weekend.

2. If Sam (1) **had** (2) **would have** attended class more often, he would have passed the course.

2. _____

3. (1) **Hopefully,** (2) **We hope that** the instructor will post our grades before we leave for the holidays.

3. _____

4. Juan used (1) **these kind of tools** (2) **these kinds of tools** to repair the roof.

4. _____

5. We were disappointed (1) **somewhat** (2) **some** at the poor quality of the color printer.

5. _____

6. We heard the same report (1) **everywhere** (2) **everywheres** we traveled.

6. _____

7. The tourists were not sure that it would be (1) **alright** (2) **all right** to travel to Great Britain this summer.

7. _____

8. Do (1) **try to** (2) **try and** spend the night with us when you are in town.

8. _____

9. The diplomat was (1) **most** (2) **almost** at the end of her patience.

9. _____

10. I (1) **had ought** (2) **ought** to have let her know the time of my arrival.

10. _____

FLASH TEST

PART 3

Each sentence contains a sexist or other discriminatory term. **Circle** that term. Then, in the blank, write a nondiscriminatory replacement. (If the circled term should be deleted without a replacement, leave the line empty.)

EXAMPLE: Every citizen must use his right to vote.
All citizens must use their

1. The male and girl students decided to form separate groups.

_____

2. Every student must bring his textbook to class.

_____

3. All policemen are expected to be in full uniform while on duty.

_____

4. Man's need to survive produces some surprising effects.

_____

5. The speaker asserted that every gal in his audience should make her husband assume more household responsibilities.

_____

6. The stewardess assured us that we would land in time for our connecting flight.

_____

7. The female truck driver stopped and asked us for directions.

_____

8. The innkeeper, his wife, and his children greeted us when we arrived at the inn.

_____

9. The repairman's estimate was much lower than we had expected.

_____

10. Everyone hoped that his or her proposal would be accepted.

_____

PART 4

Write the number of the **correct** choice.

EXAMPLE: He sought his lawyer's (1) **advise** (2) **advice.** <u>   2   </u>

1. Take my (1) **advice** (2) **advise,** Julius; stay home today. 1. _____

2. If you (1) **break** (2) **brake** the car gently, you won't feel a jolt. 2. _____

3. Camping trailers with (1) **canvas** (2) **canvass** tops are cooler than hardtop trailers. 3. _____

4. The diamond tiara stolen from the museum exhibit weighed more than three (1) **carets** (2) **carats.** 4. _____

5. The Dean of Student Affairs doubted whether the young man was a (1) **credible** (2) **creditable** witness to the fight in the dining hall. 5. _____

6. Over the (1) **course** (2) **coarse** of the next month, the committee will review the sexual harassment policy. 6. _____

7. Helping Allie with history was quite a (1) **descent** (2) **decent** gesture, don't you agree? 7. _____

8. This little (1) **device** (2) **devise** will revolutionize the personal computer industry. 8. _____

9. The professor made an (1) **illusion** (2) **allusion** to a recent disaster in Tokyo when describing crowd behavior. 9. _____

10. She was one of the most (1) **eminent** (2) **imminent** educators of the decade. 10. _____

11. We knew that enemy troops would try to (1) **envelop** (2) **envelope** us. 11. _____

12. Go (1) **fourth** (2) **forth,** graduates, and be happy as well as successful. 12. _____

13. Despite their obvious differences, the five students in Suite 401 had developed real friendship (1) **among** (2) **between** themselves. 13. _____

14. The software game created by Frank really was (1) **ingenious** (2) **ingenuous.** 14. _____

15. She tried vainly to (1) **lesson** (2) **lessen** the tension in the house. 15. _____

Answers to Exercises for: Word Choice

Part 1
(Answers may vary.)

1. The director believes that within a few months she can increase profits by 25 percent.

2. At age three I was allowed outside to play only from 8 to 11 a.m. and 3 to 5 p.m.

3. Lady Macbeth returned to the murder scene to leave the daggers beside the grooms.

4. The Bible says that we should not judge others.

5. If my grandmother were not on Medicaid, she could not afford living in her unique home for the elderly.

6. The current economy has made business deplorable.

7. Now we need to know whether the operation is beginning efficiently enough.

8. She jumped off the wall and continued down the lane to meet me outside my home.

9. The house was blue and octagonal.

10. She could hardly lose her way, because the road was very well lighted.

Part 2

1. 2	**3.** 2	**5.** 1	**7.** 2	**9.** 2
2. 1	**4.** 2	**6.** 1	**8.** 1	**10.** 2

Part 3
(First column shows words to be circled. Second column shows sample correct answers.)

1.	girl	female
2.	his	All students must bring their textbooks
3.	policemen	police officers
4.	Man's	Humanity's [or Humankind's]
5.	gal	wife
6.	stewardess	flight attendant
7.	female	—
8.	innkeeper, wife, children	innkeepers and their children
9.	repairman's	repairer's
10.	his or her	All hoped that their proposals

Part 4

1. 1	**4.** 2	**7.** 2	**10.** 1	**13.** 1
2. 2	**5.** 1	**8.** 1	**11.** 1	**14.** 1
3. 1	**6.** 1	**9.** 2	**12.** 2	**15.** 2

 FLASH TEST

WORD CHOICE REVIEW: UNIT IV
PART 1

Each sentence may contain an inappropriate or incorrect expression. **Circle** that expression, and in the blank write an appropriate or correct replacement. Use standard, formal English. If the sentence is correct as is, leave the blank empty.

EXAMPLES: He sought his lawyer's (advise) advice

The director reported that the company (was fine and dandy) had doubled its profits.

Whose idea was it?_____

1. Those sort of books are expensive. _____

2. The cabin was just like I remembered it from childhood vacations. _____

_____

3. Some children look like their parents. _____

4. I was surprised that the banquet was attended by lots of people.

_____

5. Its time for class. _____

6. You too can afford such a car. _____

7. I can't hardly hear the speaker. _____

8. Randy promised me that he is over with being angry with me.

_____

9. Irregardless of the result, you did your best. _____

10. Will he raise your salary? _____

11. Try to keep him off of the pier. _____

12. I usually always stop at this corner meat market when I am having dinner guests.

_____

13. Her presence is always intimidating. _____

14. His efforts at improving communication among all fifty staff members will determine his own success.

_____

15. Her success was due to hard work and persistence. _____

16. I'm invited, aren't I? _____

17. Their house is now for sale. _____

18. Henry and myself decided to start a small business together.

_____

19. The club lost its president. _____

20. Did he lay awake last night? _____

21. The professor's opinion differed with the teaching assistant's perspective.

_____

22. Bob laid the carpet in the hallway. _____

23. The cat has been laying on top of the refrigerator all morning.

_____

24. He has plenty of opportunities for earning money. _____

25. San Francisco offers many things for tourists to do. _____

 FLASH TEST

PART 2

On your own paper, **rewrite** each paragraph below so that it displays all the word-choice skills you have learned, but none of the word-choice faults you have been cautioned against.

1. It has been brought to our attention that company personnel have been engaging in the taking of unauthorized absences from their daily stations. The affect of this action is to leave these stations laying unattended for durations of time extending up to a quarter of an hour. In this day and age such activity is inexcusable. Therefore the management has reached the conclusion that tried and true disciplinary measures must necessarily be put into effect. Thus, commencing August 5, workmen who render theirselves absent from their work station will have a certain amount of dollars deducted from the wages they are paid.

2. Needless Required College Courses [title of essay]

   The topic of which I shall write about in this paper is needless required college courses. I will show in the following paragraphs that many mandatory required courses are really unnecessary. They have no purpose due to the fact that they are not really needed or wanted but exist just to provide jobs for professors which cannot attract students by themselfs on there own. It is this that makes them meaningless.

3. In my opinion, I think that the general consensus of opinion is usually always that the reason why lots of people fail to engage in the voting procedure is because they would rather set around home then get off of they're tails and get down to the nearest voting facility. In regards to this matter some things ought to be done to get an O.K. percent of the American people to vote.

4. Each and every day we learn, verbally or from newspapers, about business executives having heart attacks and every so often ending up dead. The stress of high management-type positions is said to be the principle casual factor in such attacks. But a search threw available data shows that this is a unfounded belief. For awhile it was universally expected that persons in high-level jobs experienced the most stress. But yet this is such a misconception. It is in the low-echelon jobs that more strain and consequently more heart attacks occur.

5. The Bible's Book of Exodus relates the flight of the ancient Jews from Egypt to Israel. The narrative says where God sent ten plagues upon the land, the reason why being to punish the rulers for not letting the Jewish people go. Moses then lead his people across the Red Sea, who's waves parted to leave them go through. There trek thorough the desert lasted weaks, months, and than years. The people's moral began to sag. However, Moses brought them the Ten Commandments from Mt. Sinai, and they emigrated safely into the Promised Land. Moses, though, died before he could enter this very fine country. Some question the historic accuracy of the narrative, but others find it entirely credulous. If you except it fully or not, its one of the world's most engrossing stories.

Answers to Word Choice Review

Part 1
(First column shows words to be circled; second column shows correct answers. Answers in some items may vary slightly. Some answers are samples.)

1.	sort	sorts
2.	like	as
3.	—	
4.	lots of	dozens of
5.	Its	It's
6.	—	
7.	can't	can
8.	over with	over
9.	Irregardless	Regardless
10.	—	
11.	off of	off
12.	usually always [or either one]	always [*or* usually]
13.	—	
14.	—	
15.	—	
16.	aren't I	am I not?
17.	—	
18.	myself	I
19.	—	
20.	lay	lie
21.	with	from
22.	—	
23.	laying	lying
24.	—	
25.	things to do	diversions

Part 2
(Answers may vary. There are approximately 80 items needing correction or improvement.)

1. We have learned that employees have been inexcusably leaving their work stations unattended for up to fifteen minutes without permission. Thus we must restore discipline by deducting fifteen minutes' pay from those absent from work stations, beginning August 5.

2. Needless Required College Courses

    Many needless college courses are labeled <u>required</u> just to provide jobs for professors who cannot attract students on their own.

3. I think the consensus is that millions fail to vote out of laziness. The government needs to mount an intensive TV "get-out-and-vote" campaign to attain a respectable voting percentage.

4. Every day we learn from word of mouth or newspapers of business executives having heart attacks, sometimes fatal, believed to be caused by high-management job stress. But a search of available data proves this belief a misconception. For a while it was universally accepted that persons in high-level jobs experienced the most stress, yet it is actually the low-echelon jobs that produce more strain and consequently more heart attacks.

5. . . . It tells how God sent ten plagues upon the land to punish the rulers. . . . Moses then led his people across the Red Sea, whose waves parted to let them go through. Their trek through the desert lasted weeks, months, and then years. The people's morale . . . immigrated safely . . . enter this "land of milk and honey." . . . entirely credible. Whether you accept it fully or not, it's [*or* it is] . . .

FLASH FOCUS

When you complete Unit V, you should be able to:

✓ Understand the basics of writing paragraphs

"Writing is the most fun you can have by yourself."

—Terry Pratchett

"There is no perfect time to write. There's only now."

—Barbara Kingsolver

"I still read everything aloud. I have a fundamental conviction that if a sentence cannot be read aloud with sincerity, conviction, and communication emphasis, it's not a good sentence. Good writing requires good rhythms and good words."

—Richard Marius

FLASH TEST

Before you begin studying the sections in Unit V, take the diagnostic test on paragraphs.

On a separate piece of paper write a **paragraph** of six to eight sentences on **one** of the topics below:

I will never do *that* again

My room (or clothes, car, etc.) as a reflection of me

If I were mayor (or governor or president) for one day

The best (or worst) film I have seen in the past year

The most unfair law

Answers to this exercise will vary.

FLASH SUMMARY

Most sentences that you write will become parts of larger units of writing—paragraphs—and most paragraphs will become parts of still larger units—essays, letters, papers, articles, and so forth. This section explains the basics of writing paragraphs.

74–75 Paragraphs
. . . .

FLASH SUMMARY

Generally, a paragraph contains several sentences clearly related in meaning, developing a single topic. Paragraphs are also visual entities that reduce a page-long mass of print to smaller units more inviting to read.

Paragraphs vary greatly in function, structure, and style. A paragraph of **dialogue,** for example, may contain only a few words (each new speaker gets a new paragraph—see section 42H, pages 136-137). A **transitional** paragraph between main parts of a long paper may have only one or two sentences. The guidelines in sections 74 and 75 apply mainly to **body** paragraphs of expository (explanatory), descriptive, and persuasive papers.

74. Paragraph Form and Length

Indent the first line of each paragraph five spaces ($\frac{1}{2}$ inch in handwriting), and leave the remainder of the last line blank. The length of a paragraph depends on the topic and its needed development. The typical paragraph runs four to eight sentences, though sometimes one or two important sentences deserve a paragraph of their own. If your paragraph gets too long, break it into shorter paragraphs at a logical dividing point, such as between major reasons or examples.

75. Paragraph Content

A. **The Topic Sentence.** Develop your paragraph around a single main topic or idea, usually stated in one sentence called the *topic sentence*. Read paragraphs 1-6 below to see how each topic sentence (boxed) controls its paragraph's content. The other sentences generally give evidence to support what the topic sentence asserts. Most often, you will place your topic sentence first—or just after an introductory or transitional sentence. You may also restate or expand upon your opening topic sentence in a closing *clincher* sentence (as in paragraph 4).

You may also place the topic sentence last (as in paragraph 2), with your supporting sentences leading up to it, as to a climax. Sometimes you may need less than a full sentence (as in paragraph 3B) or more than one sentence to state your topic. Occasionally you may just (with caution) imply your topic sentence.

Paragraph 1 (topic sentence first):

Some traditions set aside specific times for telling stories. Among my friends from several pueblo tribes, stories of Coyote are reserved for winter telling. My *compadres* and relatives in the south of Mexico tell about "the great wind from the east" in the springtime only. In my foster family certain tales cooked in their Eastern European heritage are told only in autumn after harvest. In my blood family, my *El dia de los muertos* stories are traditionally begun in early winter and carried on through the dark of winter until the return of spring.

—Clarissa Pinkola Estés

Paragraph 2 (topic sentence last):

To a well-anticipated hanging, if the victims were famous—a Jack Sheppard, a Lord Ferrers—twenty-five thousand people might come. Thirty thousand are said to have attended the execution of the twin brothers Perreau (for forgery) in 1776, and in 1767, eighty thousand people—or about one Londoner in ten—flocked to a hanging in Moorefields.* Against this may be set the extreme unreliability of Georgian statistics. Nevertheless, hanging was clearly the most popular mass spectacle in England; nothing could match the drawing-power of the gallows or its grip as a secular image.

—Robert Hughes

*Here the writer refers the reader to an endnote giving the source of his facts.

B. **Adequate Development.** All other sentences in your paragraph should support the general idea you stated in your topic sentence. Many inexperienced writers fail to develop their paragraphs fully enough; they may merely paraphrase the main idea several times or add vague generalizations instead of convincing evidence. Compare the development in paragraphs 3A and 3B below. Which writer better convinces you of what the topic sentence asserts?

Paragraph 3A

The capital of Ghana was very crowded, but that made it all the more interesting. All kinds of vehicles filled the streets. Some of these streets were broad, others narrow and unpaved. Many pedestrians added to the crowded conditions. The mix of children and adults, young women and old men, made this city a colorful one.

Paragraph 3B

> Each morning Ghana's seven-and-one-half million people seemed to crowd at once into the capital city where the broad avenues as well as the unpaved rutted lanes became gorgeous with moving pageantry: bicycles, battered lorries, hand carts, American and European cars, chauffeur-driven limousines. People on foot struggled for right-of-way, white-collar workers wearing white knee-high socks brushed against market women balancing large baskets on their heads as they proudly swung their wide hips. Children, bright faces shining with palm oil, picked openings in the throng, and pretty young women in western clothes affected not to notice the attention they caused as they laughed together talking in the musical Twi language. Old men sat or stooped beside the road smoking homemade pipes and looking wise as old men have done eternally.

—Maya Angelou

Generally, the body of your paragraph should contain enough specific evidence to support your main idea adequately, convincing even skeptical readers that what you say is true. Your support may consist of **facts** or **examples;** one or more **reasons;** elements of a **description, definition,** or **explanation;** events in a **time, process,** or **cause-effect** sequence; points of **comparison** or **contrast;** or more than one of these.

Paragraphs 1 and 2 above are developed with facts or examples. Paragraph 3B uses descriptive facts and some contrast.

Paragraph 4—developed with a reason and contrasts:

> Chief among the forces affecting political folly is lust for power, named by Tacitus as "the most flagrant of all the passions." Because it can only be satisfied by power over others, government is its favorite field of exercise. Business offers a kind of power, but only to the very successful at the very top, and without the dominion and titles and red carpets and motorcycle escorts of public office. Other occupations—sports, sciences, the professions and the creative and performing arts—offer various satisfactions but not the opportunity for power. They may appeal to status-seekers and, in the form of celebrity, offer crowd worship and limousines and prizes, but these are trappings of power, not the essence. Government remains the paramount area of folly because it is there that men seek power over others—only to lose it over themselves.

—Barbara W. Tuchman

Paragraph 5 below is also developed with reasons.

C. **Coherence.** Your paragraphs *cohere* (hold together well) when you clearly signal or imply how your ideas relate to one another—when your thought flows smoothly from the first sentence through the last (and from one paragraph to the next). You can achieve coherence by using (1) a controlling structure, (2) transitions, and (3) repeated key words or phrases.

(1) A controlling structure. Clearly showing your paragraph's structure—its skeleton—helps your reader. This structure can be as simple as labeling your reasons *first, second,* and *third,* as in paragraph 5 below (note the climactic order: the most important reason, labeled *above all,* is last). Paragraph 1 is structured around groups of people (*Among my friends . . . , My* compadres . . . , *In my foster family . . . , In my blood family . . .*). Paragraph 2 uses numbers (*twenty-five thousand . . . , Thirty thousand . . . , eighty thousand . . .*). Paragraph 6 uses a pyramid.

(2) Transitional expressions:

You may use all or part of a sentence for transition, either at the beginning of your paragraph or within it:

But the new science could not rely on these pioneers alone. . . .

. . . Despite such difficulties, . . .

Nor is depression the only effect. . . .

. . . In appearance. . . . In actuality . . .

Paragraph 5. The writer is telling why most Americans came to speak alike rather than in different dialects. Transitions are italicized.*

There were three main reasons. *First,* the continuous movement of people back and forth across the continent militated against the formation of permanent regionalisms. Americans enjoyed social mobility long before sociologists thought up the term. *Second,* the intermingling of people from diverse backgrounds worked in favor of homogeneity. *Third,* and *above all,* social pressures and the desire for a common national identity encouraged people to settle on a single way of speaking.

—Bill Bryson

Paragraph 6. Notice how this paragraph begins with a transition linking it to the previous paragraph *(Together these factors . . .)* and is held together by the italicized transitions,* which carry out the writer's idea of a pyramid:

Together these factors produced a unified national band business pyramid that affected black jazz bands. *On the top* were a few very successful national bands earning excellent salaries and fine reputations. These bands built their names through recordings and radio broadcasts, with careful nurturing by managers. This name recognition was then exploited for financial gain during national tours of ballrooms, nightclubs, and theaters. *On the next level,* less successful national bands followed the same pattern on a smaller scale. *Still lower,* the territory bands continued, but they were definitely marked as minor league, copying the styles of the national bands and losing their most talented musicians to the lure of the big time.

—Thomas J. Hennessey

(3) ***Repetition of key words or phrases*** gives your reader valuable signposts to follow the path of your thought. Repetitions may consist of the word itself, a synonym, or a pronoun clearly referring to the word. In paragraph 2 above, note the repetition of *hanging (execution, gallows);* in paragraph 4, *folly, government (public office),* and especially *power.* Repeating a familiar term from the previous sentence near the beginning of your new sentence is especially helpful; in paragraph 6, observe how repetition of *bands* and the use of *These bands* and *This name recognition* helps tie the paragraph together.

D. **Unity.** *Unity* means that no sentence strays from the topic. Look again at paragraph 4. Imagine the following sentence just after the topic sentence: *Tacitus was a Roman historian who lived from about A.D. 55 to 117 and was known as an eloquent speaker.* Such a sentence would destroy the unity of the paragraph, which is not about Tacitus at all. Look again at paragraph 6. Notice how the image of a pyramid, with its top, middle, and bottom levels, unifies the paragraph.

E. **Emphasis.** *Emphasis* means that the main points get the most space and stand out clearly, not lost in a clutter of unexplained detail. In paragraph 4, for example, the repetition of *power, government,* and *folly* not only imparts coherence but also keeps the paragraph's emphasis firmly on those three concepts and their interrelation.

*Italics added by the authors of *English Grammar.*

FLASH FOCUS

Indicate stages of thought	first, second (*not* firstly, secondly), then, next, finally
Introduce particulars	for example, for instance, in particular
Show cause or effect	consequently, as a result, because of these
Signal further evidence	in addition, moreover, furthermore, also
Mark a contrast or change of direction	however, yet, still, on the other hand, nevertheless
Show other relationships	above all, that is, meanwhile, at last, likewise, formerly, more important
Signal a conclusion	therefore, thus, then, on the whole, in sum (avoid the trite *in conclusion*)

FLASH TEST

PART 1

First, **circle** the topic sentence of each paragraph. Then find one or more sentences that violate the **unity** of the paragraph (that do not relate directly to the topic). Write the number(s) of the sentence(s) in the blank at the end of the paragraph.

1. (1)From a pebble on the shore to a boulder on a mountainside, any rock you see began as something else and was made a rock by the earth itself. (2)Igneous rock began as lava that over hundreds of years hardened far beneath the earth's surface. (3)Granite is an igneous rock that is very hard and used for buildings and monuments. (4)Sedimentary rock was once sand, mud, or clay that settled to the bottom of a body of water and was packed down in layers under the ocean floor. (5)All rocks are made up of one or more minerals. (6)Metamorphic rock began as either igneous rock or sedimentary rock whose properties were changed by millions of years of exposure to the heat, pressure, and movement below the earth's crust.

   1. _____

2. (1)Although we normally associate suits of armor with the knights of medieval Europe, the idea of such protective coverings is much older and more pervasive than that. (2)Some knights even outfitted their horses with metal armor. (3)As long as 3,500 years ago, Assyrian and Babylonian warriors sewed pieces of metal to their leather tunics the better to repel enemy arrows. (4)A thousand years later, the Greeks wore metal helmets, in addition to large metal sheets over their chests and backs. (5)Native Americans of the Northwest wore both carved wooden helmets and chest armor made from wood and leather. (6)Nature protects the turtle and the armadillo with permanent armor. (7)Even with body armor largely absent from the modern soldier's uniform, the helmet still remains as a reminder of the vulnerability of the human body.

   2. _____

3. (1)Mention the name of George Washington and most Americans envision a larger-than-life hero, who, even as a little boy, could not tell a lie. (2)However, it turns out that Washington was more human than his biographers would have us believe. (3)His contemporaries described Washington as moody and remote. (4)He was also a bit vain, for he insisted that his fellow officers address him as "Your Excellency." (5)He refused to allow himself to be touched by strangers. (6)Washington was also known to weep in public, especially when the Patriots'

   3. _____

war effort was sagging. (7)Washington was even plagued with traitors, who gave the British advice on how to beat the Americans. (8)He was not even a gifted military officer. (9)Rather than being a hero of the French and Indian War, Washington may have provoked the French to go to war by leading an unnecessary and irrational attack against a group of Frenchmen. (10)While Washington was certainly a brave man, dedicated to freeing the colonists from British tyranny, he was not the perfect man that early biographers described.

4. (1)In the mid-1800s, an apple or a pear was considered too dangerous to eat. (2)In fact, any fresh vegetable or fruit was considered too risky because one bite might lead to cholera, dysentery, or typhoid. (3)During cholera epidemics, city councils often banned the sale of fruits and vegetables. (4) The only safe vegetable was a boiled potato. (5)A typical breakfast might include black tea, scrambled eggs, fresh spring shad, wild pigeons, pig's feet, and oysters. (6)Milk was also considered a perilous beverage because many people died from drinking spoiled milk. (7)Milk really was a threat to people's health, because it was processed and delivered to home with little regard for hygiene. (8)Children and those who were ill were often malnourished because the foods with the most nutrients were also the most deadly. (9)Until the invention of the icebox in the 1840s, rich and poor people alike risked their health and even their lives every time they ate a meal.

4. _____

5. (1)Infant sacrifice must be clearly differentiated from infanticide. (2)The latter practice, growing out of economic want, was not uncommon among primitive peoples whose food supply was inadequate. (3)Even in most of the Greek city-states, in Rome, and among the Norsemen before they accepted Christianity, it was the father's right to determine whether his newborn child should be accepted and nurtured or instead be abandoned—simply left to perish from exposure. (4)In the eighth and ninth centuries the Norse invaded Britain and left elements of their linguistic and cultural heritage. (5)But in infant sacrifice a father offered this most precious gift to the gods. (6)Thus Abraham was told: "Take now thy son, thine only son Isaac, whom thou lovest, and get thee into the land of Moriah; and offer him there for a burnt offering upon one of the mountains, which I will tell thee of."

5. _____

—Constance Irwin (adapted)

 FLASH TEST

PART 2

Each paragraph below is inadequately developed. Choose **one,** and, on your own paper, **rewrite** it to develop the topic sentence (boldfaced) adequately. Use six to nine sentences, adding your own facts and ideas as needed. [You may change the topic sentence to express a different viewpoint.]

1. Young people today see how their parents act and how they feel about the world today. Since they feel their parents are wrong, they rebel because they do not want to become a carbon copy of their elders. Young people want to be treated as persons, not just kids who do not know what they are talking about and who should not express their own ideas because they are too young to understand. **Young people today want to do and think as they please.**

2. **Today's college campuses display a fascinating variety of buildings.** Some are radically different in architecture from others. Very old buildings may stand beside ultramodern structures. The variety of structures truly fascinates me on my daily walks across campus.

3. **I like the old movies shown on TV better than the recent releases shown in theaters.** The old films contain more-dramatic plots and more-famous actors. They are exciting and fast paced. The actors are widely known for their acting ability. Today's films are boring or mindless and have less-famous actors.

FLASH TEST

PART 3

In each blank, write the transitional expression from the list below that fits most logically. For some blanks there is more than one correct answer. Try not to use any expression more than once.

afterward	meanwhile	more important	however
consequently	nevertheless	therefore	likewise
even so	on the other hand	thus	in particular
formerly	finally	as a result	that is

EXAMPLE: Thousands of workers were heading home by car, bus, and train. <u>Meanwhile</u>, at home, their spouses were readying supper.

1. The night of the ball, we danced every step we knew. _____, we strolled on the moonlit beach.

2. By the late 1870s, Britons were looking forward to their weekend leisure time; _____, until the early 1890s, Americans were working sixty-hour, six-day weeks.

3. Today we take a common United States currency for granted. Money, _____, was not standardized in the U.S. until the Civil War, when the federal government produced its first paper money.

4. In postwar America people were enjoying a strong economy, which provided plenty of jobs and high wages; _____, life seemed secure and promising.

5. The term *teenager* entered the language only as recently as 1941; _____, teenagers were not really a recognized presence in American society.

6. When we speak to family members, we use an informal and intimate language. When we are speaking to a large group, _____, we are more likely to choose different words and a different tone of voice.

7. If you toss a coin repeatedly and it comes up heads each time, common sense tells you to expect tails to turn up soon. _____, the chances of heads coming up remain the same for each toss of the coin.

8. The first real movie—_____, one that actually had a story line—was the film entitled *The Great Train Robbery*.

9. American children spend about a quarter of their waking time watching television; _____, it is important to monitor what young children are watching.

10. A seven-hundred pound microwave oven, called the Radarange, was first produced by Tappan in 1955. _____, Americans were not interested in purchasing a microwave oven until the late 1960s, when the appliance was much smaller and more reliable.

11. The young singing group tried again and again to produce a hit recording, without success; _____, they struck gold with "Gotta Have Your Love."

12. Whelan's stocks soared 350 points in a day; _____, she felt that she could buy an expensive new car.

13. Some baseball records have been thought unbreakable; _____, few people expected Lou Gehrig's 2,130-consecutive-game streak ever to fall.

14. Nineteen forty-one marked the beginning of Franklin Roosevelt's third term; _____, it was the year that the U.S. was plunged into World War II.

Answers to Exercises for: Paragraphs

Part 1

1. Topic sentence: 1
    Violate unity: 3, 5

2. Topic sentence: 1
    Violate unity: 2, 6

3. Topic sentence: 2 [*10 also restates the topic.*]
    Violates unity: 7

4. Topic sentence: 9
    Violates unity: 5

5. Topic sentence: 1
Violates unity: 4

Part 2
(Answers are samples.)

1. Many young people today are jumping into the adult world for its freedoms and pleasures without thinking of its responsibilities. Let me tell you about Bruce and Kathy. All through high school they saw each other and never had an argument. After some thought and advice they decided to take the final step: marriage. All went well through the first year; but soon they had a child, and the problems began, because neither had ever really had such responsibility. Bruce left and still cannot be found, and Kathy lives with her mother in regret. Teenagers like Bruce and Kathy are impatient to marry because they want the enjoyments and satisfactions of the adult world right away but do not realize that responsibility goes along with such enjoyments. According to a recent newspaper article, more than half of teenage marriages fail. Rushing to do what older people do does not make young people more adult or more free, or solve all their problems.

2. Today's college campuses display a fascinating variety of architecture. Pseudo-Gothic Victorian towers may abut geodesic domes bulging from concrete plazas. At the State University's main campus a sheer twenty-story steel and glass tower gleams at one end of the Quadrangle; an ornate but grimy turn-of-the-century stone fortress scowls from behind massed shrubbery at the other. Between the two squat utilitarian post-World War II cinder-block dormitories indistinguishable from army barracks. Most older campuses yield similar examples. Oddly, such architectural cacophony can fascinate by its very horror.

3. I like. . . . The old films contain . . . and fast-paced. Who can forget the confrontations of Rhett and Scarlett in <u>Gone with the Wind</u>? And which of today's actors could ever replace Bogart and Bergman in <u>Casablanca</u>? No modern producer has ever tried to remake such classics, for few of today's actors could equal the originals. And most older films wove their tale in ninety minutes or so. Today we have mostly $2\frac{1}{2}$-hour plotless orgies of car-chases and explosions in which high-tech effects, not human actors, are the stars. Give me the good old days!

Part 3

1. Afterward
2. meanwhile [*or* however *or* on the other hand]
3. however
4. consequently [*or* therefore *or* thus]
5. formerly
6. on the other hand
7. Nevertheless [*or* However]
8. that is
9. therefore [*or* consequently *or* thus]
10. Even so
11. finally
12. as a result [*or* therefore *or* thus *or* consequently]
13. in particular
14. likewise [*or* more important]

FLASH TEST

PARAGRAPH REVIEW: UNIT V

Go back to the paragraph you wrote in Part 2 of this section.

On your own paper, **rewrite** it, being sure that it has a controlling structure, appropriate transitions, and repeated key words or phrases as needed to give it coherence. **Circle** your transitions and repeated key words or phrases. At the end, skip a line and **write a sentence** briefly stating what your controlling structure is.

Answers to this exercise will vary.

INDEX